T0164700

21 Allen Street

and Other Tales From the Life of Actor Paul Marin

SOL SCHNEIDER AKA PAUL MARIN

iUniverse, Inc.
New York   Bloomington

21 Allen Street
and Other Tales From the Life of Actor Paul Marin

Copyright © Tani Foger

iUniverse books may be ordered through booksellers or by contacting:

iUniverse
1663 Liberty Drive
Bloomington, IN 47403
www.iuniverse.com
1-800-Authors (1-800-288-4677)

ISBN: 978-1-4401-4787-6 (pbk)
ISBN: 978-1-4401-4788-3 (ebk)

Printed in the United States of America

iUniverse rev. date: 8/5/2009

Contents

Early Years

It was 1927; a sweltering July day on the cusp of Cancer and Leo when the first pangs of the opening pelvis said here comes the child. A carpetbag was filled and stationed at the door, so there was an unhurried rush to the hospital. My mother with my father in tow arrived early.

"Go home," insisted the emergency room nurse. "Go home! Wait 'til either the water breaks or the pains come every two to three minutes, then come back."

On the way home in a horse-drawn cab, the pains grew intense and passed the point of return. My mother and father arrived home and struggled up the stairs of the slum tenement to their fifth floor apartment a cold-water railroad flat on Dekalb Avenue, Williamsburg, Brooklyn. Water was put to boil on the pot-bellied stove in the kitchen/living/dining room. A female neighbor was called in to act as midwife with help from Hyman Schneider, husband and father. The four older children, three daughters aged twelve, ten and seven years, and the first-born son, then three years old, were shunted off to the Wald's apartment next door. At about seven o'clock that evening the howling Solomon Schneider made his appearance.

I was about six months old when my older brother, Abe, then almost four, ran to our mother yelling, "Momma, there's a rat sitting on Solly's bottle helping him drink from the nipple." I'm sure this announcement caused some consternation.

From age three I had long blond hair. Whose idea it was for me to have curls like Shirley Temple and dress as Little Lord Fauntleroy? I don't understand and probably never will, yet these curls were my identifying feature. The Wald's next door had two daughters who treated me like a living doll. They groomed me, brushing my hair and tying colored ribbons in it, even buying little dresses for me. They adored me and I them. When they were picked up for dates I would cry, as I wanted to go with them. In contrast, my older brother Abe literally ignored me. He didn't want to have anything to do with me. When I was five, I was entered into a talent contest One Saturday morning, before the one-reeler cartoons started at the neighborhood movie house, I sang Shirley Temple's "Good Ship Lollipop" with curls flying. I won first prize, a child's set of golf clubs, which Abe broke the very same day. I wore this coiffure until I registered in public school at the age of six where the principal wouldn't admit me until my curls were shorn. At home a bowl was placed on my head and its contours followed with a scissor.

When I was four my little brother Lenny was born and with his arrival he became the apple of everyone's eye including me. In order to hide my jealously for being displaced as the family's pride and joy, I became his protector.

We lived on a street of stores on Dekalb Avenue where during the day on the street level were businesses, people shopping and more people just walking. On street level of our apartment building was a green grocer who sold only fruits and vegetables. My mother giving me a nickel, with the warning," Don't lose it." I was all of five, sent me down to buy two potatoes. This was 1932. With the nickel in my pocket I ran down stairs. In the store, I looked for the owner Sam who wasn't there. The store looked empty. An old man stuck his full-bearded face out from behind the storeroom door and said he was Sam's father. Motioning with his hand to come toward him, he said in Yiddish, *kum* (come). He picked me up and we sat on a wooden rocking chair. He placed me on his knee, quickly unbuttoned and took my short pants down and played with my genitals. He did it like he was inspecting me, and I wasn't alarmed. To be very honest, he just fondled me, and there was a nice feeling, and then he pulled my pants up and asked what I wanted. I told him. He gave me the potatoes. I handed him the nickel; he gave me three pennies change, and upstairs I went. I wasn't disturbed or bothered by the old man's action. Giving my mother the potatoes, I told her that Sam wasn't in the store and that an old man who said he was Sam's father was there. I then told her as a matter of fact what his father had done.

My mother who was at the stove cooking, in our three in one, living room, dining area and kitchen, rapidly turned, and her right hand swung in an ark towards my face landing with a loud smack. I didn't know what wrong I had done or said, and the tears started down my cheeks as she looked at me with her dark brown eyes, fear written all over her face. In a controlled voice, a little too loud, she hissed, "Stop making up lies."

She was terrified; she didn't know how to handle this, or what to do. A legal Russian immigrant, she feared anything that would bring her family to the attention of the local police. She thought of them as the Kazaks who would ride at a gallop up and down the streets of Jewish neighborhoods in Kiev slashing with long swords at the people who happened to be in the streets. From that day on I knew I'd never confide or tell anything that was important that happened to me ever again.

When I was nine we moved. My sister Mary's best friend Evelyn

Gross was very rich and had a chauffeured Packard limousine. Her father was a bootlegger and had a house in Manhattan Beach, Brooklyn two blocks from the ocean. Mr. Harry Gross had a tunnel built so when a boat came to the beach to deliver contraband liquor it could be brought through the tunnel to the house undetected. The bell-pull in their living room appeared to be an innocent means of calling the maid, but in actuality when pulled it rang an alarm in the tunnel that was loud enough to be heard on the beach. When Gross was given advance notice by crooked cops on his payroll that the police were going to the beach for a bust this cord was pulled warning those on the beach to hide or get rid of the whiskey. The boat with its cargo would immediately depart. Mr. Gross was later arrested, found guilty of bootlegging and sent to prison, and the tunnel—two city blocks long—was filled with cement from the beach to the house by the authorities.

Things were so-called normal for the next three years when I came down with Scarlet Fever. Prior to Mr. Gross vacationing at taxpayer's expense Evelyn told Mr. Gross that I was sick and that we were moving. Fortunately it was a very weak case though I had to stay in bed for six weeks. Mr. Gross sent his chauffer-driven Packard Limo, I was wrapped in a blanket and placed in the back seat and brought to Bath Beach. I assume the neighbors were shocked to see this family moving out and into an apartment in a limousine with liveried chauffer no less. We must have been the talk of Dekalb Avenue and then Bay 38th Street.

We were then ensconced in Bath Beach in a five-room apartment in a two family house with three bedrooms, a living room, a kitchen, and a complete bathroom. That is, a tub, a shower and a toilet. We lived in the upstairs apartment while the Landlord and his family had the street level apartment, with Bensonhurst to the north and Coney Island to the south. Bath Beach was made up mostly of Italian immigrants from

Sicily and Jews from Eastern Europe with a few Irish families here and there added to the mix.

There was a girl named Lorraine Santangelo who lived across the street. Her mother was Jewish and father was Italian Catholic. That family was in retrospect very interesting. Her mother cooked pork and *traif* (non-kosher) food for her family while she herself ate only kosher food. She prepared it in separate pots and pans and used two sets of dishes for herself, one for dairy, the other for meat that she kept separate from the dishes and utensils she used for the family.

I loved Loraine. One day I walked across the street, knocked on her door and asked her if she would be my girlfriend. She laughed, said she had a boyfriend and closed the door. I wanted to die.

There was an Italian boy who lived two doors down from Lorraine named Antony who was very fat. His family raised chickens in their back yard. He was said to have sex with the chickens, when asked about it, he said when he was about to shoot (orgasm) he would strangle the chicken by twisting its neck till the head was completely torn off, throwing the poor bird into whole body convulsions, that caused the birds anus to contract about his penis, which he said made his orgasms greater. This was a better neighborhood than Williamsburg.

The Italian neighbors cultivated any and all vacant lots into farms and grew grapes for wine, cabbages, Roma tomatoes and vegetables. These city farmers built lean-tos and on weekends sat with their *goumbas* drinking espresso and Guinea Red wine made from homegrown grapes, and watching their crops grow. If and when those lots were sold all the grape vines and other roots and bulbs were uprooted and planted elsewhere.

Home Life

My parents were poor. My father worked two jobs, many times bringing work home to add dollars to the house. He had six kids and rent, food, clothes and doctors ate up all the revenue with nothing left over for games or summer vacations.

During the Depression my father lost his job at Peck's Upholstery where he had worked for over twenty years. I remember we ate old stale bread for three days, dunking it in hot tea. There was nothing else. There was an Italian Bakery war, and at the Italian Bakery on 86th Street a loaf was one cent. I was sent there many times. That's when President Roosevelt (F.D.R.) established Food Stamps and other work programs (the W.P.A., the C.C.C., and others).

I was never good at sports. One day at the schoolyard playing baseball I threw a ball and pulled my arm out of its socket. To this day, I can't throw overhand with my right arm, the cartilage is still torn. I went to the Police Athletic League (PAL) where I became a fairly good Ping Pong player.

I was a voracious reader. In good weather I'd read on the upstairs open porch; in bad weather, I read in the living room. I was a very lonely child and read everything I could get my hands on from Guy de Maupassant to Issak Asimov. I would lose myself in fantasy. One night my parents went to see a movie, an extremely rare occurrence. I was in the living room reading when a policeman on a ladder pounded on the window. Shocked to see him there I opened it and he said, "Are you deaf? Your parents were knocking on the door for over an hour." They didn't take a key, as they knew I would be home. I was so engrossed in my book that I hadn't heard them knocking.

I didn't make friends easily in my youth. I had a very high voice. I used to ride the subway to Manhattan and while waiting for the train I'd hum the most mournful tunes out of my emotional state. I craved attention from my mother who was a schizoid depressive I guess what would be diagnosed as bi-polar today. When she was down she'd lay in bed and cry, wishing she were dead. There was always nervousness when

I came home from school, as I never knew what I'd find. No kids were ever brought home with me. She could be on her high period when I left that morning for school. When I returned home she'd be in bed crying wishing she were dead. No one was ever invited to the house. When invited out to a celebration such as a wedding or bar mitzvah or just to visit family, either my father would go alone or with one of the children or not go at all. She would say, yes she'd go, and prepare a dress etc. When the day came, it would find her too ill to go.

Once my father's youngest brother, who lived around the corner, came over with his wife to visit. He had heard that she was in her depressive period and they came to cheer her. At first she ignored the knocking then as my aunt kept calling, "Jenny, open the door it's Becky and Benny." Annoyed that they didn't leave, my mother called out, "There's no one here. No one's home," my uncle told my father. We all laughed when we heard it, for that was one of the popular sayings on the comedy shows on the radio at that time. "There's no one here but us Chickens."

Unhappiness was like the black cloud that hung over me. I can't remember ever being kissed or held by my parents. When I was seven or eight, my mother was lying on the couch; I went over and lay down next to her. I felt immediately that she felt she had to tolerate it but she didn't like or want this, and never did it again. I had a lot of love to give and no one wanted it.

When twelve I took a bus to Philadelphia and walked the streets wanting to knock on a stranger's door and say please love me. I stood in front of row houses and once, walked up the steps but didn't knock. Just hoped someone would open their door and invite me in. I walked and walked and had no money to get the bus back to New York. Don't remember who it was exactly but some man asked what I was doing standing there. I said I live in Brooklyn and I came with enough money to get here and now I want to go back home but have no money to buy a ticket. That kind man bought me a ticket for the bus and gave me a nickel to take the subway home when I got back to New York City.

My mother used to say that life was a dream, for some a beautiful life but for others a nightmare. In my early teens I hated my father and blamed him for the way my mother was. I thought he must have done something that caused my mother to be this way. When I grew up, it was my mother who took the brunt of my anger as I realized my father stayed with her only because of us children. I knew that had it been me I would never have stayed.

I was told that before I was born my father had thoughts of leaving. He had two children at that time. He went to his older sister who lived near by, and said he had it, he was leaving. My aunt Mary was a very nice and smart woman. She said, "That's all well and good but who will feed the girls and take care of them, Jenny can't." My father left my Aunt Mary's apartment and went back home.

Before I was born my mother walked out of the house wearing a pair of slippers and the skin she was born in. Maybe it was winter or just the fact that she was naked, but a policeman wrapped his coat around her and brought her home. After that incident, she had her first electric shock treatment. These treatments were repeated a number of times during the 1940s. The treatment would leave her completely disorientated for a few days. After those treatments she'd be fine for a while and do what she had to do until it hit again in a few weeks or if we were lucky, months.

My mother attributed her illness to two events. In Odessa, Russia her parents owned a small grocery and lived behind the store in a few rooms. As a very young child she and her family were forced to hide in the second cellar for three days, while the Russian Kazaks rampaged in the store above, stealing what they could carry and destroy what they couldn't. The second event was the birth of my younger brother. She felt she had lost too much blood and it was never replaced. Even when told that the body restored blood loss in 24 hours, she refused to believe it.

When she was in her high phase she would accomplish more in a 24-hour period then the average woman did in a month. The curtains would be taken down, washed, pressed and put back up, the house would be spotless with newspapers covering the linoleum floor in the kitchen to keep it clean. Food was cooking on the stove and cakes and rice pudding were baking in the oven. The music of her voice would now fill the apartment. As a young woman my mother sang opera with a community opera group in Russia that toured the major cities of Europe. She spoke Russian, Polish, French, Italian and Yiddish but no English.

One time when sick and she wouldn't eat anything I brought a glass of milk and a piece of buttered bread to her. She wasn't in her bed; I thought she probably was in the bathroom. The room was always kept dark when my mother was ill. I went to find her thinking maybe she was coming out of her depression. Went to the bathroom but she wasn't there, and I panicked as to where she was? I went back to her bedroom and in the semi-darkness I walked around to the other side of her bed and stepped right on her chest; she had fallen out of bed. I thought I had killed her and became so frightened and guilt stricken that I threw up.

At fifteen my grades in school took a turn for the worse and my feelings of hating myself were stronger then ever. I was so depressed that I tried to kill myself. One of my neighbors had a car that was never locked with the keys in the ignition. I got a hose and attached it to the exhaust pipe and lowered the rear window and brought the hose through. All that happened was I got a monster of a headache. The window let in too much air.

The same year I got a job through an ad in the paper working for Lou Winkler in the Fur Market on 7th Avenue at 30th Street where he had an office and showroom on the twelfth floor of a sixteen story building. My function was to keep one glass full of Red Label Johnny Walker Scotch Whiskey and a second glass full of water as a chaser. I was paid fifty cents an hour for this task alone, not to answer the phone or do anything else but to keep those two glasses full at all times. In the summer it was a full time job.

Winkler sent me to Chicago with mink skins and a mink coat for Notre Dame football coach Knute Rockney's wife. My mother was definitely against my going and Winkler phoned her and promised that his friend, Chicago Mayor Richard J. Daley, would meet me at the airport; I would deliver the package and return home that same day. On my arrival, there was Mayor Daley who said that Winkler had a vacant suite at the Edgewater Beach Hotel. He wouldn't hear of my retuning immediately. He wanted to show me his Chicago. He arranged for the two of us to deliver the furs on the second day and the third day he showed me Chicago. He wouldn't let me drink anything but milk. I was only fifteen.

On bringing me back to the airport Mayor Daley gave me a package and said it was for me. It was a cashmere coat. On presenting me with it he said, "You know kid, for a Jew-boy you're a real white Jew." I assume he thought he was giving me a compliment. I considered throwing the coat down the steps leading to the plane onto the tarmac, but didn't, as I didn't want to start something with Winkler's anti-Semitic Mayor friend.

In my teen years, school got worse as I became very belligerent. Once my teacher physically pushed me and I pushed back. He slipped and fell hitting his head on his desk. He dragged me down to the Principal's office where my father was called from work and told that I was being expelled. I was then about 16 and a half. I hung around for those months in Greenwich Village until I was 17 when I could join the Navy. Until then, I found my way to the movie theaters on 42nd Street to see a double bill for a quarter. I felt very inadequate, as I was a high school dropout but that was compounded later in life even though I earned a G.E.D. in the Navy and a real diploma after the Navy at New Utrecht High night school.

New York City was amazing in those War days. It was like another world from Brooklyn especially since it was only eleven miles and took about 45 minutes to 42nd Street by subway. Before the Second World War Brooklyn was agricultural and the bedroom of the city. The city was full of Soldiers, and members of the Women's Auxiliary Army Corps (WAACs), Sailors and female WAVES (Women Accepted for Volunteer Emergency Service), Marines and female BAMs, plus European troops: young guys and gals away from home, lonely and on their own. The bars of the Village were overflowing and the Bar of the Hotel Astor on 45th Street and Broadway was a magnet for the service men and women. Every day was party time. When the Japanese attacked us and we entered World War Two, my brother Abe was drafted into the Army. I couldn't see myself in a foxhole. In the Navy, even aboard ship, you slept in a hammock or a double bunk bed one on top of the other. Lottie's husband, my brother-in-law Jack Zaimoff, was also drafted. My other brother-in-law Mary's husband, Bill Katzberg pleaded 4F or some other law that kept him out, though he was physically able.

In the Navy

I was nineteen in the Navy and stationed in Perryville, Maryland and was asked by a sailor buddy to go to a weekend party as a date for one of the invited females. I went with Kenny Burkehead in his rumble seat Model T Ford where I threw my overnight canvas zippered bag and on to Chevy Chase Maryland. After driving over an hour we arrived at a gatehouse. A man appeared from the house and opening the gate said, "Hello Mr. Kenneth." We drove in silence and after a few miles of well kept rolling hills but no houses I asked Kenneth, "Where's your house?"

"Oh, a few more miles up, what you see on both sides of the road belong to my family." We drove on. Then off in the distance was this rambling Mansion. I use the word 'mansion' advisedly. I was puzzled!

"Look there, that's my house."

"Oh…you rent a room there?"

I couldn't conceive of people living in such a big mansion except in the Movies and that wasn't real. Kenneth laughed.

"That house belongs to my family it was built by my great–Grandfather." As we drove up to a covered pillared entrance a man opened the front door wearing a tuxedo with a white bow tie… descended the stairs to the car… opened the car door for me to exit and reached for my zippered bag.

"No… No! I'll get it" and a slight 'tug of war,' began. I had no idea who he was. Kenneth called out, "I'll take the car to the garage and meet you inside."

I was petrified. "No…. No…I'll wait for you here." I went up to the front door but didn't enter.

"Please come inside," said the man who I learned later to be the butler.

"It's ok. I'll wait for Kenneth."

Kenneth appeared at the front door from the inside of the house and brought me inside. I begrudgingly allowed the butler to take my little bag that held only a change of underwear, and toiletries. A military uniform is considered formal dress equal to black tie. We then went into a room that to my eye was the size of a ballroom. It had six couches, and two large fireplaces. Placed around the room were conversational settings, a small table with two or three chairs. The room was so large that I envisioned that one person at each end had to use a telephone to communicate with each other.

Seated in a Needle Pointed back of an elegant chair was Mrs. Burkehead. At our introduction, she literally took out a pair of Lorgnette glasses and looking me up and down said,

"What a pleasure to know you Sol. Where are *you* from?"

"Bath Beach, Brooklyn."

"Oh, what a lovely area, I haven't been there since I was a girl."

I thought she must be crazy, for where I lived were the burial grounds of 'Murder Incorporated.' They had one son the eldest, already married who lived elsewhere.

"What does your father do?" Mrs. Burkehead asked.

"Oh," I replied, "he's an operator"

"I beg your pardon, what exactly does he do?" she said while lowering her Lorgnette glasses.

"He makes draperies and slipcovers."

"Oh, he's an Interior decorator." Once again raising the Lorgnette glasses and carefully inspecting me.

"No...he's an operator on a sewing machine."

With that, Kenneth rescued me. "Come on, I'll show you to your room."

This house had twenty bedrooms to help you imagine the size. The garage too, had room for twenty cars and a stable that at this time had 14 horses. In my room there were sliding door closets, which held tuxedos, sport clothes, riding and hunting habits, socks, and shoes— from kidskin for formal wear to sport shoes with cleats—in a range of average sizes, for the use of guests who arrived without a bag of clothes. My zippered bag had been unpacked and my toilet articles, to my distress were no longer in the bag and I found when looking were placed in the adjoining bathroom.

That night we all went to the Country Club for dinner. First we had drinks before a raging fire and then into the dining room. As we sat down a waiter walked over to the table wearing a chain hanging from his neck that held a key. His vest if I recall was of silver lame. Mrs. Burkehead turned toward me,

"Sol" she said, "would you please order the wine?" A blank look must have enveloped my face for she added, "Which do you think Sauterne or Champagne?" My mind froze! Champagne I heard of, the other I had no idea if it was red, white or even yellow. The only wines I knew were Manischevitz, Shapiro's, and Thunderbird. The last one was Gallo's cheapest, used by the Bowery winos. The first two were sweet Sabbath wines. Then I thought that in the movies they always drank champagne to celebrate whatever, so it left…

"Sauterne," I hesitatingly replied.

"Good choice," she countered.

I thought, why did she do that? It was obvious that when it came to wines or for that matter even simple table manners were yet to be learned and absorbed into my worldly sophistication. Years later when I thought of this, I would think, what fun could it be to riposte with someone who is ignorant of paring?

Suddenly an Admiral appeared at the table and I and Kenneth, immediately stood.

"Hello John," said Mrs. Burkehead, "You know my son Kenneth"

"Yes of course, Kenneth," "and his friend Sol Schnei…."

"No, I haven't had the pleasure."

"This is Admiral Green, Sol. I assumed you would know each other since you're all stationed at Perryville together."

There has always been a 'No Fraternization' regulation between officers and rank and file enlisted men; even with out that rule I doubt that I would have even the slightest contact with an Admiral.

After dinner the young crowd went slumming in downtown Baltimore; my weekend date was Colgate Nesbit Woodward. Colgate was named for the company to which she was heir and Nesbit for Evelyn Nesbit, Actress and wife of Sanford White an architect whom she caught cheating and shot him in the groin killing him. A socialite, Evelyn Nesbit, received lots of tabloid press and was sent to prison for that notorious crime.

We young folk went downtown to Baltimore Street, the area where there were stripper bars. The place where all soldiers, sailors and marines congregated on weekend passes, as we passed a place named 'The Silver Dollar', Coli (Colgate) asked me

"Sol, have you been here before? "

No, don't lie; I said to my self, so then I sort of hedged, "Maybe once or twice." In truth I was at The Silver Dollar most weekends when I was given a pass.

"Then lets go in."

We made quite a spectacle. The ladies wearing long dresses, those of us in service wore our uniforms and the other guys wore tuxes. The bar had the traditional swinging double doors. No sooner had we entered when one of the waitresses called out…

"Sol, you old son of a bitch, haven't seen you around. How the hell are you? With that, Coli turned, looked directly into my eyes and said,

"You left quite an impression in the one or two times that you were here."

That moment, I was hoping for the floor to open and I would just fall in and disappear. The rest of the evening we bar hoped then we all went back to the Burkehead's.

Saturday there was a touch football game; Kenny's sister came down wearing a real football player's uniform, pads and all. I thought, she looked like a truck driver and played very hard. I thought that her tackles would end up hurting one of the other players; I watched a while then went to read. When the game broke we all went to clean up and get ready for dinner at home.

In retrospect it was the worst dinner in my life. The silverware was piled on both sides of the dinner plate, even more on top of the plate. Not knowing which piece of silver to use. I focused in on Coli. She would pick up a spoon and I'd do the same. Then as I started to use that spoon, she would put it down and raise a fork. She undoubtedly thought that was funny for there was a slight smirk on her face.

The maid would bring out a platter of meat and take it to the butler, and he would take it to Mr. Burkehead to slice it. Another maid would appear and take the platter around the table. By the time it came to me it was cold.

I was afraid to use the silver, since I had no knowledge what to use on what. I ate very little thinking that Kenny's parents were wondering where this cretin was educated. The meal ended with what to me was astonishing.

The butler wheeled in a sterling silver Candy Store–a silver cart on wheels that carried ice cream in six flavors and buckets of syrups, even hot fudge. Mrs. Burkehead cautioned her daughter not to take more helpings. She was a big girl physically and she could put away lots of food and deserts.

That night after I had undressed and got into bed there was a knock at the door. Come In, I called out and it was Kenny.

"Is everything ok? Do you need anything?" He asked.

"No, but I have a question. Are we sleeping in shifts?

Kenny started to laugh, "What do you mean?" he asked.

Well, I sort of slid into my question. "When I got into bed the sheets were warm as if someone had just left the bed."

With that he laughed again and said, "Oh, my mother had the maid use warmers to warm up the bed for you."

"Warmers?" I repeated.

"Yes it's a tray with hot coals that are moved about so that the winter cold is driven out of the bed."

It was a most trying weekend of my life so far.

When I was in the Navy stationed in San Diego I got emergency leave as my mother was having one of her depressive states. I didn't have the money to fly home from California so I went to the Red Cross for a loan. To my surprise they wanted collateral. They asked me to sign over my Navy life insurance. I couldn't believe them. I said, "No Thanks" and phoned my sister Mary since Lottie's husband Jack Zaimoff was in the Army. Clara was keeping company and after the war later married Jack Miller who was also in the Army. My lovely sister Mary said, "It's not only my money; it's also Bill's." She wanted the same collateral, my Navy life insurance. She and the Red Cross were sisters under the skin. Mary was the first to marry, and I felt strongly that this was the beginning of the end of the family, as she moved out to an apartment on 21st and Benson Avenue, a ten or at most 15 minute walk from Bay 38th Street. Every time I phoned after that she would always say "I love you," but evidently not enough to loan me the fare to go home. That about sums up my sister Mary and her husband William Katzberg.

The Start of a Career

New York, after the War

After my discharge from the Navy in 1947 I decided to call one of my Navy buddies in Cleveland, Ohio. He invited me to come and stay at his house with his parents and younger brother. While there with the GI Bill, I enrolled at Western Reserve University (today Case Western) I chose design, which meant a lot of drawing and using graphs going way back to the Egyptian architecture of columns with the palm leaves. My classes on most days started at 10:00 a.m. I got a part time job at the Higbee Company, an upscale department store, in their women's window dressing department. I worked from 6:30 a.m. to 9:00 a.m. It didn't take me long to realize that I wasn't interested in design. So before the first semester ended, I quit. Staying in Cleveland was really not a choice. Now I wanted to get back home.

Back in Brooklyn I was at loose ends. I went to see the furrier I had worked for during summers in high school, Louis Winkler. When a customer came in asking for a mink or fox or whatever fur, he would tell them he's going into the vault and run to the furrier who dealt in that particular fur and bring it to his showroom, hoping he could convince the woman to have a style that she with Lou would design and to look at the skins. If she would rather have the already made coat, he'd give her a good deal.

Winkler had the habit of selling the same coat many times to many different people. One day a number of years after I no longer worked for Winkler, I ran into his brother on 7th Avenue who told me "Lou jumped from the window of his showroom. If only you had stayed with him he would still be alive today." I still wonder how I could have prevented that.

While working for Winkler, I took a TWA plane to Los Angeles to see the sights as a civilian. It was a twin-engine plane that held about thirty or so seats stopping every 200 miles or so to refuel. The stewardess's were in those days were hired for their beauty. One came to the passenger cabin and asked if anyone played Gin. I called out, "I do, but badly." She said, "That's ok" A fourth was needed. She ushered me to a closed section of the plane and there was Howard Hughes owner of TWA and two other men sitting in what looked like a small living room. Hughes was probably in his early thirties then and very nice. I won a dollar from Howard Hughes and in retrospect I should have had him sign it.

I met Arnold Weber working at Winkler's. His father was a furrier in the same building. We became friends. Arnold was a sophisticated guy, my complete opposite. He casually asked if I wanted to go to the theater and see a play. I had never been to a Broadway theater in fact I never had seen a professional play. I had been to the Brooklyn Paramount and the New York Paramount where I saw performers like Martin and Lewis, Sinatra, Nat King Cole, and others live, and then a movie. I had never seen or been to a Broadway show.

Arnold was having problems with his wife and he had tickets to see "Candida" at the Cort Theater. He invited me to go along. It was as if I entered into a world I never knew existed. The theater was beautiful and plush. Golden cupids decorated the ceiling and walls. Gilded comedy and drama masks hung in the center of the proscenium from which hung a deep red velvet curtain covering the entire stage from the top to the apron. The audience was made up of people in gowns and tuxedos and a few in business suits.

When the curtain was raised at the opening of the play, it went up in great scallop swirls to reveal the set. I was spell bound. I had never seen anything so beautiful. The star was Katharine Cornell whose husband Guthrie McClintic produced the play. Wesley Addy and Marlon Brando were in the cast. Brando's first entrance made me think that a stagehand or someone by mistake came onto the stage that was not an actor. He was so real; the others on that stage were emoting, as was the acting style then. At the first act break I asked Arnold if these people made a living at this. He answered in his best New Yorkese, "Are you kiddin'? Dey make fortunes, dey fill rooms fulla money!"

"I can do that," I said calmly. "I'm going to be an actor."

"Yeah, sure!" came the skeptical reply.

"No really, I know I can do that, that's going to be my life's work."

The next morning I phoned the Veterans Administration at 24th Street and 7th Avenue in Manhattan and asked, "Are there any schools that teach acting?"

"Yes," answered the voice.

"Are they eligible under the G.I. Bill?"

"Come here, and I'll give you a list."

Looking at the list of a full page that had a number of schools, my confusion reigned. My brother in law worked for John Hancock Life Insurance Company and wanted to get me a job there. He kept saying, "Why are you sacrificing so much as you only eat hamburgers morning noon and night." He couldn't understand that I wasn't sacrificing anything, as this is what I wanted to do with my life and knew that one day I'll do it.

Training

I wanted to go to the Neighborhood Playhouse which I heard about from other would-be-actors, but it was booked for next two years so, not wanting to waste any more time, I settled for Tamara Daykarhanova's School for the Stage. Daykarhanova and Maria Ouspenskya came here with the Moscow Art Theater Tour in 1921. When the tour continued they stayed behind and started their school. Classes met from 10 a.m. to 3 p.m. five days a week. Daykarhanova's husband taught the History of Theater, Speech was taught by Fanny Bradshaw, who gave me my love of the English Language. She also told me to buy a pitch pipe and by continually going from the high notes to the low ones, I would achieve a voice using three octaves. Later on I was always told how beautiful my speaking voice was, though I never learned to use it for voiceovers. Stage Make-up was taught by Bob(?) Buchman and dance by a member of the Moscow Art Theater.

Shortly thereafter Ouspenskya went to Hollywood where she made several Vampire films opposite Lon Chaney Jr. I remember her as the old grandma sitting next to the driver of the horse and carriage in all those vampire pictures. She was a wonderful teacher and very talented actress; I wish I could have said the same about Daykarhanova. One day in class I said that there was an imaginary sterling silver tray on a table. She immediately said that it was silver-plated. No, I said, it was sterling silver, not plated. She insisted in front of the class that sterling wasn't solid silver but only silver plated and for me to sit down and not finish the exercise. I should have quit her school then and there for her ignorance and pettiness.

In my first year with Daykarhanova, I managed to get a role in an Equity Library Theater production of Lillian Hellman's play Montserrat, starring Anne Meara, wife of Jerry Stiller and mother of Ben, then an infant. We got very good reviews so a producer was found and it was transferred to the mid-size (500 seat) theater at the Barbizon Plaza Hotel. The producer combined a few smaller parts into a character named Captain Morales, and that's how I got my Equity card, and my first paying job. Daykarhanova had a rule that first year students were not allowed to work, however, professionally or for free. Her reasoning was that they didn't know enough. Students could be expelled for taking a job. All playbills passed her desk, and if she saw the name Sol Schneider that would have been my fate. (I was naïve to believe that nonsense; she wouldn't have given up the GI bill money. This lady was now a capitalist and like all of those wanted more.) A group of us used to have dinner every night at one or another's apartment. Someone brought pasta some one else brought bread etc. On the table was a jar of Vita Marinated Herring. I can't recall who it was that said it but someone said when Saul of Tarsus became a Christian he took the name Paul. It didn't matter to me as this was a temporary name and was going to use my own name after the play ended. Then someone said, "How about Paul Marinated." Someone else said how about "Paul Ate-it." Everyone laughed. It then evolved to Paul Marin. Once again I didn't care as I was going to go back to Sol Schneider. Well that was 1954 and now it is 2009 and its still Paul Marin.

In retrospect, I should have waited for a place at the Neighborhood Playhouse, as it was a better school. I then studied with Joseph Anthony, who stopped teaching as he became too busy with directing. One of his better musical efforts, The Most Happy Fella, opened on Broadway to rave reviews. I really liked him and enjoyed his way of teaching. Trying to find an acting job was never easy, though there were far fewer actors in the 1950s then there are today.

I worked as a waiter at night from five to two in the morning, leaving my days free for class and making rounds. Auditioned and was accepted by the Herbert Berghof Studio that was taught by the great lady of the stage Uta Hagen. Now she was one of the greatest American actresses and teacher of her day. Uta played Desdemona opposite Paul Robeson in Othello and went on to win a Tony award for Who's Afraid of Virginia Wolff. Iago was played by Uta's then husband Jose Ferrer, who when he suspected that she was having an affair with Paul Robeson, turned her in to the House Un-American Activities Committee for being a communist. This committee was holding hearings to find expose and jail communists, though the Communist Party was at that time a legitimate political party. A husband like that is something else.

Uta was tough. One day after doing a scene in class, she tore into me and instead of using it as a learning experience I quit. Bad mistake, I thought I was great and only went to acting school to smooth the edges. I never said I was smart.

Looking for Work

I would make the rounds of producers and directors and casting people for TV and film every day from 10 to about 4:30 p.m. The offices would be able to set their watches as I came at the same time and day each and every week. If I didn't show, the following week when I arrived they would ask "Where were you last week?" It was my job to get to know these producers so when something came up that I might be right for, they would call me in to audition.

One day at the David Suskind Office, a number of other actors and I were waiting our turn to see Mr. Suskind, a television producer. In the waiting room, a rather large reception area with a desk in the center, sat the receptionist, a very overweight Ruth Conforte. Now remember this was in the mid-1950s. Actors made rounds in suits and dresses, working people had their clothes pressed and neat and their appearance carefully monitored.

The outer door to the office opened and in came a man in his 70s carrying a walking stick, wearing a Homburg hat, a perfectly cut top coat over his sharply pressed suit and a shirt with a not quite tuxedo collar in fashion at the beginning of the twentieth century. He wore spats with pearl buttons over his shoes.

Walking to the desk he stopped, scrutinizing her and said to Ruth, "Don't you have a comb? Your hair looks like a nesting place for rats. Shame on you! Your dress is spotted with the food you've been spilling on yourself for weeks. How dare you sit here looking so unkempt? You are speaking to ACTORS, young woman. For myself, I'll have nothing to do with office ever again." With that he turned smartly on his heel and left the office.

Cowards all, we sat there wanting to applaud but were afraid that we'd never be seen again by that office. She went on to become one of the top-casting people in the business.

One winter day I was making my daily rounds of producers, directors and casting agents' offices around the city. Walking up 6th Avenue near the Ziegfeld Theater, fighting the blustery wind, I had my coat collar up, my hat pulled down and my head and eyes facing the sidewalk. Suddenly I hit a wall, or, as it turned out, a very big and tall man. I lifted my head slightly, said "Sorry," and walked around him. He too, said "that's ok, no harm done." I walked about fifteen feet. That voice seemed to have come straight from the center of the earth. I've heard that voice before. I knew it. Who was it? It then dawned, Orson Wells. I turned and looked back. Orson had also turned and we looked at each other for about ten or so seconds. He turned again and walked to the Ziegfeld Theater and entered the side door leading to Billy Rose's office.

I immediately thought what is Orson Wells seeing Billy Rose about at ten in the morning? I continued to the building where Captain

Anderson the casting man for NBC Television. In those days TV was live like theater, and stage actors were preferred. The teleprompter was not as yet invented.

I found out about casting by/for the Networks, ABC, NBC, CBS, Dumont and independents. My first stop was to NBC where I was ushered in to meet Capt. Anderson. I thought he was kidding calling himself Captain, since in 1947 the war had been over for two years. The only people who retained their wartime titles were colonels and generals, so when we shook hands I introduced myself as "Pharmacist Mate, 3rd class, Sol Schneider."

In retrospect, I didn't endear myself to him. When he turned my 8x10 photo over it was blank. There were no credits, as I hadn't done anything as yet. He looked at the blank back of my photo, and took a photo from a pile on his desk and turned it over where there were a slew of credits. "I ask you," he said, "should I cast you who has no experience or this man who has experience?" I agreed with him. I went home and added dummy credits to the back of my photo—shows that had already closed and TV programs that were no longer on. Eventually, each was replaced with a legitimate credit.

The more I thought about Orson Wells meeting with Billy Rose at ten in the morning, the more I was certain that their meeting had to do with a new Broadway show. After lunch at the Automat, I walked over to the Ziegfeld Theater.

At this time Billy Rose was in a fierce contested divorce with Eleanor Holm, and Rose had private guards outside of the entrance to his offices, at the elevator, in the entrance way, and at the reception desk to insure no subpoenas could get through. As I entered the building I was challenged by the guard who asked, "Yes, whom do you want to see?"

"Mr. Rose," I said.

"Do you have an appointment?"

"No, but Orson Wells suggested I see him."

With that he picked up the wall phone and repeated what I just told him. He hung up and with arms folded against his chest pointed with his top hand to the elevator. "Press that button." I did as instructed. In the elevator there was only one button. I was not sure if it went up or down, as the sensation was neutral. When it stopped, I stepped out of the elevator and was at the receptionist's desk.

This woman asked, "Whom do you want to see?"

"Mr. Rose, Orson Wells suggested I see him" with that she too lifted the phone from its cradle. I heard her say, "Orson suggested…" Still listening to the phone, she pointed to a door. I thought that must be the laundry chute and when I opened that door I would be catapulted to the street outside.

On opening the door, I found there was another guard who said nothing but just pointed to another door. Through that door I found myself in a very large room with a circular desk. Sitting in the center of this desk was Billy Rose with what looked like a foot-long cigar in his mouth. "Orson suggested I see you?"

"Not exactly, I say, I'm hoping that you might have something in what ever this new show you're planning that I may be right for." With that Billy Rose looking severely at me, shaking his head. "Why do you actors lie? I don't know you and have never heard of you or your work. Do something noteworthy, and I'll seek you out, no need you coming to me."

With that I said, "Mr. Rose, I set out to see you and I accomplished my objective, may I leave my photo with you?"

"Do you pay for these pictures?" he asked.

"Oh, yeah," I replied.

"Then you had better keep it. For the moment you leave this office I'll deposit it here," pointing to the wastebasket.

"Mr. Rose, my objective was to have you see me, and I accomplished that." I then took the elevator down to Sixth Avenue and continued my rounds.

As a young man Billy Rose was a fast typist and won awards for his speed. When much younger he was employed by Supreme Court Justice Brandeis who helped Rose become rich. Brandeis later became advisor to Presidents and had a bench, which he called his office in Central Park where he sat contemplating the world. A brass plaque was placed on the back of the bench to honor the Justice Brandeis. When I met him Billy Rose was a producer and the owner of the Ziegfeld Theater.

Weeks later the musical Kismet, starring Alfred Drake and Joan Deiner, opened at the Ziegfeld. I decided to crash their opening night party. This was a black tie affair and I had my one and only brown suit. I slipped in behind people who were showing their invitations. A young guy about five or so years older than I came over saying, "I like your Tux, you from the Bride's or the Groom's side."

I laughed and said, "Neither, I crashed this party."

"Really," he said laughing, "You an actor? Well then, come with me and I'll introduce you to people who may be able to help you." As we were moving around the room, who came in but Billy Rose. He saw me and exclaimed, "Oh no, not again!"

I said, "Don't worry Mr. Rose. This is a party. I never seek work at a party."

Working

Tripping Around was the title of my Non-Equity show before I got an Equity contract and joined Actors Equity Association. Believe me we tripped; it was a kind of vaudeville show. We would enter a town; meet the town's mayor and police chief. We started down south in Georgia and did our show; move on to a neighboring town for one-night stands in the high school auditorium or on the basketball court. From Georgia we headed north. We were on the road traveling in the producer's station wagon. We were rather a small group, singing and dancing and doing skits. Mr. Bergmann drove. When we passed a school that had a quote chiseled above the door, "Work and Study Hard" he would point it out and always say, "That's worth rememberin'."

Arriving in Fairmont, West Virginia, we checked in to a hotel and a few of us actors had a meeting. We hadn't been paid in three weeks. I was appointed to represent the others and asked to speak to our producer a Mrs. Bergmann, a hard-shell Baptist from South Carolina. I went to her hotel and asked when we would be paid. She said "You don't need money. I'm paying for your hotel rooms. You'll get it when we finish the tour." I said we needed money for food. She countered that we should come to her hotel, eat in the restaurant and sign the tab. What about our laundry? "Bring it over to her hotel and have the Nigger woman do it." I left there frustrated, as I couldn't pry her loose for some cash. Walking back to the hotel I saw the Mayor, whom we met when we arrived. He seemed like a nice man about late 40s or early 50s, unmarried and living with his sister. Unbeknownst to me, Mrs. Bergmann had phoned the Mayor and said that I was the shepherd leading the sheep astray. She asked him to teach me a lesson. Fairmont, West Virginia was a dry city in a dry state–no liquor or beer–but behind the rear wall of every restaurant was a speakeasy. A narrow eye slot was opened when you knocked and if you were thought not to be state police you were admitted. I invited the Mayor for a drink. He said, "Thank you son, but my sister was waiting on me for dinner maybe another time. Where you gonna be?" I pointed to a restaurant over there.

We parted, and I walked into the restaurant. There wasn't any one in there. Going to the back wall and knocking on the door, the slot opened and like Sesame, the door opened to music and gambling and a bar full of people. Taking a seat at the bar I ordered a beer. Before it was served the phone rang and the bartender called out, "Is there a Sol Schneider here?"

I said, "over here."

As he brought the beer he said, "You got friends in the restaurant wanting you to come out."

I put a dollar on the bar next to the beer and went out without taking a sip. Nobody was in the restaurant. I thought it strange, why didn't they come in? Then figured that maybe they were outside. It was now dark. When I opened the street door spotlights from two police cars lit me up. Two cops got out of their cars with guns drawn and asked, "You Sol Schneider?"

"Yes."

"You're under arrest."

"What for?" I asked.

"You're drunk"

"What?!" I didn't even get a chance to take a sip.

"We can't talk to you. You're the Mayor's baby. Git in the car," said one of the cops. This was the answer to every question.

I was taken to the police station and my shoelaces, tie, belt and all my valuables, watch, wallet etc. were taken from me and I was put into the Drunk Tank. The putrid smell of vomit and feces was overwhelming. There was another inmate asleep on a bare cot. I wasn't booked, just put into the cell. I found myself in jail for the next three days.

When my cellmate came out of his drunken stupor asked me, "You a preacher?"

"No," I said. He wouldn't believe me.

"You must be a preacher. You're wearing a shirt and tie."

The food for those days was two slices of white bread and a thin slice of bologna for breakfast, lunch and dinner. I ate nothing giving it to my cellmate. I wouldn't drink out of the sink as it was encrusted with you name it.

I had no idea if any of the guys from Tripping Around knew I was in jail, and the jailhouse was on top of a cliff at least on the jail side. There was a window about ten feet above the cell floor and I would scale it to peer out the window, and, since there was no glass, I would yell at people passing below. Of course I was in jail and as far as they were concerned I was there for some good reason. I managed to throw out a note to call the hotel and tell them where I was. I didn't know that Mrs. Bergmann phoned them saying I was in jail and unless they behaved they would follow me.

One of our guys was a Southerner and he found a dentist who was in the political opposition. The dentist said he was "waiting for the Mayor to do something as stupid as this," and he got me out of jail and got us our money. When the police were returning my belongings, my release, according to this desk cop was contingent upon being "out of Fairmont by noon, as it was now ten a.m. or you'll be back in jail for a lot longer." The actor who had gotten my release had a car so we went out of town to a fish BBQ. As we walked in, there were the Bergmanns having lunch. Mr. Bergmann jumped up and ran outside to check and see if we slashed their car tires. Not only hadn't I though of that, but it was definitely not my style; it was, however, the mentality of the Baptist Bergmann's.

I worked in "What Every Woman Knows," in the 1954, revival starring Helen Hayes and Co-starring Kent Smith. We played the City Center Theater that is a Special Contract theater (read: less pay). Miss Hayes had to be treated as the First Lady of the American Theater. Though there were others thought of as First Ladies. Eva La Galleon,

Uta Hagen, Lynn Fontanne, Katherine Cornell. Only in America do theater royalty share the same crown and throne.

Miss Hayes was, in my estimation, a Professional Catholic, no profanity such as Hell etc. and no one dared to say Christ. The result was she would have you fired. During rehearsals of a scene between Miss Hayes and Kent Smith, Kent said the word "Damn." Immediately Miss Hayes stopped, throwing down the gauntlet by loudly proclaiming, "Is that one of Sir James Barrie's Lines? I don't recall it being so." Well, the tension on the stage was like a spring tightly wound and ready to snap. We on stage and those watching in the house, waited for Kent's reaction. Though very well known not only in theatrical circles but also to the theater going public, Kent was not a star of the same magnitude or caliber as Miss Hayes. He stood there on the stage and looked at Miss Hayes with eyes that were saying, "Who the hell do you think you are?!" A gentleman, he said nothing and continued on the line that he stumbled on.

Our director, John Stix, was hand picked by Helen Hayes. She would do something and say, "This was the way we did it originally in 1934. Is that ok, John? "Of course," he would answer. In essence Helen Hayes directed this revival as it had been done, with John Stix saying "Yes, Miss Hayes" to all her commands. Instead of directing he was a traffic cop seeing that no one bumped into the furniture.

This First Lady of the American Theater would throw her head up and make her entrance to thundering applause and do the same physical action on exiting after each scene to signal the applause. That was the action of actors of her generation who found it was a true and tried reaction from any audience to garner applause, before and after finishing a scene.

When she arrived in the wings, if anyone was seated they had to get up till she passed. One night when she exited the stage, a supernumerary (in the theater we never called them extra's) a young guy was sitting in a chair as Miss Hayes made her exit. Since he didn't stand on her arrival, she stood there in front of him and just looked at him. The very next night he was no longer in the company. It was rumored that she had him fired.

Helen Hayes was a member on the council of Equity. She was very short, and they cut the legs of her chair so her feet could touch the ground. When I was elected to council of Equity, I inherited that chair with my knees touching my chest. As the newest member, my life and Helen Hayes's continued to be interconnected.

The only time I had seen her as a woman and real person was when her husband the playwright, Charles MacArthur, drove in front of the stage door at the theater, which faced the street, to pick her up. He sat in their chauffer driven limo. Sitting in back with the passenger window down, drunkenly shouting, "Helen, for Christ sake get your ass out here, I'm waiting." Coming out of the stage door she became Mrs. Charles MacArthur and running out to the car trying to quiet and placate him, the star was replaced and she became the dutiful and loving wife. So much for the First Lady of the American Theater. She was a star and won Tonys, Oscars and TV awards. We all play many roles.

Now for sad news, on Wednesdays when I wasn't working I was a volunteer at The Motion Picture Actors Home in Woodland Hills, California for people who are connected to the Movie Industry. One day a number of years after I no longer helped out there, it was 20 miles away from my place in West Los Angeles. I went there to visit friends who were now living there. These were people I worked with or friends that I met as fellow members of the Academy of Motion Picture Arts and Sciences, the Oscar Organization that I was elected to in 1983. I walked into the area of the dining room (it's a very big place with a full hospital) and sitting in a chair about thirty feet from the dining room, was Kent Smith. With a big smile on my face I said, "Kent, How wonderful to see you, I didn't know you were here." He didn't answer or react. His face showed no sign of recognition and his eyes were blank. He didn't know me from Adam. I then realized he was suffering from Alzheimer's. So sad, as he was such a fine talent to end losing his mind.

I met Lilly Lodge in that company of What Every Woman Knows. She was the daughter of John Lodge, Governor of Connecticut and niece of Henry Cabot Lodge, the then American Ambassador to the United Nations. Lilly at that time was living with Helen Hayes in Nyack, New York. Lilly asked me to audition with her for the Actors Studio. We rehearsed an original comedy piece of a girl who goes to a dance club for singles looking to find a husband or at least a boyfriend.

Before we went on to perform, we were called to the stage to tell about ourselves. In essence it was Lilly's audition yet both of us were there on stage. Friend Alba Olms a member of the Actors Studio privately directed us. She later became a well-known director and actor in English and Spanish theaters, also director and actress in Miriam Colon's Puerto Rican Spanish Theater Company. Miriam as mentioned before was a mutual friend of both Alba's and mine.

Our judges were Tamara Daykarhanova, John Stix, the director, mentioned above, whom Lilly and I both were working for at the time of the audition. The last but not least to pass judgment on us was Lee Strasberg. Lilly, 5'9" tall and built rather like a footballer. I was 5'8" and weighed about 145 lbs.

John Stix was the first to question, "Lilly, tells us whom you're living with? A perplexing look showed for an instant, then came the answer, "Helen Hayes in Nyack." Then he asked where she had studied. RADA (the Royal Academy of Dramatic Arts in London, England) came the answer. Other personal questions were about her father and uncle. Lee Strasberg ended the questioning with "all right, go get ready and start your five minutes." I was totally ignored. I had studied with Daykarhanova for years under the G.I. Bill. Daykarhanova asked nothing not even acknowledging that I had been a student of hers. After Daykarhanova, I studied with Joseph Anthony, the director of "Most Happy Fella," with Uta Hagan, who was quite a remarkable teacher. She charged three dollars a class and those actors who didn't have any money as most student actors don't, paid nothing or what they could afford. Even up to the twenty first century she only charged six or seven dollars a class. She was a remarkable actress, teacher and human being. After Uta I studied with Paul Mann.

Before we left the stage we described the set. An imaginary banner was hung at the back of this dance hall ballroom. It had painted on it "Every one here is supposed to be Friends." A window, on the left stage wall and a stool towards center left. The opening line was mine. Lilly was directed to be looking out the window at the street below. When I entered there was Lilly sitting on the stool. I said, "Excuse me is there a girl in here? Her line was, "Read the sign, Mister, every one here is supposed to be friends." She just sat there and didn't say a word. I walked to the stool and looked into her eyes and could see that she was totally up and obviously frightened. Trying to relax her, I took out my cigarettes and said, "Do you smoke? Have a cigarette." She just shook her head no, and said nothing. This went on, with me ad-libbing for the time that we had.

Then I heard a voice say thank you. We left the stage and went to the street. Lilly apologized while I tried to comfort her. A week or so later I received a letter saying I was not accepted and that Lilly was. I was dumbfounded. Lilly phoned to invite me to lunch at the Yale Club. That place was furnished like an English men's club with leather easy chairs and a large fireplace, to sit in front of for a drink before entering the dining room if one chose. We were ushered directly into the dining room where now all the tables were occupied. Every one was talking yet not a sound was heard as the insulation in that room was meant for all conversations to be private and not to over hear some tidbit or financial remark.

After apologizing profusely saying she has no control over the questions that were asked at the Actors Studio and she was sure that she was chosen as a member because of her attachment to high-society which meant an entrée to money and donations. She then said, "Look around this room, the people having lunch their conversations were of what we will pay for bread, milk or meat tomorrow," the Yale, Harvard and the New York City Athletic Clubs plus a few others were where these economic decisions were made. These people with their old money didn't care who was in the White House. What was eight years to families who came to the New World on the Mayflower? They could wait until the next election when their chosen politico would be ensconced in the White House and the Halls of Congress.

One day, Lilly and I went to visit a close friend of hers, Kay Medford, a very talented Broadway actress. Kay lived in a cold-water flat on the lower East Side with the bath tub in the kitchen. The tub had a porcelain cover that doubled for her dining table. Lilly also lived in a cold-water flat though I had never been there. In conversation she mentioned that she was living without financial help from her family, though at the Yale Club she had signed her father's name to pay the bill. Its one thing to live without hot water, a bathroom etc because there wasn't another choice. But to do so with signing tabs with your father's name at Bergdorf's, Saxs Fifth Avenue, restaurants, or other emporiums, when you can at any moment decide to go back home to a life of luxury is very different. For me, I had no choice. I had yet to get my first Broadway show.

She mentioned that when she moved there, needing a small table to fit in her entrance hallway and had seen one at the Duchess of Windsor's apartment in the Waldorf Astoria Towers. So she phoned and asked the Duchess if she was still using it. The Duchess said, no, it was in storage. Lilly asked to borrow it and the Duchess said of course, I'll send it with the chauffer. I came to the conclusion that poor people buy a needed piece of furniture while the rich borrow. I guess that's why they have money. Lilly did not pursue the acting profession as far as I know, as I've not heard of her in many years. Last I heard was that she had married to a New York City Official. A nice girl and I hope her life is/was rewarding.

Twenty-five to Qualtla, Mexico

Through Alba Ohms an actress and close friend of my future wife, Doris Luper, I heard of a group that was planning to go to Mexico to form a Repertory Theater in English using the Michael Chekhov method and bring it back to the States to perform here. Why Mexico? Finances. We were twenty-five young actors who formed this group. Two guys traveled down from New York to Mexico City to search for suitable quarters for housing. They traveled in a station wagon filled with the theater books we had each donated to our future library, some filched from New York's Public Library.

The town of Qualtla, in the State of Morales, was seventy miles south of Mexico City, a small town near the Emiliano Zapata home which was then inhabited by farm animals. Qualtla had this Hotel, Posada de Rio, (River Bridge) with a running brook. It had an annex with twenty-five rooms separate from the main hotel, plus a large room for classes, and meetings. It was perfect for our group.

Most hitchhiked, some took buses and we were told to go to the American Express office in Mexico City where directions to the hotel were posted on their message board. I hitched down. I had twenty dollars for the trip plus my share for the school, $180. We all had to come up with $180 to cover our stay of six months. Thirty dollars a month covered three meals a day, daily maid service, laundry, etc. The exchange rate was eight pesos to one dollar. In 1954 one peso bought a carton of cigarettes, (came in a wrapper of six packs) eggs, toothpaste, and other things. Personal items were our own responsibility.

My first lift was a by a fuel truck driver from Manhattan to outside Wilmington, Delaware. From there a large Cadillac Sedan towing a boat picked me up. The driver was in his late forties or early fifties, I guessed. He said he had the monopoly on macadam for three states Delaware, Pennsylvania, and Maryland. He was on his way to Tyler, Texas. He told me that his wife had been killed in an auto accident, and he had been thinking of divorcing her but hadn't broached it to her as yet and then the accident. I guess it's easier to confess to a stranger and rid one of guilt. At our stops for food he graciously would not let me pay. This driver (I can't remember his name) then made me an interesting proposition. When you plan a trip, he said, you take your car to be checked so you know it won't cause problems. He was going to Tyler (to a clinic similar to the Mayo Clinic) to be examined for three days, and if I agreed, he'd pay for me for the three days, and then drive me to Mexico City. I said "Let me think about that, and I'll let you know when we get to Tyler." He was very bright, intelligent and obviously very rich. When we arrived in Tyler, I thanked him for the ride and his generosity and decided to keep going on my own. I wanted to get to Mexico to start my studies with this Repertory Theater.

Crossroads: who knows where my life would have taken me if I had said, "Yes I'll go with you. It's only three days," instead of "no." I wouldn't have had to worry about hitchhiking in Mexico.

In Tyler was picked up by three young guys who at first said they would take me about five miles but after I got into the car and we chatted, they invited me to a party. I decided to go, and it was a good time. As we entered the bar there was a man sitting at a long table. He said, "Gentlemen your guns please." My five new friends took out their guns and laid them on the table. To say I was surprised is an understatement. When we left they lined up to retrieve their guns and placed them in their hidden holsters.

After the party we slept at one guy's home. The next morning he drove me about twenty miles. We said goodbye and I went on toward the Laredo, Texas border crossing. With many short rides I reached the border. At the crossing I met a young couple driving to Mexico City for vacation. Luck stayed with me for these American tourists took me with them. Once there I found the American Express office, the message board with instructions how to get to Qualtla, Mexico by bus and directions to the hotel.

The director of our group was Alex Horn. We studied the Michael Chekhov method of placing centers, internally, externally or wherever, in creating physical characterizations plus acting classes. One of his exercises, as an example, was where would you put the center of a West Point Cadet? The answer to that was in his backside: an iron pipe going up from there along his spine.

We studied Shakespeare, American classic plays, British Restoration, Comedia del Arte, fencing, etc. We started at first light up on the roof doing the Michael Chekhov method of becoming frogs, trees, pigeons, or what ever we chose, until about 9 a.m., then down to the main building dining room for breakfast. After breakfast we went on to different classes on all phases of performing. Then lunch, classes, dinner more classes till about 11 p.m. This schedule was seven days each week.

One morning up on the roof we were seen by the Parish Priest and the very next Sunday we were his Sermon. Unfortunately, he warned his congregation that we were some form of devil cult worship because we were up there with the rising sun, and warned them to stay away from us. We immediately became nervous for a few months prior to our arrival we were told two Mexican government surveyors were murdered because they were thought to be putting a spell on their land.

This company started badly. In the first days Alex called a meeting and wanted us to swear we'd never do Broadway or commercial theater. I stood up and asked who had ever worked or been offered an acting job on Broadway or anywhere else? Not one of us had, so I said, "It's easy to say I swear I never would. But if offered a Broadway show I'd take it in a second." Alex's girl friend a member of the group always defended him lashed out at me.

A few weeks later, Alex asked those who were homosexual in the group to swear they would become heterosexual. I got up incomplete disgust and said we came here to establish a repertory theater not a psychiatry clinic. With that Anne said, "Don't you dare talk to Alex that way or I'll slap your face." "Really?" I said, "You do and I'll slap you back so hard you'll never raise your hand to anyone again."

The day I arrived, while I was unpacking there was a knock on my door. Sitting in a wheelchair was this American ex-patriot wounded in World War II who said, "I hear you're Jewish." I said, "Yes, I am. What can I do for you?" He said there was one Jewish family living in Qualtla. He gave me their phone number and told me to call them. He himself was not Jewish. I said I was there to study and would be busy around the clock, that I wouldn't be able to. He persisted, coming by to the hotel until I relented and said, "Ok, give me their number."

I phoned and was invited to dinner the coming Thursday. Their name was Dichter. The family consisted of Grandfather Dichter, his wife, their daughter, her husband, and their children, one of whom was Issak, a young man my age. Five languages were spoken at their dinner table: Spanish, English, Russian, Yiddish and Polish. Knowing two, Yiddish and English, I was able to follow the conversation. They were far from observant Jews. At one party to which I was invited there was a baked full-sized pig with an apple in its mouth on the table. The party was lovely, with plentiful food and drink and Mariachi and dance bands that played alternate sets.

It turned out that Señor Dichter was from the same town in Russia where my father was born. He knew my Grandfather and knew of my father though had never met him. Señor Dichter had a sister in Brooklyn who, second surprise, was my sister Clara's landlady. Small world. They were a lovely family, and it became a Thursday night ritual. Señor Dichter insisted I come this one Sunday and even though I said I couldn't, he was adamant. He wanted me to meet his niece from Mexico City for a possible match. "Matchmaker, Matchmaker."

I didn't go and he was furious though I continued to be invited. From then on Señor Dichter addressed me through his grandson never talking directly to me as I had disobeyed him as he felt that since my parents weren't here, he was responsible for me. The biggest point was there weren't many eligible Jewish young men. Then there were only eighty Jewish families in Mexico City.

Crossroads: who knows where my life would have taken me if I had gone that Sunday. I might have married this niece and settled in Mexico City and worked in Señor Dichter's building supplies factory. Can you imagine that? I can't.

One Thursday dinner I expressed my fondness of a painting on their living room wall. The next day it was delivered to my hotel. I was stunned. I sent it back as I couldn't accept such an expensive gift. Only after explaining that by my accepting it forces me to stop taking classes and get a proper job in order to send them something of equal value which would end my studying. With that he agreed to take his gift back.

Our attempt at creating a Repertory in English lasted about six weeks and disbanded with everyone going his or her own way. One of the members said, "He was going to South America to eat grass. Cows do it and survive." He forgot or didn't know that cows had two stomachs to process the grass.

Mary McAuliffe a member in the group was a teacher, wanted only to spend the summer learning acting to help her teach. She a few others and I took a bus to Acapulco. She was a devout Catholic; I suggested that we share a room to conserve our finances. She immediately squelched that idea with, "My Mother would have a heart attack if she ever found out that I shared a room with a man." She found a cheap room at a small hotel.

The next morning I got a call from one of the actors who said that Mary wasn't in her room and hadn't slept in her bed. We found her at the local police station. She went for a walk on the beach at about one a.m. and was arrested for prostitution. I couldn't believe that, knowing Mary. We rounded up the money to pay the bribe-fine and got her released. To this day I believe the charges were trumped up.

A few years later I received a phone call from Issak Dichter who was in New York and invited him to my home. We had dinner, and he played with my daughter Tani who was about three years old and that was the last I heard or saw any of the Dichter's.

Marriage and Family

In returning to the city I got a job at a drug store that had a coffee and short order counter with about twelve stools. The drugstore was across the street from the Ziegfeld Theater and that's where I met my future wife, an aspiring actress. She worked at the Ziegfeld as an usherette at night so she can see the plays and musicals. She'd come in before she'd start work for coffee, with a co-worker usherette Alba Ohms (later a working actress and director, and member of the Actors Studio).

Doris and I dated and she moved into my apartment. Well not exactly. She lived with me from Sunday to Thursday nights going home to the Bronx for Shabbos. She told her mother she was staying with her best friend Rose Ostro. Her mother, an observant Jew had buried her three husbands, all rabbis. I think her last husband was also a kosher ritual slaughterer whom she married when Doris was under a year old. He died when she was about nineteen. Doris and her older sister Ethel as well as their mother always referred to him as That Man. I leave it to you the reader to discern this strange relationship. I never knew his name other than That Man.

Doris's co-worker usherette Alba Ohms was maid of honor at our wedding by a judge at City Hall in December 1954. The judge who performed the wedding had seen too many bad actors playing judges in films. It was a hoot. He stretched out each and every word pausing between each, in singsong, "Dooooo youuuuuuu taaaake this woooman…." I couldn't stop laughing. Doris was furious with me, saying that I ruined her wedding. Alba changed her reaction from laughter to sobbing tears.

We lived in a cold-water flat on Canal and Allen Streets where I was the janitor, so my rent was low. Originally for the one room apartment where I had lived since 1951 my rent was $11.23 a month. Cold water meant that there was no hot water, heat or bath. The guy in the front apartment died, and I took it over and broke the adjoining wall that now connected the two kitchens. The rent went up to $22.46 a month.

Doris and I used the public baths further up on Allen Street which were immaculate and washed down with a germ killer after each use. The men were on one side and women on the other. The baths were individual marble enclosures. When on entering the bath you went into a marbled room section with attached showers. Each individual room was rectangular having a marble door. Inside was a place to hang your clothes, a marble bench and a marble wall with an opening separating the dressing area from the shower. The cost of ten cents was for a towel and soap. If you brought your own it was free. That's what we did, brought our own every morning winter and summer. Then I would go to make the rounds of producers and directors offices. Doris went to work in an office on 57th Street. I worked as a waiter as many aspiring actors do, for waiters were always in demand and if an audition came and it was a choice between the possibility of getting an acting job or waiting on tables, the waiters job will be the one to lose. There were always more restaurants that needed waiters then acting jobs.

In early 1955 Doris miscarried and was at Flower Fifth Hospital. I was sitting with her when her Uncle Sam arrived screaming that she was a whore. Told we had been married at City Hall he replied, "I didn't know that rabbis perform weddings at City Hall," and demanded that she have religious wedding. I said, "You want a religious wedding? You make it!" Make it he did. After the miscarriage we had our religious wedding in June of 1956, honeymooned in Montréal, Canada and Doris came back pregnant.

In 1956 someone I knew told me of a 20-gallon water heater that was free for the taking. My younger brother Lenny and I went and picked it up. I went to the public library and took out a book on plumbing and installed it. Now we had hot water in the kitchen I also took out the toilet in the new connecting apartment since we had one in the old one. I built waterproof walls and built a small low wall made of bricks that I also waterproofed with tar to hold the water in. That shower I named our Tar-B-Que pit.

One day there was a knock on my door and answering it a man in his late thirties or early forties said, "Excuse me but I heard you are an actor."

I said, "Well I want to be, as I've yet to get my first professional, (meaning Broadway) job."

"Oh" says he, "I also was told that you put in a hot water heater, may I see it."

Being proud of my accomplishment I said, "Sure come on in." I took him to where the heater was, in the other kitchen, which was now my infant daughter's room. Looking at the heater he asked, "Where did you learn how to do plumbing?"

"I took a book out at the library."

He was astounded; "You mean you learned to do this from a book at the library?"

"Isn't that where one goes to learn things?" I said.

He looked at me and said, "I'm a city plumbing inspector, and I'll be right back I want to get something from my car." I almost died, he's probably going to write me a summons and I'll have to tear it down. Then a knock at the door and he returned with a long wrench and plumbers wick, saying, "You did a great job I only want to put plumbers wick on the gas intake to make sure it doesn't leak." With that done, he left saying, "From the library, boy! Good luck kid."

On February 9, 1957, my daughter Tani was born at Flower Fifth Hospital. The water heater helped keep her room warm during the winters. At that time I was in a non-union play, which meant very little or no pay. It was a Wednesday, a matinee day. My kid brother Lenny met me at the hospital, and we went up to the delivery room. Doris wanted natural childbirth and refused to take pain blockers. When I arrived and heard what was happening, I told the doctor to give them to her. Tani resisted entering this world, even after sixteen hours of labor. They used forceps to help her out, and Tani's face was pushed in and her chin was pushed under. She was all nose with flaming red hair. I turned to Lenny and said, "I think I just won the Oscar for the Ugliest Baby born this year." The doctor said that her facial bones will return to normal in two weeks or so, and when that occurred she was beautiful and is to this day. Tani was born at 6:16 and taken off to the nursery to be cleaned and swaddled. I had to get back for the evening performance but Lenny insisted that I eat something before going back to work. We found a hamburger shop near the hospital and ordered. Lenny asked, "Are you nervous? "No," I replied. Lenny looked at me and said, "Then if you're not nervous stop putting ketchup into your coffee." It was one of the best days of my life, despite my sweet sister Mary who counted the months between our honeymoon and the birth in front of me to satisfy herself that Tani was legitimate.

I was now very worried as to how we were going to make ends meet with a new baby and another mouth to feed. Doris said something that turned out to be true. "Every child brings its own luck." and 1957 brought my first Broadway show.

In May 1957 Doris and I were in Sean O'Casey's, Red Roses for Me, when Tani was three months old, she was carried on stage making her Theatrical Debut in the riot scenes. She held by Doris, at that age they don't move around and as long as she felt her mother, she felt secure and never once cried.

Raisins and Almonds

Raisins and Almonds, was an English translation of a Yiddish play. This was done before there was an Off-Broadway or an off-off Broadway. It was a sweet play about a husband and wife and their troubles with, children, making a living, etc. Nothing earth shattering but a very good character parts for both the man and woman. I played this with Ivy Bethune a very good actress and we've been friends since. We were playing in a loft that was on the third floor walk-up in the Chelsea

District and it seated about 30 people. We normally had about 15 to 25 at each performance. This one night in came Gertrude Macy who was the stage manager for the producer, Guthrie McClintic whose wife Katherine Cornell (one of the First Lady's of the American Theater, along with Eva LaGalienne, Uta Hagan and Helen Hayes, all First Lady's). Gertrude Macy came back stage after the performance and was effusive in her praise and gave me her card with "Come see me tomorrow." The McClintic office was a busy one and I was rather excited as the play I was doing paid zilch-nothing. Here was a possibility of a paying job.

The next morning I took the subway from the Lower East Side to Uptown Manhattan to the McClintic Office. Upon entering the office there were actors seated and standing all holding and working on scripts. Walked over to the receptionist and introducing my self-said, "Miss Macy had asked me to come by." She phoned the inner office and said, "Please sit, after Miss Macy is through with her appointments she wants to see you." Sitting there and watching these actors one by one going in, I thought why don't they give me a script to work on while waiting then I'll be able to give an intelligent reading, this I felt sure, was the reason she asked me to come in. Finally, the last actor made his exit from the inner office and I waited to be ushered in. The receptionist, a very pretty young girl answered an inner office beep and said, "You can go in now."

Sitting behind her desk and rising as I entered was Miss Macy. "How nice of you to come, please sit down, as she shook my hand, you were so wonderful last night, It was a thrilling performance," She had said those same things the night before though nice to hear I was more interested in what she called me in for. So I interjected with, "Those actors here when I arrived were all reading scripts, obviously they're auditioning. Is there something that I'm right for in it?"

"Oh, no," she said, "there are no Jewish roles in this play."

"I don't play only Jewish characters," said I.

"Unfortunately you're not right for anything in this."

"Then I don't understand, why did you ask me to come to your office?"

"I wanted to tell you how wonderful you were."

"You told me that last night, do you know that it cost me a nickel to take the subway here and another nickel to go back? I have a baby at home and that dime would buy food for her. It's not that I don't appreciate your admiring my work but a paying job is what I need, not flattery." I never heard from her again. One lesson that I've never learned was not to burn bridges.

I don't intend to be short with people but there is something in the way I speak that intimidates people. While working in Kansas City, Missouri, I was the Equity Deputy, the liaison between union and management. When there was a problem I was called upon by the actors to talk to Equity or if possible to remedy the situation. Each time I would call the producer in regards to something or other, he told me later, that he would "quake in his boots."

I was cast in a TV show on the Dumont network called Crime Photographer starring Darren McGavin. I was cast as an Under 5—meaning fewer than five lines—and the pay was for that designation. In rehearsal the director kept adding lines to my part, and when we filmed, it was a featured part. When my paycheck arrived it was for an Under 5. I phoned the office and after saying the check was wrong, was asked to come in. After asking this casting woman to please watch the kinescope and you'll see it was now a featured part, this casting lady said, "Yes I had seen it and you are right but I had only money for an under five. If we can overlook this I will make it up to you." A young actor not wanting to make waves I said "Sure." I was never cast in a Dumont show ever again. That was an AFTRA show and the American Federation of Television and Radio Artists then as now, a dreadful Union.

Another lesson, promises, promises. Get the TV salary for the character you ended up playing, not what you were originally cast for. The producers signed the contract and knows the rules. They demand the actor follow these rules and so should they.

Light Up the Sky

I was cast in a play entitled, Light Up the Sky, at a theater in Fort Lee, New Jersey. The producer was Robert Ludlum. A producer for hire, his responsibility was basically to oversee how the monies were spent; he hated it. After the dress rehearsal's final curtain on the afternoon of opening night, Ludlum called me to come off the stage and into the orchestra. All the actors had left and it was just the two of us. He looked at me and said, "If we weren't opening tonight I'd fire you, you're awful, you're terrible... the worst actor I ever hired, etc!" I was playing Sidney Black, the producer in the play, which was a lead part. To say I was devastated is putting it mildly.

I left the theater and went to an Italian restaurant nearby and was seated at a table. When the waitress arrived I ordered a martini, a shrimp cocktail, a filet mignon rare, coffee and a cannoli with the instructions to bring it all at the same time. She looked perplexed and I repeated, "I want it brought all at the same time, drink, everything!"

She did as instructed and placed everything on the table in front of me and for the next hour and a half I sat there just looking at the food and drink. Not touching or even taking as much as a sip of the Martini. The waitress came by and asked if something was wrong? No, I said, and please bring me the check. When she returned, I put some money on the table and told her, I didn't touch anything and she should take it home or do whatever and to keep the change. I then left and walked slowly back to the theater. Went to my dressing room and put on my makeup and waited for the call, "places please." I really don't remember that performance, but when the final curtain came down there was wild applause and the whole cast and I got three curtain calls. I was in my dressing room taking off my makeup Ludlum came in carrying a magnum of champagne saying, "You were wonderful! Thank you, thank you."

I looked at him and said, "Get out of my dressing room, I don't want to talk to you, you destroyed me, keep your champagne."

Then Orson Beane came in, the actor whom I didn't know, who said some lovely things and then asked, "How are you getting back to the city?"

"I'm taking the train."

"No you're not, I'm driving you."

Of course the reviews came out and one with the headline "If you came to see Mindy Carson, Paul Marin took over to the exclusion of everyone else," and more words to that effect. Mindy who had star billing didn't speak to me for two weeks as if I had written the review. We played to full houses until we closed.

I was told by Bennis Marden, another actor in the cast that one day Ludlum told his wife that he wanted to quit this job take his two young children, twelve and nine, out of school and move to the Island of Bimini in the Caribbean and write. "What," said his wife, "Are you crazy? You never even write a letter, what are you talking about? Take the kids out of school, that's crazy." Ludlum said, "I feel I can write, and I think that's what we should do. After much discussion that is what they did and the rest is history. He became a marvelous writer of intricate espionage, many best sellers, and was a mainstay on the New York Times fiction best sellers list. Some of his books were made into films (The Bourne Identity, etc.).

Paul Mann

I enrolled in Paul Mann's Actor's Workshop. I liked Paul, who was a fine teacher though he was an avowed Communist and went to Russia and Poland quite often. He was Black-listed in films and TV. He told us he had a three picture deal with Warner Brothers and had finished the first one when Jack Warner called him into his office and holding up Paul's contract tore it in half as Paul entered and said, "The film you just finished will never be shown; it'll be put up on a shelf, never to be seen. Now get off the lot." That was in the early 1950s. That ended his film career until he played the Butcher, Lazar Wolf, in the film version of Fiddler on the Roof, in 1971 for director, Norman Jewison.

In my opinion, the film was dreadful. Jewison hired Topel, an Israeli actor who played Tevye in London to great reviews. I thought he missed the boat. Topel as far as I know was a Sephardic Jew (Spanish origin or a secular Israeli) and very different then the Ashkenazi Jews who lived in the *shtetls* (tiny hamlets or ghettos), of Eastern Europe and were mostly observant Jews. In the film, I loved Leonard Fry as Motel the Tailor. In the Broadway show if I remember he played the bookseller. The original Motel was Austin Pendleton who was memorable. He and Zero played off each other to the comic limit. What a joy it was to see them on stage. For me, Fry and Mann were the best in the film. Norman Jewison the director might have Jew as part of his name but was a Christian and didn't understand the material.

Paul Mann's career as a teacher took a downward spiral due to his involvement with under-age female students. He told them in order to open their throats they should give him a blowjob and, stupidity after stupidity, he took Polaroid pictures of this. These photos found their way into some of these students' hands. They in turn got them to the press. When those photos were published in the *Village Voice*, the scandal hit the daily papers. I flew in to N.Y. from Los Angeles, where I was working on a film to have lunch with him at the Gaiety Delicatessen and offer moral support. He died shortly after that. I was always fond of Paul Mann though his politics used to piss me off when he'd spout them in class. His stupidly taking Polaroid pictures that ended up in the Village Voice, was for me, incomprehensible. Once again human frailties surface and destroy what we build.

Rita Gam and her Brother

I was at Sidney Lumet's sister Faygie's apartment for a small party. Faygie was a classmate at Daykarhanova's, Sidney a TV director was married at that time to Rita Gam. Those parties were rather sedate with discussions of theater, politics, religion, etc. Sitting on the floor against Sidney's knees was Rita. I knew Sidney and Faygie's father, Baruch Lumet as we played together on TV. They came from a very famous acting family. Rita besides being exceptionally beautiful, I thought was very bright. Later, on reflection, I realized that she hadn't said one word during the discussions. That's where I learned that when one wants to appear intellectually bright, you let the others do the talking then you seem as bright as the clever people there.

Rita and I didn't meet again until I was cast in The Frog Pond a very famous book at the time on psychiatry now written as a stage play with Mindy Carson, Betsy Von Furstenberg, Rita Gam, and others. One night while we were playing there, in this Summer Theater, Rita was supposed to make her entrance when all of a sudden in came Rita on all fours thru the fire place, sending the audience into convulsive Laughter.

In an earlier scene she had come in through the bathroom, which led the audience to wonder how long she had been in there. Her reason for these obviously wrong entrances was she couldn't find the wings. Our director was quite upset and assigned an assistant to take her by the hand to the wings and to push her on if necessary when her cue came.

Rita was from a very wealthy Main Line Philadelphia family. At Sidney's and Rita's wedding Luther Adler (who told this to me) hired four black little people walking behind him carrying a large box. Luther wore a black cape and large brimmed black hat and on command from Luther (clapping his hands together,) the box was lowered to the floor. Then these little people opened the box and took out sandwiches from the Stage delicatessen. Then they ran around to the tables, distributing them to the guests. Of course it was a sit down dinner with a number of courses.

The Gams were furious since they were against their daughter marrying into this Theatrical family in the first place. But the worst was yet to come, according to Luther Adler. The ring bearer, dressed in a Little Lord Fauntleroy outfit, walked down the aisle smiling as he was whispering to the people sitting in the aisle seats, "Fuck you, and fuck you, and fuck you too." Arriving at the rabbi and the *chupa* (the four cornered canopy) he loudly proclaimed "and fuck you too." That marriage was not made in heaven nor destined to be forever.

Then there was Rita's brother, when I helped at the Theater De Lys on Christopher Street in the Village, he was working there. The story goes that he was mentally ill and his parents hired this nurse to watch him. She was Israeli, and was offered One hundred thousand dollars to marry and take care of him. She agreed. One night she awakened with his hands around her throat attempting to strangle her. That was her last straw; she left for Israel in fear for her life. I guess that marriage was annulled or they divorced.

So his Father, the story goes, paid the Theater de Lys to hire him and paid his salary. They placed him on the lighting board as all he had to do was to follow the written cues placed in the script. I really don't know what provoked it but he literally destroyed the lighting board, with its dimmer switches et al. Obviously he wasn't kept on. Interesting family

Speaking of the Adler's, when I was in The Tenth Man, Jay Adler, brother to Luther was a replacement of one of the original cast. He told me this abhorrent story. At the turn of the Twentieth Century, men always carried their wallets in their jacket breast pockets. When he was a young man he and some friends would go downtown to the Wall Street area where there were public bathrooms. Men would use the stalls and hang their jackets on the door. In those days there were no locks, according to Jay. They would push the door in so hard that it would hit the occupant in the head stunning him while one would grab the jacket and take the wallet out of the breast pocket and throw the jacket back. He and his fellow thieves would also stand at the urinals and when a homosexual or so they thought, would stand at the connecting urinal, they would impersonate plain clothes police officers and demand money as not to arrest and bring them to the Station House for booking. These unfortunate men in order not to be part of this scandal which would ruin their lives and jobs would immediately empty their wallets and in some cases give in to Blackmail. He was so proud of this despicable behavior, thievery is what it was, and it can't be called anything else.

Off-Broadway

I was determined to get a paying play and I heard that The Theater De Lys on Christopher Street in the Village was preparing to do this play, Moon in Capricorn. I hung around and ran errands did all what was asked in expectation that if there were a supporting role or even a lesser one, they would give it to me. Unfortunately, the play didn't do well. Mr. DeLys paid me a dollar a day because I had to spend money on the subway and lunch for myself and he felt guilty for having me work there for nothing. I felt it was worthwhile for I thought that with the very next play I'd get a part. Unfortunately, Mr. DeLys sold seats to the public with their name on a plaque attached to the back of each seat, then absconded with the proceeds. The Theater DeLys was no more. Much later Lucile Lortel's husband bought it for her and renamed it The Lucile Lortel Theater.

I did Shakespeare's Othello at the Cherry Lane Theater, also in the Village; directed by an English professor from Brooklyn College who really should remain nameless. He knew his Shakespeare but he didn't know theater or directing. We got terrible reviews and closed shortly after we opened.

Then I did a play, The Silver Cord by Sidney Kingsley at the Provincetown Playhouse, also in the Village. This production and I were terrible. I was working as a counter man in a drugstore on 6th Avenue making things like ham, tuna, egg sandwiches, malteds, coffee etc. when in comes a customer and sits down at the counter. We started to chat and he said he saw the worst production of a play he ever had seen. Every thing about it was awful including the actors. Oh, said I, what play was that? The Silver Cord, said he. I thought about it for a few seconds and then said, "I'm in that play," he sat there nonplussed not knowing what to say. He rapidly finished his sandwich and coffee and made a quick exit. One has to learn somewhere.

There wasn't an Off-Broadway yet, that came later when Geraldine Page opened in Tennessee Williams, Summer and Smoke, at the Circle in the Square Theater on Seventh Ave South in Greenwich Village. She created a sensation for when it had played on Broadway it was a flop. During that time period I was in a play, "He Who Gets Slapped," by Andreov, with Robert Culp. We opened at The Actors Playhouse across the street from the Circle in the Square Theater. Culp was wonderful. Culp, later became famous for the TV show, "I Spy," starring both Culp and Bill Cosby. Now with two hit shows in Greenwich Village the critics came, That started Off Broadway Theater. Culp was wonderful. Now with the playing of two hit plays in Greenwich Village that received excellent notices, the critics took notice and that was the real beginning of Off-Broadway.

On opening day, we had bought seats from a movie theater that was refurbishing. I was screwing in the seats into a cement floor with cement screws. The rent for that theater was $105 a month. Last I heard back in the 1990s, The Actors Playhouse was renting for $7000 a week.

In the late 1950s Off-Broadway was ruined for aspiring actors when Franchot Tone, one of the founders and financial backer of the Actors Studio. Tone was a film star who the off-Broadway producers paid $100 a week while the off Broadway actors at that time were making $35 a week for eight performances.

That brought in all the unemployed Hollywood names. Off-Broadway was established with the primary reason that unknown actors could draw attention and be hired for Broadway shows where the pay was a hell of a lot better.

Broadway

The Great Moss Hart & Fair Game

My first Broadway show was rather a fluke. I was reading the morning New York Times, where I saw in the inner pages on theatrical news in a one-inch announcement that a Play had been optioned by the production company of Moss Hart and Joe Hyman called Fair Game, written by Sammy Locke. That was the total extent of the announcement. Being young and very inexperienced I looked in the Phone Book for the offices of Hyman & Hart and mailed in my 8x10 photo and promptly forgot about it. Then about two months later I received a phone call asking me to come to the office for an interview. I was in an off-off-off Broadway show at this time; I was performing in Sean O'Casey's Red Roses for Me. I was playing an Orange Man, a Protestant in Northern Ireland. The play was Red Roses for Me, by Sean O'Casey. I grew a Hessian Beard for the character I was playing. It was at The Stella Adler Studio in Manhattan.

Going to the Hyman & Hart interview as I entered into the inner office, sitting there was producer, Joe Hyman, stage manager Porter Van Zandt and Author Sammy Locke. Joe Hyman after Porter introduced me looked at me quizzically and said. "You're so young; from your photo I thought you were much older." I replied, "Give me a reading."

Mr. Hyman replied, "You are much too young. Thanks for coming in."
Sammy Locke said, "That's an interesting beard; I had one just like it
when I was in Africa."

I learned that when you wanted something from someone you let
the person interviewing you talk. When a lull occurs, you try to cue
them into continuing. That person then thinks this guy is a wonderful
conversationalist. After about ten or so minutes Sammy Locke turned
to Joe Hyman and said, "Give the kid a reading."

Joe Hyman looked at him, "What for? He's too young."

"What is it, five minutes? Give the guy a reading." Mr. Hyman
finally relented, and said we'll call you and I left figuring that's the end
of that.

About six weeks later another phone call to come to the Plymouth
Theater for a reading and to come to the office to pick up a script. Now
no cast list had been made public. I get to the office and the part I was
to read was for the lead. I told Doris that the part they wanted me to
audition for was the lead, I who never had a Broadway show. Doris
said, "You go read what they want you to read, and if you get the job
you'll do it." This was very practical advice. I went to audition on a
bare stage of the Longacre Theater, with only the work light on and
finishing the reading heard from the darkened orchestra, "Thank you."
As I was walking to the wings to leave, the next actor to audition was
ushered in by Porter.

This was repeated, five times over as many months. The last time I
read was with Shirley Ballard, an actress, who said to me, as I walked on
stage and stood on her left side, she pulled me over to the her right side,
saying, "I already have the job, they can see you better on the right side."
What a wonderful thing for her to do, so unselfish. After finishing the
reading, once again I heard "Thank you." I crossed in front of Shirley
and walking again into the wings I wondered, what is this game they're

playing? When the second part of their thank you penetrated my brain, "We're gonna use you, come to the office tomorrow to sign contracts."

I was already off the stage and in the wings. I had used a big fat cigar for the audition and it was clamped in my teeth and I laughed with hysterical joy, all the way to and in the subway. People passing must have thought I was a madman. Stopping at 14th Street station, which had a public phone on the platform, I called my wife and then my mother to tell them the good news. The next day I was told my job was to Understudy Sam Levene who was playing the lead and to play the Waiter in the third act. I was disappointed for I really wanted the lead part, but consolation, I got my first Broadway show.

Fellow actors warned me that Sam Levene was a very tough actor to play with. His reputation was that of a very good actor and a bastard. I found that this was nonsense, as he was a very nice man and out-of-town in Philadelphia, every night after work we would go to Bookbinders for something to eat and became friends.

Sam Levene was starring and his co-star was Ellen McRae, (later Ellen Burstyn). She later was elected President of Actors Equity, Oscar and Tony winner and star, plus being an exceptionally good actor. Our out-of-town tryout opened in Philadelphia at the Forest Theater. That theater was extraordinary, it was built without dressing rooms for the actors to change into and out of their costumes or put on their make-up. A house was bought across the alley where a tunnel was built to use during inclement weather or to run across in the spring and summer. Whoever the architect was, a theater architect he sure wasn't.

Our first director Paul Roberts was a fish out of water, for he was a TV commercials director, and it was bantered about that he was Ellen's boyfriend. Every time our director, got lost and wasn't sure what to do next, he sat in the empty theater about 15 or so rows back from the stage, he would put up his hand and say, "take five." Then Paul Roberts lifted a brown paper bag and took a drink.

Robert Weber, a featured member of the cast, standing behind Roberts, a few seconds prior to Paul's raising his hand saying the magical "take five." Weber anticipating Roberts being lost would raise his hand with the five fingers extended pantomiming take five.

We opened without ever rehearsing or blocking the third act. We actors not knowing where to move made sure that we didn't bump into each other or the furniture'

Needless to say, Roberts on opening night right after the final curtain was fired. Then we heard, more drama, for he threatened to jump out of his hotel room window. Moss Hart who was the other half of Hyman and Hart, at the highpoint of his career for he had directed My Fair Lady, which as we all know, was a smash hit, came to rescue their investment.

Mary Alice Bayh and I met in 1957 at the first rehearsal of Fair Game. It was my, also Mary Alice's and Ellen McRae's, first Broadway show. Ellen had co-star billing with Sam Levene. Sara Cunningham wife of John Randolph was also in the cast and a wonderful woman. Sara, a good cook, Mary Alice, Sally Gracie and I would on Sundays eat in Sara's hotel room as Philadelphia in 1957 was a Blue Law state. Nothing was open: no room service, no restaurants, no stores, and no playing games of any sort. Sunday was a church day. So we shopped on Saturday between matinee and evening performances for food to be eaten on Sunday.

The very next morning we were all assembled on stage sitting in a semi circle. I was sitting next to Sally Gracie (who was then married to Rod Steiger) when walking in from the wings was this man radiating success, who looked as if he was dipped in gold. His suit appeared to have been sewn on him, his face a burnished tan. I whispered to Sally, who is that? She looked at me as if I was slightly addled and said "That's Moss Hart our producer and now obviously our new director. Walking to the center of our semi-circle, saying "Good Morning," he told us that he will redirect and be prepared for new scenes to be handed out and rehearsed that afternoon while playing the old scene that night but putting the new ones in the next day and that will be the procedure.

The very next morning he called us all together again and called the names of four of the ladies in the play to meet with him in the lobby. Mary Alice was one of the four. Saying he did some rewrites and handed them out.

Fair Game took place in a furrier's office and showroom. It had four beautiful actress's playing models. Moss told the four ladies that he had written them out, but not to leave Philadelphia as he wanted to see if his cuts worked. Needless to say Mary Alice Bayh, (sister of Indiana Senator Birch Bayh), being a first timer like myself came directly to me from the lobby to commiserate. She was in tears. Her first Broadway show and she was written out. Comforting her I said, "Come on, in this business, this is an every day occurrence and it had nothing to do with her acting as she was quite good."

"You don't understand," she retorted. "We in the business know that happens in new plays out of town, but what will I tell my psychiatrist? He says that every thing that happens to us, we bring upon ourselves. We know that's not so, as there are many variables that we have no control over," and a new flood of tears erupted.

Moss handed out the new scenes, we rehearsed them that day and played the old version that night. The next day the new scenes were in. Moss came back stage, and we were told a rehearsal was called for 10 a.m. The next morning after all assembled, Moss came on stage, brought back the four ladies he cut and said, "Ladies and Gentlemen, I had a dream last night, God called the Archangel Michael to him and asked, 'By the way, where is Moss Hart?'

'He's in Philadelphia,' replied the Archangel. 'He's rescuing a new play and doing magnificent work. His rewrites are brilliant. He fired four of the woman. Oh, he's such a major talent. Just what Fair Game needed. He's a genius.'

'Really!' said God.'" Moss raised his middle finger and said, as God, "Give it to him."

"People," Moss continued, "I've been got. Ladies you are now back in the play, as the brilliance I infused did not work. The play makes no sense with out you. New rewrites will be handed out. The same procedure I outlined yesterday will be followed. We shall rehearse the new scenes by day and do the old version that night and the new scene will be put in the next night."

Then turning to Ellen, Moss said, "Let's rehearse this scene where you're in the showroom of the fur shop. Since we have very little time, I'll show you what I want. With that he takes the mink coat that Ellen would be wearing places it onto his shoulders, takes it off and throws it on the stage couch. The mink just opens in a flair covering the couch. Then gracefully he falls down with his back on top of it. He gets up, hands the coat to Ellen for her to do it. She looked at Moss and sarcastically said, "You do that much better than I. Why don't you play the part?"

The whole company on stage and in the house watching was shocked by her talking to the great Moss Hart that way, especially since this was her Broadway debut. Everyone was waiting to see what would happen. Moss being the gentleman he was, looked at her and said, "We really don't have the time for that. I'm sure you'll do it beautifully."

The office of Hyman and Hart got their revenge. During the run Ellen was offered a film in Hollywood for six weeks. Ellen went to see

Joe Hyman to ask to be allowed to take the six weeks off for the shoot, and then return to the show when the film was finished. Joe asked what she was getting paid for this. She said $60,000. He said that's a lot of money (it was 1957); all right you can go but what I want to release you for the six weeks is $100,000. Ellen replied, I just told you I was getting $60,000. Yes, Joe said, I heard you, and you get the point, don't you! There are very few secrets in the theater and it was repeated many times.

The first time I saw a mink-lined raincoat I was watching rehearsals in the audience and in came Moss's wife, Kitty Carlyle Hart wearing this raincoat. And she promptly opened it and turning around and around again, modeling it for those there saying, "I brought my mink to the furrier to get it Hollanderized," a process, used then that brings the life back to older furs. The furrier said to her, "Why bother, this fur isn't worth spending money on it, instead leave it with me and bring me your raincoat. I'll line it with the mink fur. It was the very first one in the city. A mink-lined raincoat.

Joe Hyman was very fair to me, as this was my debut on the Broadway stage and I was hired as understudy and as the Waiter in the third Act where as I said, had three lines. When I went to his office to sign the contract, I was being paid minimum, my salary $85 a week for eight performances. At the signing, Joe said, I was told you're married and have an infant, if we're successful I shall give you a raise."

Well I can't say we were successful but we were running. After a few weeks I called the office to speak to Mr. Hyman to request a raise. On arrival to the office (this happened twice) he took me to the public bathroom on their office floor and he stood at a urinal and urinated. I stood at the back wall of this john, each time looking at his back and very embarrassed. Both times he gave me a $50 a week raise. I guess he hated giving raises it was like he was pissing money away, my Freudian interpretation.

Opening night Joe Hyman and Moss Hart hired a makeup man to do Ellen's makeup. Ellen came out of her back stage dressing room in the St. James Theater for the "places please," call. Ellen was stunning. As I was passing Ellen's dressing room, an obvious flamboyantly gay makeup man, followed her out, he stopped out side of her dressing room. As Ellen headed towards the wings, I coming down the stairs from my fifth floor closet, read dressing room, no window, no sink, and worst of all no air conditioning. This make-up man said, to no one in particular, "Why do I get the dogs to do? You should have seen her before I did her. What terrible eyes." He said with an effeminate lisp and swinging his hands in the air.

Sally Gracie was from Little Rock, Arkansas and had a lovely soft accent and was obviously having difficulties with Rod Steiger, as he would fly in from Hollywood to see her. She loudly proclaimed in front of everyone backstage, "Rodney go back to Hollywood. I want a divorce."

Steiger pleaded, "Oh Sally, I love you and want you."

"Really?? Then who is Claire Bloom? I don't want to see you. I want a divorce." One Saturday night after the performance Rod was waiting at the stage door. As I came out he said "Paul, let's go to Downey's." Downey's was a bar and restaurant on 8th Avenue where working actors went after their shows. Stars generally went to Sardi's. "Sally will meet us there," he said.

We were having some food and drink when a very pretty girl came over to the table and sat next to Rod. I was asking her what she wanted to eat or drink when Rod picked her hand up onto the table top and said "Paul tell your friend to keep her hands to herself." I was astonished, "My friend? I thought she was your friend!" With that Jim Downey was called over and the girl was escorted out. Because Rod was a big film star all she had to do was claim molestation and any judge would assume that he had taken advantage of her. He could be sued: the price of fame.

For Fair Game I had to use the bathroom on the fourth floor for making up and putting on my costume. I was only an understudy with three lines. In 1957 only the starring actors, Sam and Ellen had air conditioning. Of course the audience had a/c and when the curtain was raised in came a blast of cool air that made the stage comfortable to play on, though the cold air did not go up to the dressing rooms: only hot air rises.

One summer night it was so stifling up in my closet that I brought my costume down to stage level to change. Porter Van Zandt, the stage manager, came running over with "What are you doing? You can't dress here. Go up to your dressing room."

"No," I said, "I don't even have a fan up there and it's so hot one can fry an egg." Porter said he'd see if they can get a fan. Promises, promises. "Really" I said, "until there is one I'll stay down here." In ten or so minutes a fan materialized and was brought up to the closet.

Returning from Philly, on the bus to New York we had a betting pool where we all put in a dollar, as to how long this turkey would last. Every one wanted 'closing in one night,' numbers were put into a hat. I being the last to pick, disappointingly, got number nine that turned out surprisingly, to be the Winner. We opened to lukewarm reviews, except Ellen and Levene. She got Richard Watts of the New York Post. Watts fell in love with her beauty and devoted his complete column to her. The play was practically ignored. On the strength of Levene's reviews however we ran nine months. So the nine I picked and the nine months made me the winner. My wife Doris, who came to Philly to watch the closing night performance, rode back to New York on the bus with the cast, whispered to me. "Don't worry, you got this show, you'll get another one. This play is very bad it will close opening night."

As a prophetess, Doris was no sibyl. Opening night on Broadway was mainly with an invited audience; the play took off and came to partial life. Sam was on and excellent. Later Doris said, "This wasn't the play she saw in Philadelphia." It was the fact we were on Broadway, which in itself affects all actors who tread the boards here. It's that unknown quality, knowing this is the pinnacle of the acting profession and brings out the best in all.

On opening night my brother-in-law Bill and sister Mary came and when the final curtain came down, Bill ran up the stairs to my closet and on entering proclaimed, "Kid, I knew you'd make it." After all those years when I was studying acting and working as a waiter, Bill with his ritual of "Why are you sacrificing, I can get you a job at John Hancock." Later when remembered, "Kid, I knew you'd make it." I would laugh as I had only three lines and had to take off my make-up in a toilet on the fourth floor.

An aside: Diana Millay one of the beautiful actresses in Fair Game had an unwanted admirer, Tommy Manville, sole heir to the asbestos fortune. He had the same seat in the front row at the evening performances. Every night flowers were sent to Diana, which she had instructed the stage doorman to send to Roosevelt Hospital. There were bracelets of emeralds and diamonds sent to Diana that she refused to accept. Tommy had already been married and divorced 13 times and it was said that one marriage lasted a huge seven minutes. One evening before a performance a visitor came back stage to Diana's dressing room. It was Mrs. Tommy Manville the eighth. She brought a proposition. Tommy wanted to marry Diana or at least sleep with her for one night and he was willing to give her $100,000 if she would agree. Then she said, "Oh Honey, it's the easiest and fastest money you'll ever make.

Number Eight then said, "Tommy lies in a glass-covered coffin and all have to do is straddle the glass cover and defecate for the money." With that Diana, now in fury said, "Leave my dressing room immediately or I'll call the police, and if you or anyone else of the Manville group bother me again I'll have all of you arrested for pimping." I must confess that I wasn't there but it was bandied about openly back stage. In contrast to Paddy's morality, good for you Diana!

During the run I learned two very important lessons. One day Sam after a scene he played with Robert Webber and Jason Evers. Asked me what I thought. I was naïve enough and inexperienced not to know better. When an actor in your cast asks for the truth of himself and those in the scene acting with him you never tell what you think. I told him. I saw immediately that it was a mistake and never did that again. They only want to hear compliments.

Then there was an episode that taught me a greater lesson. One of the actresses told the stagehands and I who was also there, that she had slept with Sam the night before. Then she put up her hand with only the small finger extended then with her other hand pantomimed by bringing the index finger of the other hand across the little finger cutting it in half as to the size of Sam's penis. True or not, the stagehands roared. That taught me never, never to screw where I eat.

On our closing night we were invited to a closing night party being given by Stella Adler. I think she was Ellen's teacher. Stella borrowed a Park Avenue penthouse and gave the party there. There were a number of her male students as I heard that she showed preference to the male students and was very difficult with the females.

Stella sat on a couch and these young men sat on the floor around her feet while she held court. She favored décolletage dresses that just about held in her breasts. The cut was so low you thought her bosoms would explode out of her dress and her nipples would fire away. Stella was known for her low cut dresses.

Now this had been my first Broadway show and I stationed my self near the table with the food. I just kept stuffing my mouth when Doris came over. "Get away from that table," she whispered. "You're acting as if you never ate." I looked at her "I feel this was my last job and like a squirrel I'm stocking it away for I'll probably never work again." Later I learned that all actors feel that way when their shows close.

Sammy Locke the author of Fair Game and I became close friends. Sammy's sister Katherine Locke was married to the writer and director Norman Corwin, when I worked in Los Angeles Sammy and I met often. One night Lynn Wood and I were one of six couples invited to a dinner party at Sammy's house. Buddy Hackett the comic was also there. Now comedians are a different breed. They are bottomless pits and need to be filled with attention of everyone all their waking hours. At this dinner the conversation like all normal dinner parties was the latest show business gossip, politics, relationships etc. Hackett wasn't content so before we sat down to eat he got up and literally started to pound on the wall for attention. When asked to stop and sit down he continued to demand attention until Sammy said "Buddy why don't you go home" and he left miffed. As I said, "Comics are a different breed."

Tyrone Guthrie

In 1959 my agent sent me to an audition The Tenth Man, a new play by Paddy Chayefsky. I arrived at the Variety Arts Studios on 47th Street between Broadway and 8th Avenue in New York. The stage manager David Cantor came out of the audition room to where a few other actors sat waiting to be called. He had a list and checks off the new arrivals. When it was my turn, I followed the stage manager who introduced me to a man sitting in a straight back chair at an old kitchen table. "Dr. Tyrone Guthrie, this is Paul Marin." I walked to the table and put my right hand out to shake. Dr. Guthrie started to stand. He was six foot seven, but I didn't know. I saw that my hand was in the vicinity of his crotch. He continued to rise and I raised my hand too, but the proximity of my hand to his crotch remained the same. Now I was flustered. When he reached his full height he said, "Please sit down and tell me about yourself." I was so embarrassed and thrown that my brain went into self-destruct. My mind was totally blank. Trying to save the audition and get this job I said, "Let me read my resume."

"No dear boy," said Guthrie in his trilled British accent, "I want to hear the timber of your voice." Again I said, "Let me read my resume." He looked at me, then stood and said "Thank you for coming in."

I walked out cursing myself and kicking myself down Broadway. I was disgusted with myself for screwing up the audition. I cursed myself to the subway and all the way home. Well, I thought, there goes the possibility of working with one of, if not the greatest director in the English-speaking world of his day.

A few days later I got a call from the stage manager that I was hired. Unbeknownst to me Guthrie loved it when people were intimidated by his height. My hand in his crotch area must have convulsed him. If I had known I probably wouldn't have gotten the job for I would have tried to play it. I later learned that Guthrie doesn't read actors. He talks with them.

Rehearsals for The Tenth Man were indeed an eye-opener. The first day the whole cast assembled on the stage sitting in a circle, ready to read the play out loud, each character reading his part. In walks Dr. Guthrie saying, "Hello everyone, I assume you all know how to read so we'll dispense with the reading of the play so let's get on with the blocking." The chairs were removed and down to work.

He had brought a Jewish actor, Arnold Marley to play the old rabbi.

Marley had escaped to London from Hitler's Europe. Gene Saks a fine actor who later became famous as the director of Neil Simon's plays on Broadway played the young rabbi. Arnold had worked for Guthrie before in London where he had played in Shakespeare's Coriolanus. The rest of the cast was George Voscovec, also a refugee, from Prague, Czechoslovakia. Jacob Ben Ami, Lou Jacobi, Jack Gilford, Donald Herron, David Vardi, Alan Manson, Paul Marin, Tim Callaghan, Martin Garner and the only girl Risa Schwartz, who was the daughter of the famous great Yiddish theater star, producer/actor Maurice Schwartz. Marty Garner who created the role of the 82 year old man (the part I later took over when Marty quit the show) was quite a character.

One day during rehearsals at the Amsterdam Roof Theater Marty started to shake and silently tears began to roll down his cheeks. What's the matter I asked? He said, didn't you see someone go onto the stage and give David Canter, the stage manager a pink piece of paper, that we sitting 40 feet away Marty knew was a pink slip meant for him as he was being fired. Of course it wasn't so but that was Marty Garner.

On opening night after the performance, Maurice Schwartz stood out side of Risa's dressing room door shouting, "Risa, come on, I'm tired of waiting." The next day I asked her what her father had said as she was the only woman in the cast and actually one of the lead players. She said "Nothing, not a word about the play or her performance." My interpretation: a cruel, egotist and jealous father.

The Tenth Man takes place in a synagogue. Arnold Marley, in one scene being rehearsed had these lines. "Halleluiah, Halleluiah, Halleluiah, Oh, here are the cookies." Guthrie had directed him to be at the lectern and sing three Halleluiah's and then find the cookies in the lectern's lower shelf.

Arnold, the only actor in the company who called Guthrie "Tony" called from the stage, "Tony, I've an idea may I try it."

"Of course," came the voice from the back of the house.

With that Arnold started singing Halleluiah while turning in large concentric circles, crossing the stage from the audience's right stage to stage left in religious fervor repeating the Halleluiahs. Just before he reached the bookcase on the left wall Arnold tripped and fell against it exclaiming, "Ah, here are the cookies."

Running onto the stage Guthrie exclaimed, "Arnold, that dear boy was wonderful," then Guthrie lifted his left hand to his chest level, and slapping his wrist with his right hand and in a loud voice, exclaimed "Tish Tosh, that is so much better then I had thought of. I wasn't doing my homework. Of course dear boy, let's keep that."

I have been in many plays and worked with many directors since, and not one American director would ever say something like that. I think their ego's get in the way.

Then there was David Vardi an Israeli actor who played the Sexton, didn't speak one word of English, his wife who he brought along acted as his interpreter. He learned the part phonetically.

Arthur Canter was the press representative during The Tenth Man. One day in rehearsal Arthur came and sat next to me in the Amsterdam Roof Theater. I was sitting watching, Arthur asked me if I understood Vardi's English. I was thinking about that too, but unwilling to bad-mouth another actor I said, "Don't worry. We still have to go out of town." Before we come in to New York he'll be fine, I thought. When we opened at the Booth on Broadway David Vardi got rave reviews. He was adorable. The critics and audiences loved him.

While The Tenth Man was out of town in Philadelphia, I received a phone call from director Morton Da Costa to join his production of The Wall. The Tenth Man had Paddy Chayefsky and Tyrone Guthrie; The Wall, starred Herbert Berghof, husband of Uta Hagan and partner in their acting school. I decided to stay where I was and lucked out.

The Wall ran 167 performances or about five months while The Tenth Man ran two years.

Once, at the Forest Theater in Philadelphia, I was watching rehearsals and sitting next to Mrs. Guthrie. She's was 6' 4" tall and wore the same plaid fabric as Tyrone, only hers a jacket and skirt and his of course jacket and pants. While we were sitting there, a five-minute break was called. Now we could talk, so I asked her, "Where did Dr. Guthrie get his doctorate?" She said, "It was an honorary doctorate, actually he has two and really should be called 'Doctor Doctor,' but that's a bit ostentatious don't you think?" So very British.

About nine months into the run of The Tenth Man, Marty Garner who created the role of Harris quit. Marty was David Vardi's understudy for the part of the Sexton and thought he'd never get to play it, as Vardi was strong and healthy. A few weeks after Marty Garner had left David Vardi became ill and as my wife Doris and I were sitting down to dinner the phone rang. It was Arthur Cantor the stage manager who said, "Vardi is ill and I know you're not his understudy, and since Marty left there wasn't an understudy for the Sexton and since you're never on stage at the same time, you are the only member of the company who can play your own part and the part of the Sexton at the same time. If you decide not to do it we will have to cancel tonight's performance and possibly a few more until we can find someone who will play it."

"Arthur that's not fair to make me responsible for the curtain to go up, I'm not Vardi's understudy." "It's up to you," said Arthur. Now I'm feeling responsible for we don't get paid for cancelled performances and monies will have to be refunded to the audiences, so I said, "Ok, I'll come at once.

I lived very close to the East River and as I walked to the subway I thought if I go right I'll jump into the East River and if I go left to the subway and the Booth Theater. I was terrified. Was pinned into Vardi's costume and his part was made easier as his scenes were separated by intervals of ten or more minutes, so I learned each scene prior to going on. Changing from his costume and make-up to mine to play my own part and back again a number of times that night. That lasted a full Eight performance and then was asked play it and play my own part of Harris while he was ill and to be his understudy. Paddy was very nice and said he'd take me out to dinner as payment. I laughed and said, "Oh no. It will have to be a raise in salary." And so it was.

When we did our Actors Fund performance and I playing only my part of Harris and when the curtain came down to wild applause. This audience is like no other as its all with our peers out front from all the other Broadway shows sitting there. I'm in my dressing room when the back stage doorman shouts up the stairwell to me that Bette Davis wants to come up to see me. I laughed and said "Sure send her up," thinking it was a friend playing around. Miss Davis was playing in the Tennessee Williams play, The Night of the Iguana. There is a knock at my dressing room door and I call out "Come in." It was Bette Davis holding an autograph book that she asked me to sign. She was a collector and said that she loved my performance. Flattered is not the word, I was flying high to think that Bette Davis that great star of film and stage walked up four flights for me to sign her autograph book.

The Tenth Man slowed, and we knew this wonderful play, in which, most nights, it was a joy to act, would close, and we would be on the unemployment line once again. I don't think I met an actor who didn't wonder if that was his 'real last' job. I'm on the line waiting to swear to the state that I looked for work so I could collect unemployment insurance when I see Alan Manson coming into the unemployment office. As he gets closer I see he's crying; tears are rolling down his face.

"Alan...what's the matter?"

"My wife died this morning."

"What?! I don't understand.... What are you doing here?"

"I had to do something normal." The tears were really coming now.

"Alan, Alan," and I put my arms around him. I feel terrible for you. Oh my condolences. Alan can I do anything?"

"No! No! Thank you. I'll be fine." If a writer had put that in a film, people would say, come on, never! I knew then that this is one of the moments in life that not only will I never forget but also one that I often remember.

A few weeks after The Tenth Man closed the phone rang and my wife answered it. She puts her hand over the speaker end and says, "It's Tyrone Guthrie." "Sure," I say, thinking its one of my friends playing a joke, and pick up the phone, "Hello."

The voice on the other end says, "Paul Marin? This is Tony Guthrie, are you engaged for coming season?"

"No," I say, having recognized his trilled R.

"You are now. I'm on my way to Brookline, and I'll drop off the script. Be there in half an hour."

"No. That's not necessary," I said. "Tell me where to meet you and I'll pick it up."

"No, dear boy. I'll be passing your house and will see you soon. Ta ta." Immediately I told Doris to go to the bakery and buy some cakes. I set the coffee up and arranged things in the Living room. Doris returned and while prettying the table there was a knock on the door. Here was Tyrone Guthrie at the door. He hands me a manila envelope while I'm saying, "Come in."

"No, no dear boy, I'm in a bit of a rush, See you in the fall, ta ta," and he was gone.

One day I was walking on Broadway when I see Tyrone Guthrie,

"Paul Marin," with his trilled R's, he says "so good to see you. Tell me where can I find a European Barber Shop?" Not knowing what he was looking for, "What do you mean, European Barber Shop?" I asked. He said, "You know, where they charge one dollar for a haircut." I then understood and told him that on 42nd Street was a Barber School and he said "Right" and "Ta Ta" and headed that way. Not that he was cheap, but he never bought cigarettes. He would just put out his arm and open two fingers of his hand till someone put a cigarette in it.

Broadway Camaraderie

The Booth Theater was next to the Shubert Theater in Shubert Alley. The Shubert Theater had a larger house and played mainly Musicals. There was a connecting staircase leading to the backstage area of both theaters. That where I met Valerie Harper and Arlene Golunka. We would sit on the stairs and talk waiting for our cues in our respective productions. Valerie was in Take Me Along and we became fast friends. The Tenth Man played two years and closed in June 1961.

Valerie became a star on television with the "Mary Tyler Moore Show" and then as "Rhoda." On stage, she played Golda Meier and in 2008 played Tallulah Bankhead at the Pasadena Playhouse; she was astounding. Going back stage to see Valerie after her performance, she was surrounded by a number of people that had gone back stage, as soon as she saw me she screamed "Paul," broke away and came running throwing her arms about me with a big hug.

A reporter acquaintance I knew had interviewed her one morning a few months before, and my name came up. In 2005, on a trip I took to China, I was on a ship that traversed the Three Gorges. I met this reporter, and it turned out we live very close to one another in West Los Angeles.

I get a phone call from this reporter to meet him that day at Marie Callendar's for lunch. Unbeknownst to me, in he walks and trailing behind him is Valerie. What a joy! And a very big surprise. It's very typical of people in the entertainment business, we might have not seen each other in years but after the initial reaction of hugs and kisses the warmth and screams, etc. it was as if we have seen each other just yesterday and the friendship is picked up immediately. Back to Tallulah, I said to her if she could come to see Marin at Marie Callendar's then Marin could go to Pasadena to see Harper and we both laughed. Besides being a marvelous talent she is a wonderful human being.

Interlude: A Visit to Cuba

I had been asked by a cast member of The Tenth Man if I wanted to house-sit in Mexico in the town of Taxco, made famous for its silver filigree jewelry. A writer friend of his who owned this house had gotten a contract to go to London, England to work for the BBC for the summer. In Taxco the house had a staff—cook, gardener, etc.—but wanted someone to be there so it wouldn't be looted. I readily said yes and booked passage on a Spanish registry passenger ship leaving for Vera Cruz, Mexico stopping in Havana, Cuba for three days.

Arriving at the dock on 45th Street in Manhattan and boarded the ship. This was early June 1961. After settling in my compartment I went on deck. There, hundreds of ex-patriot Cubans were on deck unfurling a massive red flag with hammer and sickle over the side facing the city. We were still at the dock in Manhattan. They were all shouting "Cuba, Si! Yankee, No!"

It seems they were actually two hundred Cubans most had been residents in the U.S. and were voluntarily giving up their alien papers and a few native born U.S. citizens of Cuban ancestry who also were giving up their citizenship. Their leader was a native born Chicagoan who collected all these people and was going to Cuba to help Fidel Castro build his communist utopia, this was a few weeks after the Bay of Pigs invasion by the anti-Castro Cubans who were living in the U.S.

Standing there and watching this spectacle I was introduced to the leader. After we sailed I was in the bar when in he came with a few of the others. After a few drinks were exchanged I asked him if it was possible for me to go into Havana. I told him I was an actor and just closed on Broadway in Paddy Chayefsky's play called The Tenth Man and was booked for the next Paddy Chayefsky play entitled Gideon, with Frederic March to go into rehearsal in October. He was duly impressed as he knew of Paddy and had seen Frederic March in many films. March had been a stage and film star since 1927.

I told him, "I come with an open mind and heart," and I wanted to take advantage of being in Havana and see for myself. He said he'd make inquires and let me know as it was three days away before we reached Cuba. These ex-patriots were a lively crew with much drink and song. The next day I was paged to go to the purser's desk and there was the leader (sorry, I can't recall his name) who said he'd been in touch with the Cuban State Department and they said "No." I replied that I'm an actor not a politician.

The rest of the trip was uneventful and we docked a mile out of the port of Havana. There was an interesting live picture. The statue of Christ with open outstretched arms on a hill in Havana Harbor while nestled underneath these arms was a large Russian freighter with the hammer and sickle flag unfurled. I sent that photo to Newsweek and Time magazine who replied that they only publish photos from professional photographers. What nonsense!

Now that we were in the harbor I'm once again paged and told that if I still wanted to see Havana I was welcome to enter Cuba. I was given my passport and told to wait for a launch. The gangplank was lowered and from a Cuban motor launch up came four young boys between twelve and fourteen year olds carrying Russian machine guns. Two boys walked in front of me and two behind me down the gangplank to the launch. They proudly said that their machine guns could fire six hundred rounds a minute better then the American machine guns.

A Mexican Army Captain was shouting at me from the deck 'Not to go as they can throw me into a prison and that Cuba has no diplomatic relations with the U.S. I yelled back that I'm coming with an open heart and open mind and why would they want to do that? We were seated in the motor launch and sailed into the Immigration building dock. All marble and was then taken into an Ionesco marble waiting room with marble walls and marble benches. No pictures on the walls or any other adornments. I was left to sit there with the Mexican Captain's words echoing in my brain.

A gentleman finally arrived and introduced himself as a member of the Cuban State Department who told me he had just spoken to Raul Roa the Cuban Ambassador to the U.N. who had said, 'No Entrada.' His reason being that he didn't want an incident to occur that will entail a diplomatic problem, but as a consolation they would like to take me into Havana for lunch. I said I would love it but I had no Cuban money and that the U.S. money I had with me was illegal. He said not to worry, as I'll be their guest for lunch and laughingly said, "You will not be searched."

I was escorted into an upper class restaurant—white cloth tablecloth and white cloth napkins. The lunch was good; while desert was ordered my host went out for a moment and returned with an armload of magazines and newspapers in Spanish. One magazine was a Russian one in Spanish was extremely clever. On one side of the open magazine was a story and photo of one of the arts, (ballet, theater, film, dance, opera etc.) and on the opposite page was a photo of heavy industry, housing, hospitals, schools etc. We had another drink and a bit more talk and was taken back to the launch, given the magazines and newspapers and returned to the ship.

It was very hot in Havana for the ship had closed down the air conditioning to save fuel. Those days in Havana Harbor was made bearable if one sat in a shaded area and hoped for a breeze. Finally we left Cuban waters and a day or so later entered Vero Cruz Harbor. Disembarking I left my luggage in the city square and went hunting for a hotel for the night or two and then by bus to Taxco. On my valise I had a Time magazine and my camera. Returned two hours later and there was everything as I had left it. Nothing had been touched. Maybe I was naïve but it was a totally different world then.

That summer was lovely and made use of the time by writing a dramatic play. Received a phone call from my wife (she worked for the City of New York as a social worker and couldn't accompany me) that the FBI had called and informed her that my passport had been found and had she heard from me?

What? I have my passport with my papers and it was never lost. I figured what prompted that phone call. When I was leaving the ship in Havana Harbor coming down the gangplank into the Launch were Cuban reporters and a TV crew was filming me. Being an actor I know when the red light on the TV camera goes on and I'm the subject. This presented a problem. If I smiled it will look as if I'm happy to be in Cuba. If I scowled, why did I come to visit? I tried to keep a neutral look. Undoubtedly it was seen in Miami and the FBI thought they now had a turncoat and told Doris that on my return I'm to phone their office, they left the name of agent Callahan if I remember and his telephone number.

On my return I was furious that the FBI had frightened my wife and phoned and told them so. My passport had never left my possession. I was given a lame excuse and never heard from them again.

Gideon and Frederic March

My next Broadway show, Gideon by Paddy Chayefsky, would star Frederic March as God and a Canadian actor, Douglas Campbell, as Gideon. Douglas was a fine actor and a wonderful artist. He did a charcoal drawing of me as Zalmunah, King of Mideon in the play Gideon that graces my Ego wall. In the play Gideon, God only talks to Gideon and Zalmunah, whom God creates. That's in a cast of about 40. This was my second Broadway show directed by Tyrone Guthrie. Douglas Campbell and I were the only ones that had scenes directly with March who played God. Campbell played Gideon and we rehearsed our scenes for four weeks prior to opening. The rest of the cast played the Mideonites and Israeli Armies and townspeople. We opened November 9, 1961 at the Plymouth Theater.

March had spoken to no one during rehearsals other than Tyrone Guthrie and Paddy Chayefsky. During the performances the wardrobe mistress would talk to me and complain that every time she passed March's dressing room, his door being open, he would come out and grab her breasts. I said tell Arthur Cantor who for Gideon was our producer. She looked at me as if I was retarded. "He's the star of this show. Cantor is not going to even mention it to March and I'd get fired." Her intention was to grin and bear it.

March had a reputation of being a womanizer. He was married to an equally talented and famous actress, Florence Eldridge. Prior to the 1970s before hoodlums and muggers were plentiful, the curtains went up at 8:30 p.m. and came down before 11:00 p.m. If it were a minute after, the stagehands would have to be paid one-hour overtime.

The actor's call then for the performance was 8 p.m. our half hour to make up and put on your costume, curtain at 8:30. This was later changed to half hour for the actor was 7:00 p.m. and curtain at 7:30. All Broadway shows did as they still do eight shows a week but then, all shows were dark on Sundays. The ticket buyers complained that it cut into their dinner hour so now its half hour at 7:30, curtain at 8:00 p.m. although some start a bit earlier.

One Monday, Mr. March came in to work with a big swollen cheek. What was told to the cast was that he had a very bad toothache and couldn't find a dentist. Incredulous! Frederic March was a mega star. He became a full-fledged star in 1927 the year I was born. It's like the President of the United States needing medical or dental attention. A dentist would open his office or carry his dental chair on his back to care for March.

Then, the true story came out. March went out after the show every night to the watering holes in the city. This past Saturday night he chose, The Versailles, favored by high society and other famous people for supper and a drink. Star entertainers performed there. A beautiful woman walked past and he pinched her (bottom, breasts?) I wasn't there. This lady's companion, I assume her boyfriend or husband who was walking slightly behind her, turned and punched March in the jaw. That was the reason of "the toothache." From that night on Florence would be at the theater stage door to pick up her husband and went with him or took him directly home.

Those were the days when the Broadway season was June to June. Rehearsals began September/October. Sometimes November. Rehearsals were four weeks for a play, six weeks for musicals, to opening. Either out of town, for a shakedown cruise, so to speak, the contracts can be renegotiated in June unless signed for X amount of months or the run of the play.

One night after we opened to a great success. March was like the great organ in St. Patrick's Cathedral with all the stops pulled out. Unfortunately for the audiences, he played full out five times. Opening night, the night Carlo Ponte and Sophia Lauren were there,

The Actors Fund benefit performance night and another night when friends or family were there and lastly his closing night performance. He left, and then a month later we closed. With Mr. March we did sell out, and SRO business. Douglas took over the part of God and Stefan Gierasch played Gideon. Campbell one night after his performance as God, said to me, "I'm not bad in this role, and Stefan and I play well together, I know that. Yet business has fallen off tremendously. They were both very good but no one could have followed Frederic March. The audiences came to see Frederic March and now that he no longer is playing… in four weeks we were gone.

Mr. March, every one called him that except Guthrie and Paddy. In fact March, never spoke to anyone during rehearsals except those two. I made my entrance from the musicians pit as I had eighteen inch feathers on my head coming out of my turban and wore a shift that was down to my ankle's I was asked by Dr. Guthrie during rehearsals if I could look as if I floated up onto stage level. Of course, there was a staircase. It took me three weeks to achieve that appearance. I had jeweled armbands and costume jewelry applied onto the shift I wore. A black beard with wig of black hair down to my shoulders, and Arabian Night shoes of gold with the toes turned up. It didn't have little bells at the end of the toes but I sure did make an impressive King.

Frederic March most nights timed his entrances from a speaker in his dressing room and would leave when he heard what he set as his cue and walked without pausing onto the stage. One night in December, I was standing in the wings watching some of the action when Mr. March suddenly appeared next to me. It was early for him. Quietly he said, "Smoke?" We weren't allowed to smoke in the backstage area, though some did. We were Always on the look out for the Firemen from NYFD who were assigned to the Theater District and if caught would be ticketed and fined. "No thanks," said I. It wasn't my brand.

The pack had bout three or four cigarettes, which he then pushed into my hands insisting that I take them. I put the almost empty pack into my pocket that the costume designer had put in for valuables. "Thank You." We both stood watching for a minute or so when March said, "Thank you for your Christmas Card." "You're welcome, but it wasn't me. I'm Jewish and don't celebrate Christmas or send cards." "Oh," said he, then after a short pause. "You'll have to forgive me, but you all look alike to me." A bit unusual since as I said before, just Campbell and I had scenes with him. Strange, yet at the time I thought amusing. With that he heard his cue and walked onto the stage. I went off to the basement for there was the entrance to the pit and waited for my cue.

One night in January I'm in my position in the pit, bent over in half, to make sure my feathers weren't seen, when Alan Manson, an actor in Gideon who I also played with in The Tenth Man, was at the door to the pit and we spoke very quietly while I was awaiting my cue to float up to the scene where God tells how he will create me and on my arrival orders me to go to Shechem. Later in the battle I'm killed. Alan and I were in conversation when I hear Mr. March say, "I am God! I command you. Come forth. I am omnipotent. I am omniscient. I command you. Come forth."

"What's wrong with March tonight," I say to Alan. I think he went up. My cue was "Look there in the Divide...etc." That was the second time he repeated that line that was supposed to be said once. Then, I realized that in talking with Alan I missed my cue and that night I came in not fourth but last. I literally ran up the steps not bothering to float up. On getting to stage level began my lines, and March also spoke, we both stopped and started and again we did a duo, and in unison. I then stopped and let March bring us back to the scene. When we finished that scene I am killed by a spear thrown by the Israelites. Being on a stage that was raked to 15 feet with me on the top of the incline when speared I fall backwards off the mountain. To be caught by another actor standing on a couple of mattresses in case he missed. Which he never did.

I immediately went to the wing that March will exit from. When he came off stage I stopped him to apologize for missing my cue. I really thought I did it this time, and will be fired for causing March to ad-lib, making him appear that he screwed up his lines. He very magnanimously said. "Oh forget it, that's what makes live theater exciting and keeps one on his toes. Needless to say I never did that again.

While out of town in Philadelphia Dr. Guthrie tried many ways to make my being speared look real. First wore a bag filled with a red liquid to simulate blood. That didn't work for when speared it didn't squirt out but ran down my chest under my costume. Then a chest plate made of a metal with a two inch cork overlay. One night during the performance when Douglas Campbell threw the spear it went through the cork, through the metal and the two pronged metal spear end went into my chest I felt the blood running down under my costume. Douglas felt it going through and blanched white through his makeup. It wasn't serious but that too didn't work. I suggested that we do it the way actors have done that being knifed and/or speared by catching it with my upstage armpit then falling off the raked stage to be caught by the actor waiting on the mattress, and that worked, looked real and satisfied Dr. Guthrie.

One actor in the company was George Segal and he was memorable. He was playing a soldier and Guthrie had him crossing the stage as I remember, George on making his entrance stumbled on across and garnered applause every night. Talent will out. He also had a talent for remembering songs his mother sang to him when he was two years old. He gave us renditions of, "I Didn't Raise My Son to Be a Soldier" an anti-war song of the First World War.

A number of us shared a dressing room and one of the actors Amnon Meskin, an Israeli whose father was an Israeli stage star. Amnon was a member of the Actors Studio. One night this woman came to our dressing room to see him. She wore no makeup and had a babushka on her head tied under her chin and he introduced us to Marilyn Monroe. If you passed her in the street looking this way you would have passed her by and not a head would have turned to look.

Amnon Meskin was a strange guy. When I was in Israel on my tour with the International Theater Institute's blessings I looked him up and we met. In discussing the state of the Israeli theater he was one of the avant-garde of their off-off Broadway movement (so to speak). His body language and his discussion of working there in Tel Aviv were entirely negative. Needless to say we never met again.

After Gideon closed in 1962, I got a call from Luther Adler who knew I was in the original Broadway production of The Tenth Man. He was doing a production to open in Kennebunkport, Maine, then to Miami and then back to Broadway. Luther was to play the old rabbi. Since that part was not very big he took scenes from Ansky's Dybuk and added it to his part of the rabbi. We never got to Miami or Broadway as we closed In Kennebunkport.

Paddy Chayefsky and the Union

Paddy was a friendly man and since "Marty" (the TV show and Oscar winning film) he was thought of as the writer of the people. He had written other things films i.e.; "Hospital," "The Goddess" with Kim Stanley, etc. She was marvelous though Paddy felt and said she ruined his screenplay. We The Tenth Man received unanimous raves. In 1959 there were seven newspapers in New York City and each one had a theater critic. In addition, the TV and Magazine critics gave it unanimous raves. The dean of critics was Brooks Atkinson who wrote for The New York Times.

When we had opened in Philadelphia the critical consensus was "They didn't know how to criticize this play and that the public should go and see for themselves." Business was all right but not SRO in Philadelphia. Other well-known writers came to Philadelphia to help. Paddy was adamant and sent them back to New York. He said this play will stand on its own and if it fails, it fails as a Chayefsky play. Not a word was changed. Guthrie staged it and oversaw David Hayes' lighting, which also garnished a Tony award, and it was magnificent. You could stop the action at any moment and the stage looked like a Rembrandt painting: so very beautiful.

As soon as the New York reviews came out the very next morning there was a line to buy tickets from the Booth Theater on 45th Street to 8th Avenue to 44th Street down to and across Schubert Alley and back to the Booth. We ran for two years which at that time was unheard of for a non-musical to run more then one season (June to June).

We opened in the fall of 1959. The Equity contract with the League expired in June of 1960 In order to get a salary hike from $85 a week to $125 and also start a pension for all in the professional performing arts, Screen Actors Guild, the American Federation of Radio Artists and Stage Hands, etc.

In April of 1960 I'm walking up Broadway when Paddy Chayefsky and his agent Bobby Sanford stop to say hello. Paddy says "What's this I hear that Equity is planning a strike?" I say, "I know the same as you; it's what I've read in the Times." With that Paddy says, "What's this strike about. There's nobody in our company that makes minimum. It's those chorus cunts. They're only in this business to find a rich husband. It's those fuckin' cunts" plus other choice descriptive words. With that, he takes out a black jacketed notebook from his inner jacket pocket and says, "I'll lose $10,000 a week if you guys go on strike, see this black book, all you guys will be in it. I will see to it that none of you get another job."

Now Bobby Sanford takes Paddy's arm and gently pulling Paddy to walk away, "Leave the kid alone, says Sanford, he's just a member and has to do what his union tells him." Sanford still trying and Paddy resisting being pulled away. "No, says Paddy, It's only those chorus cunts. Paul, I'll see to it that you will never get a Broadway show again. Finally Sanford succeeded in pulling him away, Paddy called back over his shoulder; "You'll never work again Paul Marin" I was thoroughly shocked. This from "the writer of the people." Remember Diana Millay and her reaction to the eighth Mrs. Tommy Manville, what a contrast in morality.

In June of 1960 Actors Equity Association, the Union that covers the stage actors, whose contract with The League of New York Producers and Theater Owners, had Rule One that said the Union could call a Meeting with the actors at any time. Equity called this meeting at 8:00 p.m. on a Monday night, which, in 1960, was half hour before all the actors in the play had to be at the theater to sign in. Since we were the only company called to this meeting we went to our Union's offices at Actors Equity Association's little house on 48th Street. In retaliation the next night The League locked out all actors from all the shows on Broadway.

The next meeting took place on Tuesday in the Edison Hotel that proved too small and we moved over to the Grand Ballroom of the Astor Hotel on 44th Street on Broadway. In the company were a couple of Black-listed actors, Alan Manson and Jack Gilford. They both believed in social reform and either joined the legal communist party or were thought to be members. The House Un-American Committee listed them, ending their careers in TV and films, but not in Theater as there were no corporate sponsors that could be pressured into withholding monies for the productions. As we sat there, the Union officials gave uninspiring speeches. I felt that it needed a speech that would inspire, so, being young and stupid, I got up and said that I was proud and honored to be part of The Tenth Man company called on to represent our fellow actors. That I had a wife and an infant daughter and was worried how we were going to make ends meet for we don't know how long this lockout will last, but it was necessary for not only a salary increase for the rank and file member but a pension to be to be started and if my Union felt that we should stay out, I'm proud and honored to be in the company that was called, etc.

On arriving home my wife said, "What did you do tonight?"

"What do you mean? I was at the Astor Hotel where Equity had called a meeting."

"This phone hadn't stopped ringing all evening from Reporters from the Times, The Daily Mirror, The News, Journal American and others. All left their numbers for you to phone when you got home. I told them when you came home you will call them. I took the phone off the hook. "What did you do?"

"What did I do? Nothing!" I didn't return their calls, for I didn't want to get into more hot water with my bosses.

The next morning The New York Times headline on the front page in its column on the lockout read, in big bold letters, "Actor Says He's 'Honored'" then went on to misquote and embellish what I said. The next evening when I went to the stage door of the Booth Theater at 8 p.m. Guilford and Manson both immediately said "Don't stand near me, as I have enough trouble already." These were actors who were on the black list: so much for social reform and for the unity of workers.

This lockout lasted thirteen days. I personally received two telegrams, one from Paddy and the other from the producer Arthur Cantor, each suing me for one million dollars. It was settled when the City of New York agreed to donate the tax on each ticket to help start the Pension fund and the producers also agreed to contribute I think, an eighth or a half of one percent of total salaries and the lockout ended. Rule One said that Equity could call a meeting at the time of its choosing, with the settlement was forever stricken from future agreements. The rest of the cast members and I, who were sent telegrams, those suits were also dismissed as part of the settlement. When I had received the telegram I called friends asking to borrow $25 or $50 to make the first payment.

That encounter with Paddy and Sanford made me an active union member. I joined committees and eventually ran for election to the Council of Actors Equity. My tenure as an elected Counsel member, the governing body of Actors Equity, ended in a slight dispute as I served in New York and also California on the WCAC (West Coast Advisory Committee), WAC (Western Advisory Committee), WAB (Western Advisory Board), and as a Counsel member since elected in 1965. When in 1986 I had decided not to run for re-election as I felt after all these years on the governing body of AEA it was time to give way to the younger group of actors who hopefully will have fresh ideas. The powers at that time felt that my service in California was not to be included. Only Counsel in N.Y. and that they felt was only 13 years. My parting gift from AEA a plastic paperweight inscribed with the Equity Logo and 13 years of service, that from a national union that I had served for over 21 years.

My union, which I renamed Actors Concessionary Association, for if a producer wanted to mount a play he/she would come to AEA under funded and even the BOND that was supposedly sacrosanct, was not demanded and plays that closed without having a bond and owing the actors pay were then paid by using AEA dues money.

As a member of council I was appointed by council to go to a production that was being shown in Greenwich Village for donations only; the producer of course, didn't share these donations with the actors. In California Joseph Ruskin, a fellow Council Member came up with a plan for allowing plays limited to theaters with 99 seats and then the actors weren't paid or paid $5 a performance for three, four or five performances weekly. The logic behind this was that the AEA members wanted this and in fact held large rallies demanding this with the encouragement of producers. Some even used this venue to try out new plays before going into full production. No pay for actors = a cheap way to see what works.

My argument was that this would destroy all contracts, as the middle-sized theaters in Los Angeles then would cut back to 99 seats. And behold, that's what happened. Of course the Mid-sized contracts then paid a living wage, not great, but one could pay rent and buy food.

With the 99-seat theater paying $5 a performance one had to have another job to survive. Now in 2009 actors playing in 99 seat theaters can make $15 a performance and with gas prices now, it won't even pay for that. Since most of these Theaters play five performances, and a small car gas would cost $40 or more to fill it up.

One evening I went to the Freud Theater at UCLA to see Lynn Redgrave in Shakespeare for My Father. While waiting in the Lobby for the Theater to open its doors, James Brodhead who had been a member of the Western Advisory Board when the 99 seat Theater was on the Agenda was violently opposed to my argument feeling that the membership were demanding it. I said then and still say today, "We were elected to lead not follow." Jim Brodhead walked up to me and said, "Paul Marin, I owe you an apology, everything you said would transpire has, and the stage actor in Hollywood will never make a living here. All Equity contracts here now are 99 seat waiver contract, meaning no money. Unfortunately there was no pleasure for me in this vindication. Thanks Joe Ruskin.

The Odyssey Theater has three 99 seat theaters on Sepulveda Boulevard in west Los Angeles in one building all owned by one producer who drives an expensive car and lives I was told in an expensive home. All on the backs of the cotton picker actors who think that agents and casting people will see them and they'll get paying jobs. In 1980 I did a study of all the 99 seat theater productions in Los Angeles, which totaled without exaggeration 800 productions. With that amount of plays you'd think some actors being seen would get a paying job in TV or film, One did, that's right only ONE.

Today in 2009 it remains the same and very few agents or casting people ever bother to go. Some casting people under the guise of classes in cold readings charge to see actors. When that's their job to see and cast actors. I assume some even aspire to teach acting since their background before becoming a casting person was receptionist in a casting office.

My very next job after The Tenth Man closed in June 1961, was Gideon by Paddy Chayefsky, directed by Tyrone Guthrie with rehearsals starting in late October 1961 "You'll never work again," the threat remark that Paddy flung at me didn't have the last part of that threat, "Until we need you."

During one or more of my terms as a Counselor of Actors Equity, Theodore Bikel was President of AEA Each year I would receive Holiday cards he would send out. One day many years later, Bikel and I now in Hollywood and both of us elected members of The Academy of Motion Picture Arts and Sciences. I when viewing films sat with Robert Clary and others. It seems that we're territorial animals so we always sit in the same seats. Bikel came over to chat with me and I introduced him to Clary. Now he no longer comes to speak to me, he just waves or a gratuitous "Hi" but makes a beeline to Clary who's has had some success with New Faces of 1952 and Hogan's Heroes.

The Summer Season at Venice, Ca.

The bandshell at Windward Avenue in Venice, which was built on the beach, was an open to the sky theater. It never rains in Southern California in the summer. It was leased for one dollar from the City of Los Angeles. It had 1025 seats. Producer Herb Alexander, and director Max Miller, picked the four plays. We opened with The Seven Year Itch, starring MacDonald Carey and I co-starring. We received good reviews, did good business and played out our two weeks. We did have minor lighting problems. One night all the lights went out except one, directed onto the couch. It was very funny as MacDonald Carey and I fought for the light.

One night Hershel Bernadi who was scheduled to play Jake, the Grandfather in Awake and Sing, the third play scheduled, came back stage to my dressing room after a performance of Seven Year Itch to tell me he couldn't wait to play with me in Awake and Sing as he thought I was wonderful etc. I love flattery but then who doesn't. As when I played in the film "Private Benjamin" that was produced by and starred Goldie Hawn. After I finished a scene Armand Asanti came over to me (he was co-starring) and said, "God, you were wonderful, how do you feel? It's like having a ten course meal at Chasin's or Sardi's isn't it?" Flattery from a fellow actor is the best. Goldie phoned my agent and said, "That when this picture comes out, your client will not stop working," That was very nice, but it didn't happen.

The next play was Room Service, an American classic comedy. This play had Morry Amsterdam and Professor Irwin Corey, and me playing the hotel manager plus others including Tony Bill. That was a disaster. The two stars Morry and Corey were Night Club comics and on opening night, Morry is on stage and waiting for my cue was stunned to hear Irwin Corey on stage ad-libbing. I was, according to the script to come on before Corey. He came on before his cue and one of his many ad-libs, said to Morey "What do you get when you cross a Jew with a Popsicle?" Amsterdam answered, "I don't know, what do you get when you cross a Jew with a Popsicle?" "You don't know what you get when you cross a Jew with a Popsicle? You get a Jewsicle." It fell like an unexploded bomb with a dull thud. In vaudeville comedy, you repeat the line three times like in Shakespeare, to make sure the audience gets it. Then he said, "What do you get when you cross an Italian with a Popsicle? A Wopsicle." Then a third Popsicle joke. Falling with deafening silence on the audience. It didn't even get a chuckle. Corey then stood upstage at the rear wall and acting as if urinating, being an open-air theater, said something about the wind blowing urine into his face.

When the reviews came out, one worse then the next. The essence was, maybe in a nightclub where people are drinking though in bad taste and insulting to those groups, it may be funny. To add these lines to an American classic comedy is dreadful. We did very little business and happily closed after the two weeks.

One day before a performance I'm walking on the boardwalk in Venice to the theater when I see Corey famous for his string tie and sneakers and known because of his appearances on "The Tonight Show." There was Corey going up to young women and saying something to them, then pinching or grabbing a feel of their breasts. Laughing and walking away. Don't know if he ever got slapped but he sure as hell should have. I guess being a TV personality he thought he could get away with anything.

The joy of that season at the beach was the Clifford Odets play *Awake and Sing*, with Hershel Bernadi as Grandfather Jake, Harold Gould as Uncle Morty, Sal Mineo as my son Ralph, me as the father and husband, Ruth Waschafsky, as my wife and mother. Our producer Herb and his wife Ruth Alexander played the roomer and the daughter respectively, plus others. We opened to rave reviews. We were extended for two more weeks, playing to standing room only audiences and turning away two to three hundred people a night. We could have played a few months more but Bernardi had a previous engagement and couldn't stay after the extended two weeks. That was a wonderful production and a joy to play. I had taken a flat in Venice as I was living in North Hollywood on Barham Boulevard and the commute was too much to travel each day.

Then came the mother of all disasters. We were in rehearsal for our next and last play Othello starring William Marshall, playing Othello. He was 6' 2" or 3" tall and was over 230 lbs. He had a great deep beautiful voice. There were rumors that Marshall and Danica D'Hondt, playing Desdemona, that they were having an affair. True or not I really don't know, as I wasn't there at their private rehearsals. I also didn't know if friction developed between them. She 5' 7" or 8" tall weighing about 115 lbs. were both rehearsing privately and also with the cast.

On dress rehearsal night with an invited audience in attendance, suddenly Marshall was choking her, literally to kill her. Our director, Henry Scott 5' 6" or 7" tall ran onto the stage and jumped on Marshall's back to dislodge him from his stranglehold.

Marshall and Scott were childhood friends. Scott being a very light-skinned Black who could pass as white and Marshall who was a very dark-skinned Black, I was told by a fellow actor, Marshall resented Scott for his having a White wife, which made very little sense as Marshall had two families, a White wife in one and a Black wife in the other. Once again I don't know whether they were simultaneous. Marshall threw Scott off his back into the first row of seats as if tossing a ball. Then Bill Wintersole and I plus a number of other actors ran on stage and also were thrown from him as if we were just pesky flies. Finally with enough of us we dislodged him from his stranglehold on Danica. Then Marshall ran down into the audience and began to pummel Scott while Scott's leg was caught in the bench like seats with the backs held to the seat with attached slats.

That finished the dress and the curtain was brought down. Danica refused to play opening night saying that her husband was adamant and threatened that if she continued in this production he would kill their baby. Another actress, Adrienne Ellis, was found who had played a condensed version of Othello before. During rehearsals with the new Desdemona in came Scott with knee bandaged and using a cane shouting from the back of the band shell, "I'm directing this play." With that Marshall shouted "Like Hell you are." Now this is day of opening night and we are all frantically showing Adrienne her blocking and the curtain was brought up on opening night.

As the Equity Deputy I had to report the grizzly happenings that took place and it became a case of charges and counter charges being brought to the Equity Council.

Then the city of Los Angeles broke with their policy of trying to extend the Arts to the Western part of Los Angeles. They were quoted, "The city didn't want to deal with crazy actors ever again" and vowed never to have another acting company use the bandshell again. I don't know if the city or Marshall were sued, for this took place on their property and the city was the landlord. That play unfortunately was cursed now and I was happy when we closed though we did good business for the remainder two weeks. Though a fine actor, Marshall's presence made the rest of the company uncomfortable, as he had too much baggage since the dress rehearsal night fiasco. There was always the possibility of another flare up to put it kindly.

as the Messenger in 'Othello' 1953

'Fair Game' with Sam Levene, Ellen McRae
Burstyn, Robert Weber and Ed Bryce. 1957

Paul circa 1960

charcoal of Paul Marin as Zalmuna in Gideon by Douglas Campble 1962

Poster 'Fiddler On The Roof' 1965

as Lazar Wolf in 'Fiddler On the Roof', 1965

With Kathleen Freeman in 'Cabaret' 1970's

Carricature of Paul Marin in 'Cabaret' by Dick Gautier 1970's

Paul circa 1975

With Lucciano Pavarotti and Bette Midler on set of 'Yes Georgio' 1982

Pavarotti and Paul Marin in 'Yes Georgio' 1982

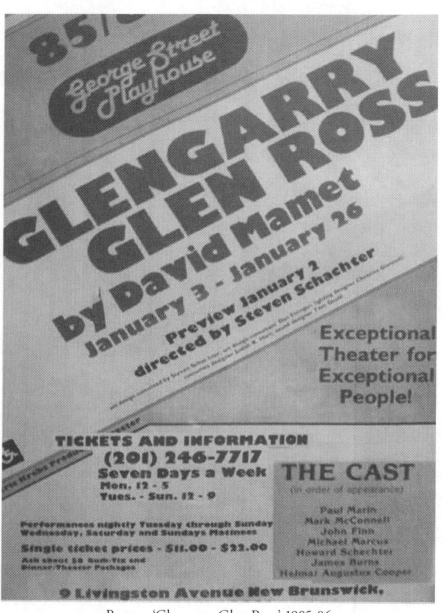

Poster - 'Glengarry Glen Ross' 1985-86

Poster of film 'The Choice' 1988

In 'My Pretty Pony' by Stephen King, 2009

1965

Fiddler on the Roof

Now I come to the most painful part of my career, this was the most difficult time in my life as an actor I will try tell it as it transpired. Fiddler on the Roof opened to great reviews and was a tremendous success and a very hot ticket. I went to see it at its first Actors Fund performance and was thrilled. Zero Mostel and Austin Pendleton stole the show as far as I was concerned. Maria Karnilova, Bea Arthur were cliché characters, though Karnilova won a Tony award for her portrayal of Golde. That was the part that Helen Verbit understudied.

In 1965 Helen Verbit phoned me and said they were casting for the touring company and that she had spoken to Jerome Robbins about me and to call the office to set up an audition for the part of the Butcher Lazar Wolf. Since Helen knew that I didn't sing, she said don't worry, you can talk sing that part.

Since I wasn't signed to anyone I called Jerry Kahn who was Helen's agent and he agreed to represent me and arranged the time and place for the audition. I picked up the script, took it home and worked and worked and worked some more on it. The day came for the audition. Off I went to the Majestic Theater and finding the stage door entrance walked in. Sitting there at the entrance to the stage on steps leading up to the dressing rooms and standing in the wings were actors who came to audition for many of the male roles.

My turn came and walking on to the stage was introduced to the darkened theater by the stage manager. An upright piano was right stage with a man sitting in front of it. I later learned he was Milton Green, the conductor. When I finished reading I stood there waiting for a reaction of some kind like 'Thank You' when I heard a voice say, "Did you give your music to the man at the piano?"

"Oh, was I supposed to? No, I didn't bring any music."

The voice out of the dark said. "You do know that this is a musical?"

"Yes, but… I was told this was a non-singing part."

Another voice called out, "Do you know 'The Star Spangled Banner?'"

"Yes but," I sheepishly said, "I don't know the lyrics."

"Do you know 'Happy Birthday?'"

"Yes"

"Sing that for us."

My rendition of "Happy Birthday" (I'm sure and hope) was forgettable. Another voice rang out from the black void.

"Will you do the scales for us?"

"I'd be very happy to, if I knew what they were."

This same voice said, "Milton, play them for him." Milton dutifully played: do re, me, fa, so, la tee do. I must have had a look of complete mystification for the voice again rang out.

"Milton, you just heard the man say he doesn't know what they are, play them…. one at a time!" Which Milton did, and I sang, one at a time. This time another voice said, "Would you work on a song and come back and do it for us."

"Yes, sure!"

"Call the office when you're ready but not later than two weeks, will that be enough time?" Before I could answer "And thank you." I called Helen to thank her and tell her the good news and she said, I have a friend who is a composer and he has songs that he will be happy to teach and work with you on it.

That's what I did. I always had a lot of confidence and even though I was always told at school, "You're a Listener!" I not only couldn't stay on pitch, I didn't even hear the pitch. My speaking voice was very good as I trained it to speak in two to three octaves. People were always saying "What a beautiful voice you have." One draw back, I never learned how to use it professionally.

A strike was called by the city's transportation union. All the subways and buses stopped running. I was apartment sitting in the Bronx, an actor friend who was a fellow elected member of Counsel of Actors Equity that is the governing body I was then elected to. He had gotten a job to tour and asked me to watch his place while he was away. Now due to the strike I couldn't get there from the city, and this composer, this wonderful man, unfortunately Helen's dead and I can't recall his name, but he offered me his couch. We worked hard on a number called "Needle Needle," about a little Jewish tailor. It changed tempos and keys. I memorized all the tricks and turns talking my way through. When I went to the audition I was really into the song. It seems that my body took on a life of its own. I danced and sang and moved across that stage with ease. At one point it was like someone else.

On finishing, to a "thank you" from Hal Prince, the producer and Jerome Robbins, the director. I smiled and walked off. Was it Truman Capote who wrote, "Answered prayers? One must be careful what one wishes for. One might get it"

As I got to the wings, an actor who was waiting to go on to audition and watching from the wings said. "It's yours! There's no one here to compete with you. You were great, the part is yours!!!" It's always nice to get a compliment, I felt like I did a good audition but I've felt that way before and didn't get the job. The strike, finally over and I took the train up to the Bronx.

By the time I got to the apartment and made coffee the phone rang. It was Jerry Kahn. This time I got the job. Of course Jerry Kahn wasn't the worst of agents but far, very far from the best. The George Abbot Office (the production office with Hal Prince) wanted to hire me to play Lazar Wolf, the Butcher and understudy Tevye. Jerry Kahn was ready to agree to a deal of two hundred and fifty dollars a week for me to play Lazar Wolf.

"I said No!"

'You'll lose this job. Take it." He counseled

"I want a grand a week!"

"You'll lose it!"

"So, I'll lose it."

Jerry was worried more about losing his ten percent of a big twenty-five dollars a week, rather then negotiating to get me more money. I dropped down to seven hundred and fifty and the Abbot Office came up to three fifty. They let Jerry sweat awhile then settled for five hundred a week plus a thousand each time I went on to play Tevye. My compromise.

Bette Midler played the 18 year old Tzietel, whom Lazar wanted to marry. It was a very funny and sad scene where I'm asking Tevye for his daughter's hand in marriage and he thinks I'm asking to buy one of his milk cows. Bette's stardom that came later. After performing, she would go to a bathhouse and perform there. That was the start of her super stardom.

Rehearsals were in a few places. Dancers and singers were at the

Variety Arts Studios. The book was rehearsed at the theater where Fiddler was playing. I enjoyed rehearsals though I was extremely nervous of the singing. The butcher has six numbers. "Tradition," with the complete cast, the duet with Tevye, "L'Chiam, To Life" and bits here and there culminating in leaving Russia for Chicago. The dress rehearsal was set for an afternoon before we were to travel by air the next day to our first city, San Diego. Where we'd rehearse a week on the stage of the Civic Auditorium Theater there and play for two weeks. The audience for the dress rehearsal was made up of working actors from the shows on Broadway, plus other guests of the producers. It was a doubly tragic day. My eldest sister's husband Jack Zaimoff died that morning and according to the Jewish religion he was to be buried that same afternoon. I decided to play the dress. "The show must go on!" The second disaster was, after the final curtain of the dress rehearsal came down, Ruth Mitchell the production stage manager came back stage to the dressing room I was using and said, "You were terrible. If we weren't leaving tomorrow, we'd replace you." I mumbled something like, "My brother-in-law died this morning and instead of going to the funeral...." "Oh, I'm sorry, I didn't know..." she said. She then mumbled some sort of condolence and quickly left. I sat there taking off my makeup, numb, shocked and not knowing what to do. Some people sing, "The best is yet to come, Oh, won't it be fine." Unfortunately for me the lyrics change.... "The worst is yet to come! And it's all mine."

We assembled in front of the Majestic Theater our steamer trunks were already at the theater having been picked up a few days before. On to a chartered bus much laughter and talk from the cast though I was full of foreboding and off to the airport. That plane trip was something in it self. The young man who played Fyedka the Russian, who loves and marries Chava, was a wild actor who thought of himself as a cross between Brando and James Dean. Not that I led a sheltered life but I wasn't into drugs. A couple of drinks of rum and coke or an occasional Alice B. Toklas brownie when some one brought one.

We are now in the air towards San Diego. I'm working on the script of Tevye; we're thirty two thousand feet in the air when I feel a hand covering my mouth and a vial held to my nose and forced to breathe in. I thought I was having a heart attack. He was holding a broken vial of poppers to my nose. That's Amyl Nitrate for those who are not initiated (I wasn't). It's used when people have angina attacks to help stabilize their hearts, or as the fad then and still, though now it's Butyl Nitrate, used during sex to heighten the experience. I wanted to kill him. Later on in the tour He would prance around back stage buck-naked. I wonder what had happened to him. He might even be dead by now. I rather liked him. We stayed in San Diego for two weeks and then up to Los Angeles and on to the Dorothy Chandler Theater.

The Dorothy Chandler had just been built and the sound system was awful. In order to correct it, to try and make it a bit better, baffles were built. It did help some but later I understand it was fixed. There were all kinds of parties during that seven-week period.

I asked our conductor for musical rehearsals for Tevye, I knew that the vocal part of the role was where I could run into trouble when and if I get to play him. I have a tendency to go off pitch and change keys without even knowing I'm doing that. One excuse after another was given.

"You already have two rehearsals each week."

"Yes but that's for the whole company, we do a complete run through. It's a musical rehearsal I want." The understudies had normal rehearsals before the matinee's on Wednesdays and Saturdays. So then we'd set a date and time to work together. I'd get to the theater to rehearse and the conductor wouldn't be there. That night at the theater when I'd ask what had happened. The answer came back, "I forgot" For someone who sings as I do, off pitch, wrong key or many keys, all on only one note. To say I was unhappy is putting it mildly and the weeks went on. After seven sold out weeks we flew up to Seattle.

Here we played in the shadow of the Space Needle. Ever been to Seattle in the fall? Rain and more rain. One night after work I went to a bar for a drink. Sitting next to me at the bar was a young guy in his late twenties. We started chatting and he turned out to be a Seattle policeman, off duty of course. He said, "It rains all fall and winter and that it's so depressing that on the Seattle Bridge, there are so many suicides the jumpers to keep it orderly have to take numbers as to who is next." It has its benefits, however; every thing is green. Two weeks up in Seattle in their liquid sunshine and we were ready to leave for San Francisco.

I stayed at a small hotel around the corner from the Geary Theater. We opened to wonderful reviews. San Francisco as someone had said is a small New York. It certainly is, but it also has fog, lots of fog. There were parties and picnics. One remains in memory. It was held out on an island in the bay where we took a ferry there. We were a group of us from Fiddler and there was Bobo Lewis, an actress I knew from New York, who was in town with a play plus others from her company. We brought hamburger meat and chops etc. Someone brought Alice B. Toklas brownies. After we ate the brownies, before we cooked the meat, we also smoked some weed. It must have been a good combination as we all fell fast asleep. When we awoke it was dark and the last ferry had left. If I recall we shouted at a passing boat and he contacted a boat that came and brought us back to the city. It was every ones day off so no harm was done and the sea gulls had our planned picnic hamburgers, raw.

The part of Tevye was played by Luther Adler. Luther had replaced Zero Mostel who had contracted for the first season only. Luther opened to greater reviews then Zero, which in my opinion was ridiculous. Zero created Tevye, like a person going into a virgin forest and blazing a trail. From that moment on everyone who travels the forest uses that trail. If another actor had created Tevye in Fiddler, it would have been a different Fiddler. Zero, bless him, was a great actor, His Rhinoceros is still remembered by those of us lucky enough to be alive then and had seen it. To this day every Tevye uses Zero's path. With Zero it was musical comedy, with pathos and humor. In my opinion, Luther Adler played it like it was Chekhov's The Lower Depth that is, *sans* comedy. Most of the comedy was left on the written page. He was let go after he said to Hal Prince that Fiddler was a heavy show with eleven songs and like Uta Hagan who was in Who's Afraid Of Virginia Wolff, Uta was doing only six shows a week with the understudy doing the matinee's. He felt that he should have the same. Luther, when his contract was up found out he was replaced when he read it in the *New York Times* that Herschel Bernardi was his replacement.

He was furious that Hal didn't tell him and he had to read it in the Times. However, he got his revenge, when due to his Broadway reviews when he did Tevye was asked to do the Tour, I understand not only did he get a great salary but also a percentage of the houses we played. Always to full houses.

Luther and I had worked together before, when Luther produced and starred in a revival of Paddy Chayefsky's The Tenth Man and I was in the original Broadway production. We were rehearsing in the Edison Hotel's very large banquet room. Luther felt the part of the old rabbi was too small so he took a scene from Ansky's, The Dybuk, and incorporated it into Paddy Chayefsky's The Tenth Man. We were finishing our second week of rehearsal when in came this man in a three piece suit carrying an attaché case. He said, "Is the producer of The Tenth Man here?" With that Luther said, "I guess that's me,

I'm really half the producer. What can I do?" This man then said, "I represent Paddy Chayefsky and we were told that there were changes and additions made to The Tenth Man. I am here to inform you that if one word is cut or added, we will see you in court. Good morning." With that he turned and was out the door. Luther looking chagrined said, "Well, we'll have to go back to the original script and the two weeks we already have invested will have to be thrown out and start over.

Luther was something else, a selfish scene-stealing actor. He used the other actors as props and always used whichever actor was on stage standing near the wings as Luther made his entrance, he would grab the actor's shoulder and pull himself on even if it meant pushing the actor almost to his knees. He was far from a giving actor as he tried to steal every scene. In my scenes Luther played with his leather boot, scratching it as if the inside of the boot was making him itch. One night he was doing that and I had had it, as he had been doing it to get the audience watching him instead of the scene. I slapped the table we were sitting at, forcing him to focus on the scene. When we both were in the wings, Luther said. "Why did you slam the table?" "Why," said I, "did you scratch your boot so the audience's eyes are on you during my scene? If you do it again, I'll do it even louder." " Why are you so excited," said Luther, but he never did it again. Luther got his revenge. When the first touring company was put together, Luther negotiated for $10,000 a week plus a percentage of the house. One time at the Actors Fund performance when all the working actors on Broadway buy seats to see the show on their day off and the proceeds are donated to the Actors Fund. The actors in the show work without pay the producer gives the monies for that day to the fund and the theater is the theater owner's donation. During the Christmas week a pitch is made to the audience to donate to the Fund and the actors in the show go through the audience with baskets collecting what people who want to donate give. As one of the actors who made the pitch from the stage after the first act curtain came down said, "This is for indignant actors not indigent ones." A wonderful line.

The Actors Fund takes care of actors who have run into hard times. Rent, utilities, money for food, etc. Not as a loan but as grants never having to pay it back though many actors do when they get their next show. An actor who was never a star or name actor at the turn of the twentieth century left a legacy to the Fund to buy shoes once a year for stage actors as we make rounds, walking mainly to producer's, director's and casting offices for stage and TV jobs. I too used the shoe grant many times in between shows. The only proviso then was that you were a working actor who happened to be unemployed.

The weeks were going by and all was fine when I got a message from Bob Currey the stage manager of Fiddler that Luther Adler was ill and I'd be going on that night. I didn't have time to be nervous as I was dressed or more accurately pinned into the Tevye costume. My recollection of that evening is bare. I was told that very few people asked for their tickets exchanged or their money back. I remember clearly doing the Chava Ballet number with me on my milk cart singing about her going off and marrying outside of the faith and tiny bits and pieces. When the final curtain came down there was a smattering of applause from the cast during the curtain calls. Some of the company asked me to join them at the Curtain Call Bar and restaurant across from the theater. It was a lovely celebration and when I went back to the hotel there was champagne and snacks in my room sent up by the management of the hotel. To say I was high was an under statement, I was on cloud nine. I phoned Helen; it was four thirty New York time and told her the good news. Coming down a bit I now went to sleep.

The screaming ring of the phone awakened me a little after nine the next morning; it was Bob Currey the stage manager. Telling me I wasn't playing Tevye that evening or ever again and that they were flying in the New York understudy who had played it many times before and to be at the theater at noon for rehearsal, as I'll be playing my part of Lazar.

At first I felt confused, then shock, and resulting fury. Why? Why the party? The champagne was sent up by the hotel. Then it hit. The party was by a few of the cast not the reps of the producers nor for that matter Bob Currey the stage manager. My first reaction was not to go to the noon rehearsal; I really just wanted to disappear rather than have to see members of the cast who all knew that I was removed as understudy and they would be playing with my replacement. How could I face them but then my head came to play as I knew that Equity would bring me up on charges if I didn't show up for a rehearsal when called.

Actors are strange people, if thought to be not talented you would be treated as a non-person. Worse some would have nothing but contempt for you. Dolores Wilson, who played Golde, was such a great individual. Best not to say more about her. Use your imagination. I played Lazar for a few days more then was sent back to the Broadway company where I played Lazar.

A few weeks had past when a member of the touring company, I think it was Mickie Pollack, sent me a letter with a review of my performance. It was written by one of the small town paper reviewers bordering San Francisco. This reviewer happened to be in the theater that night and headlined her review "A Star Is Born." She went on and on.

Here was my justification! I phoned the press office that represented Fiddler and asked them for a photo of me as Tevye which they happily supplied. I took the photo to daily Variety (an entertainment trade paper) and we worked up an ad with a copy of the review plus me thanking Hal Prince. Pointing out that this review would never have happened without his faith in me. Of course it was a slap at him. Everyone on Broadway knew and interpreted it that way. The Abbott Office had a clipping service and they undoubtedly had known of this review.

When I arrived at my dressing room that night I found a telegram on my table informing me that a Retraction was demanded or I will be sued. Then the company manager paid me a visit to tell me Hal was furious and that I was to take an ad equal to my half page ad. Sure I replied, what do you want me to say, "Hal, I don't want to thank you" Realizing that it would be worse and the talk of Broadway, it was then forgotten. A few days passed and Helen Verbit came to my dressing room to tell me the Hatchet Lady (Ruth Mitchell) was in the theater and was there for the express purpose to see my performance and if not up to par to fire me. Not only was I good that night I got applause from the orchestra, which only happened to me twice.

The Broadway company of Fiddler was invited by the Abbott Office to see a dress rehearsal of Flora the Red Menace starring Liza Minnelli. On my way there I see Hal Prince. As we come abreast of each other Hal says, "Paul, Why?" referring to the Variety ad. "I sent Ruth Mitchell to see your performance with the instructions that if you weren't good she was immediately to buy out the remainder of your contract. She reported that you were very good." We then reached the theater and separated. That was the last time he spoke to me. My contract expired the first of June. I was offered a cut in pay to stay in the show which I refused and on the last day said goodbye to some of the cast. There was a small party and a wonderful camera with all kinds of lenses given to me by the actors. The residue of that experience was, it destroyed my confidence and it took years to rebuild. Interestingly when I think of that, it still hurts. I was so hurt and humiliated that I couldn't walk down Broadway for fear that I'd see someone who knew me and knew the tale of Fiddler so I ran off to Europe and stayed fourteen months. I'm sure that when I run into people that knew, they remember and after I leave talk about it.

The Greatest Story Ever Told

This was a film for which I was hired to play The Crying Man. The great George Stevens was directing. It had every star and name in Hollywood saying one or two lines from John Wayne, who played a Centurion, to Shelly Winters. You name them and you'll probably be right. Max Von Sydow was playing Jesus and the only actor with blue eyes.

Lynn Stalmaster was the casting agent on this film. I originally was supposed to be cast as one of the disciples, but as the weeks went by, I heard nothing I began calling my agent. After a few of these calls he said to me "I have an actor who gets $100,000 for his part and I get $10,000 for you who do you think I should push?" I was very upset by that. Any way I went to the Columbia back lot on my first day on the set. As I drove thru the gate I was asked my name and was told to follow the crowd and park my car and then follow the arrows to a tent where I was to hang my street clothes and get my costume from a costumer. At the entrance to this tent, this assistant told me that the metal pipes hanging above the benches both had corresponding numbers. "Remember them" for there are 500 extras and forget where you dressed and it will be a long time till you find your street clothes. I was given rags that looked like what desert Arabs wore. I dressed and followed the arrows to makeup where I was painted with body makeup. Following the arrows, I met one of the six assistant directors who told me to go up on a roof facing a square where the action was to take place.

On arriving on the roof an actor came up to me and asked, "You a Waver?" I looked at him and said, "I don't know what I'm supposed to do as they haven't told me as yet," waving my hand. "No I mean waiver," spelling it out. I didn't know what he was referring to when he saw the perplexed reaction on my face and "You a Principle?" he asked. "Yes," I said. "Let me stand next to you he said, so when they do the close-ups I will have to be in the shot and then I'll get another days work. Then in the evening George Stevens, sitting on a crane camera seat, used a bullhorn to announced that everyone should remember where they were and be in the same place tomorrow morning. The next three days every morning I'd go up onto the roof and wait till I was told what to do.

On this third day over the loud speaker system I hear, "Is there a Paul Marin on the set?" I call down from the roof that here I was. "Who told you to go up there," was the next question. "Come down from there." I found the assistant director who was looking for me. He said, "Who told to go up there? Where did you get that costume? You never went to your dressing room. Where are your street clothes?" "In the tent" I said. "Tell me the number and I'll have someone get them and bring them to your dressing room." My trailer was between Max Von Sydow's and Donald Pleasence's. From that day on we would lunch together every day and Peter Lorrie's ex-wife Celia Lovsky made up our fourth.

About two or so weeks into the shoot we infamous four were having lunch when Donald Pleasance asked me, "What character are you playing?" I said, "The Crying Man." "The Crying Man," he repeated, "I don't recall that character in the script." Then to relieve my anxiety he said, "It's undoubtedly an added character. "Did they give you a script?" "No," I answered "not as yet." Then I began to get nervous for they will probably knock on my dressing room door with scenes and say learn these, as we will shoot it in an hour. Thankfully that never happened.

One day as I was watching the shoot, it was on The Road to Calvary, when an extra fell down onto the street in an epileptic attack. Since my sister Mary had epilepsy I immediately went over to the guy and turned his head to the side so that he wouldn't swallow his tongue. Mr. Stevens now on a bullhorn from the boom camera was ranting about losing $8000 a minute and to move that guy away so he can finish shooting. Here we were making a picture of The Christian, half-God Jesus, and our director just wanted that ill person removed. One of the assistant directors came running over and I asked where was a doctor or nurse as the SAG contract called for a mobile hospital when there were so many actors and extras on the set.

With that, Assistant number one warned the other assistant that I was a principle, not an extra. Of course there wasn't a field hospital though by contract there was supposed to be. Finally an ambulance arrived and the poor man was taken away and the work continued: so much for morality in Hollywood.

On the close of the sixth week there was a knock on my dressing room door. Standing there was assistant number five who said, "Thank you Mr. Marin, it's a wrap for you." "A wrap," I said with disbelief, "I haven't worked yet or stepped in front of the camera." He looked a bit incredulous. "Well you go home, and I'll check the front office he said. If it's a mistake I'll phone you at home and we'll see you Monday, if not then thanks a lot. Bye and good luck."

Thank you George Stevens for subsidizing me that year. I get a residual check every year since "The Greatest Story Ever Told" is shown every Easter.

My Tour of Europe with the ITI

When the International Theater Institute (ITI) an apolitical group with offices in every major city in the world , had a meeting in New York, Actors Equity Association (AEA) hosted a cocktail party at

Lincoln Center and I met a few of their members. I was an elected council member of Actors Equity Association's governing body, unpaid but prestigious and a lot of work. There were perks such as seeing every play on Broadway free as we voted for the Tony Awards. When I mentioned I was planning my trip, Ralph Bellamy, president of AEA at that time, suggested I contact the ITI which had offices in the Theater Guild Theater building on 52nd Street near 8th Avenue. They gave me a book listing names of the executive secretary's and address's and phone numbers plus a letter of introduction with instructions to send a note or card two weeks in advance of my arrival.

I knew a flight attendant who worked on KLM airlines. When in New York, he would come to Joe Allan's where the working actors came for something to eat or a drink at the bar after work. He said, "Book your passage with KLM and I'll upgrade you." I booked my economy passage on his flight and was seated in First Class with all its amenities and was fêted with caviar. On landing he gave me an open tin of it as it couldn't really keep.

On arrival at Schiphol Airport, Amsterdam, I called the ITI office from my hotel and was invited to a party that night. A car was sent for me, and when I walked in a man greeted me in English, "I know you." "No, I'm afraid not as I just arrived here in Amsterdam this afternoon." "Well I still know you, and I saw you seven times." He was the producer of Fiddler on the Roof in Holland and saw me in the Broadway show prior to mounting Fiddler in the Netherlands. We chatted for a while and he wanted me to play Sancho Panza, in Man of La Mancha. I was flattered, but to play a Spaniard that means using Spanish-accented Dutch and especially since I don't know Dutch, I declined his offer.

My next stop was the Scandinavian Countries. In Oslo, Norway I wasn't too impressed with the theater. Also, the bars closed at odd hours and the patrons set themselves up with three and four drinks and then could barely walk out. This inevitably resulted in fights among friends. One day, leaving my hotel I saw these five guys all pretty drunk walking with their arms about each other. Suddenly one of them reached out and socked another of his group. I had had it. Since I arrived all I saw in the streets were fights. I went over and I tried to stop the fight.

One of the group said in English "You don't understand. One of the guys kicked the other." One of the fighters wore a heavy ring. I said, "You will end up cutting the others face and then you'll stop when the blood begins to flow. Then you'll throw your arms around him and both will be sorry, so stop now." Of course they didn't and what I had just prophesized happened as I had said. I left Copenhagen, Denmark and flew to West Berlin. The American Counsel in West Berlin advised me not to go, but if I went to come back to West Berlin to sleep. He cautioned me that there was no diplomatic exchange between East Berlin and West Berlin; therefore if I was arrested I would essentially be alone. I said "Thank you but I'm sure that I'll need no protection, as I am an actor and going to see Plays and rehearsals etc. I go with an open mind and open heart."

In the Eastern Bloc of countries I was met at all the airports with flowers and taken to anything I wanted to see, ballet, opera and theater. As a guest of the Berliner Ensemble Company I spent two weeks in East Berlin. Going back to the West each night and heading East through Checkpoint Charlie every morning. Berlin was divided into East Berlin, (Communist, Russian influence) and West Berlin, (Western, American influence) gave my passport to the *Vopos*, (East German Border guards) and told to sit and you will be called. When for the first time I went through Checkpoint Charlie I waited from 8 to 11:30 a.m.. I kept saying that I was invited to see rehearsals that started at 10 a.m., to no avail. I would sit there waiting to get my passport and was kept there for hours. To tell the truth I was very nervous. Why was I being kept at the checkpoint, are they duplicating my passport? All sorts of crazy thoughts were shooting through my brain. I would complain bitterly that I was missing a rehearsal but the East border guards had a deaf ear. Finally after two to three hours of cooling my heels they would signal me to come get my passport and make my way to the theater. I was allowed entry to East Berlin but first had to buy the minimum of $5 of East German Marks that were worthless anywhere outside of the Soviet Bloc. There were times that I waited only an hour but always waited.

I saw the Berthold Brecht's Theater production of Shakespeare's Coriolanus. The sets were way overbuilt, as every thing was functional. A bookshelf had real books. The ceiling had real beams. Here in the good ole USA we painted them onto the walls or scrims. In that production, however, when the battlements are stormed it was thoroughly believable: one army climbing a wall fighting to get over it and another army defending the wall was extremely realistic. The Berliner Ensemble Theater Company was known for their realism. The Three Penny Opera with Lottie Lenya starring was very stirring.

One night the cast invited me to a supper after Coriolanus. The restaurant was elegant and there was French Service, one waiter stood behind each guest refilling the plate as the food was being eaten and the wine glasses after each sip. One of their young lead actors asked me "How do you feel to be enslaved?" Enslaved? I answered, trying to be diplomatic that we are all enslaved it's just that I had a longer leash. Again the subject was raised. "Well, I can come to your country as long as I have the money to travel," I said. "Can you do the same?" He looked at me as if I was feeble-minded, and said, "Why would I want to." I said, "Yes but if you wanted to travel, could you? Once again the same answer, "Why would I want to? I don't want to leave this paradise." I wanted to say "yes but you're not answering the question: *could* you?" I let it drop. This same actor told me that the two packs of Marlboro cigarettes a day cost about $3 U.S. each, this I assumed was to tell me how good life was there in the East, that he made a lot of money and could afford American cigarettes.

Sitting next to me on my left was an actress in her upper twenties or early thirties. The actor opposite me raised himself off his chair leaned over and grabbed my head and planted a big wet kiss on my lips. To say I was nonplussed is putting it mildly. For a moment I was in shock. The actress soothed the atmosphere and just said "Forgive him, he thinks he's a clown and loves to shock people."

All in all it was a lovely supper and then a few walked me to Checkpoint Charlie and in no-man's-land between the two Berlins. The actors from the Berliner Ensemble Company (the Berthold Brecht Theater) and I sang songs from Broadway and German musicals. From that time on my entrée was instantaneous, without being forced to buy worthless Marks. When I'd get to Checkpoint Charlie, the *Vopo* I handed my passport to would hand it to someone behind a bank teller-type window. An officer would come out and in German say *"Wilkommen Shouspieler"* Welcome actor.

My overall impression was the acting and plays they did were really wonderful. Case in point, I had seen Strindberg's The Father in English many times. It never made sense that he would allow himself to be straight jacketed without putting up a fuss. In the Berliner Ensemble production in the very first scene the old woman housekeeper walks over to him while he's at his desk working and without as much acknowledging her she removes his suit coat and replaces it with his smoking jacket. All the while he keeps working. From this one action the audiences is led to believe that this is a function that she's been doing for years. When in the last scene she puts the straight jacket on him you see the shock, disbelief that she would do this to him.

Munich, Germany: I kept a daily diary that was stolen from my hotel room with all my money, letter of intro, the camera that was my goodbye gift from the Fiddler company, passport and my portable radio. Many three star hotels didn't have radios in the rooms. I was showering then stepping out to shave. I was going to the Munich Opera House that evening. On opening the bathroom door, it was very silent. I thought, damn the batteries died. I'll have to ask at the desk as to where I can buy them. After finishing bath and shave I stepped into the room and lo and behold! I didn't have to worry about replacing the batteries. The radio was gone. With every thing that was on top of the chest of drawers of value and bedside end table including my cigarettes except one thing, the booklet of ITI addresses which I found later was in my inside jacket pocket.

I immediately phoned the desk and told them to call the police as my room was burgled. When the plainclothes detective arrived he spoke English. I told him what had transpired and then he said in German to the uniformed officers "Isn't this the same room that was hit three weeks ago?" Since I spoke Yiddish I understood a great deal of the German conversation. They wrote down what had happened and left. To this day I feel it was an inside job done by one of the employees who had ready a built in reason for being in the room if confronted, could deflect suspicion: 'I came to turn the bed down.' They probably had a pillow case and swept off the end table and the top of the chest all that was there and swiftly departed. I can't prove that but whoever did it didn't break in but used a key.

Now with out money or passport etc. I immediately went to the U.S. Consulate. The Marine guard after I told my story gave me his pack of cigarettes and took me into the commissary and bought me breakfast until the Consul arrived. He took me to lunch and after I told him what had happened and that I need a passport in order to get replacement of my American Express traveler's checks. He was very clever, during lunch he casually asked what was on Broadway before I left for Europe, and what did I, a Brooklyn Dodger fan, feel when they left for L.A. and who the manager was. I passed all the tests for he told me to go across the street from the U.S. Council to a photographer and get two passport photos and handed me a 5-mark note to pay for them. Saying you'll return it when you get your money. A half-hour after I returned with the photos I had a new passport in my pocket.

Now to the American Express office in Munich. This turned out to be a trying experience. "What were the numbers of the checks?" I was asked. I didn't know, as all was taken with the check numbers, letters of introduction, booklet of names of presidents, secretaries and addresses of the ITI offices etc. were in two wallets and both were stolen. I had over fifteen thousand in traveler's checks. I was told that the main office for stolen checks was in Vienna.

After much arguing and then threats to take an ad out in the English language Herald Tribune and picket their office here in Munich I was given six hundred dollars in traveler's checks and was told the rest will be given to me in Vienna. In Vienna I learned that the restitution office had moved to Paris. It just so happened that I was planning to go to Vienna next. But... what would have happened if Vienna were not on my itinerary?

As it turned out there were a lot more arguing and threats that ads will be taken out in the New York Times, Chicago Sun Times and the L.A. Times telling of the false claims of the American Express Company: "If checks are lost or stolen, they will immediately be replaced without hassle." Not true. Over six weeks passed before all my money was returned, and I had to stay in Vienna all that time. It is not one of my favorite cities, and I couldn't wait to get my money and leave. German-speaking Austria and Germany twenty-three years after the Holocaust had too many awful thoughts for me. The German speaking countries are so full of superiority (read, inferiority) complex that an incident that took place in West Berlin illustrates this.

I was in a restaurant in West Berlin at a table alone when the *Maître d'* placed a young man who turned out to be twenty-two years old at my table. I said hello in English. He immediately said "American." "Yes," I answered. In our discussions on politics expressly, Russia and The Soviet Union, he said, "If you Americans gave us the atom bomb we'd know how to use it." I answered, "That's precisely why we won't give it to you." The Germans then were still denying their Nazi past and all were saying they had no knowledge of the Holocaust. Even those living in the shadow of the smoke with the stench of the burning bodies thrown into the ovens, all claimed, "No, they didn't know, they saw and smelled nothing."

Austria- two memories stand out. I was at the Opera House that is beautiful, but I found out the reason people in classic plays and operettas hold handkerchiefs to their noses, the body odor there was gagging. I assume they perfumed the handkerchief so they didn't have to suffer their fellow patron. In Vienna I had an expensive blue blazer cleaned and it came back smelling from gasoline or turpentine and I couldn't get the smell out of it so left it in the hotel. I recall walking down the Austrian streets and seeing stout dumpy woman sitting at the outdoor café's with their Tyrolean hats and skirt suits eating mountains of whip cream deserts.

Hungary: In 1967 and Soviet soldiers were everywhere and the hotel had a female concierge sitting behind a table on every floor to jot down each person's comings and goings. I was assigned a guide, a college student, (KGB? secret police?) who would escort me only to places that I was allowed to go to. Where, I asked, was a synagogue? He said he'd check and the next day when I asked again was told he was waiting for the information.

One day he told me he had exams and he wouldn't be able to escort me so he wrote out instructions to show to a taxi driver to take me to the theater with instructions to pick me up after and bring me back to the hotel. Since I don't speak, read, or write Hungarian I decided to take a city bus. I got the number of the bus from the hotel clerk. Getting on the bus, I showed the guide's paper with the theater's name on it to the driver. She answered me in Hungarian. I was back to square one, as I now didn't know what she was telling me. An old woman wearing a babushka and peasant blouse and skirt, who I figured was about seventy, was sitting on the bus. I said "*Sprechen Sie Deutsch?*" and then in German she said, "*Ich vill dir tzeigan.*" (I will show you) I said "*Danke*" "*Nisht tor fa vus,*" she answered. My ear went up when I heard this Yiddish, and she asked me to sit next to her. (Yiddish is basically *Platz Deutsch*, Low German that the Jews took with them when they were expelled from Germany in 1605. They developed the language by adopting words from all the other countries languages that they went to. Present German is *Hoch Deutsch*, High German.) She told me that life there was terrible and that she worked six days a week in a factory ten hours a day, and if she went to the synagogue she would be fined a days pay. Her husband was dead, and she had small children. She said that she was 40 years old. I couldn't believe it. She looked so old. She asked me to come with her to her home, as she needed to talk to me. Should I or shouldn't I go. I had a ticket to a play and this was basically why I was there. Is she a plant by the State Police set up to see what I'll do, as to why my guide was made unavailable? The U.S. State Department advised me before I went a) not to go to the Eastern Bloc as the U.S. had no diplomatic relations with the Communist governments and b) if I should get into any situation they wouldn't be able to help me. To my regret to this day I did not go with her, even if it was for nothing more than allowing her to vent to a fellow Jew. Her life was tough.

In Europe a theater ticket enables one to check coats. During intermission I had my cigs in my jacket pocket but my lighter was in my coat. I saw a man about thirty who was smoking so I pantomimed needing a light. He immediately took a lighter out of his jacket and lit my cigarette then took me by the elbow to the bar and ordered two cognacs, I tried to pay but he wouldn't let me.

He took me over to meet his sister and her husband. She spoke German, so we had a language in common. Now we could speak I understood one of every twenty words. She asked what I would like to see in Budapest after the theater. *Tzgyna* (Gypsy) music was my answer. We got a cab and off we went to Pest where by chance, at the restaurant a Gypsy wedding reception was taking place. It was wonderful and we danced and sang, without words of course. We had two bottles of wine and lots of food for which I paid. When the bill came I couldn't believe it. It equaled two dollars and change.

Since they lived in Pest she told her brother to escort me by taxi to my hotel in Buda, if I went by myself she said the driver would overcharge me. It was a memorable evening. I stayed there in Budapest about eight or nine days went to the zoo, saw ballet and folkdance performances and plays. Dance was easier to follow because things that are not said but shown with body language etc. I might have sold myself a bill of goods and thought the play I was seeing was the author's but in reality it could have been something totally different. Yet if the acting was good it was entertaining, if it was bad I dozed off, and since I didn't snore no one knew. I always went back stage to congratulate the actors and often was invited to go with them for a drink and food and talk of Broadway theater and Hollywood. They knew of the vibrancy of the Broadway theater of the 1950s and 60s.

Under Marshal Tito, Yugoslavia was in bed with Moscow. Behind the Iron Curtain I was met with a red carpet at the airports and taken to a hotel. I paid for my hotels and also for my reciprocal dinners, plus a gift of a book on New York theater. I was invited by the then President of the Actors Union to dinner at a club, with his secretary, her husband, a woman from Moscow who held the purse strings for the Arts Grants from Russia to Yugoslavia plus a few other guests.

In conversation I asked, "Who are the men I see on the streets wearing white skullcaps, from down just above the eyebrow to behind the ear, covering the whole top of the head?" "Oh," said the President of the Actors Union, "those are our Niggers." I was stunned, so I said "that word in English is derogatory and…." Before I could finish he said, "I know English very well and I chose that word carefully. You see they are Albanians, and they do the same kinds of work that the Black man does in the U.S." Oh, I thought then, Karl Marx was probably spinning in his grave. I wasn't too thrilled with their theater, mostly liked their vaudeville type theater. Time to move on.

Greece was in the hands of the four(?) Army Colonels' military dictatorship junta. Arrival at the Athens airport was not the same as behind the Iron Curtain. No one met me though I knew my hotel so took a cab there. In the room I phoned the ITI office but found that the number had been disconnected: strange. I had the desk clerk write out a map to the address he found in their phone book. I got off the bus and walked up to the building. The door and windows facing the street were covered with boards. Stepping back to make sure I had the right address I noticed two men to my left, one leaning against a lamppost and the other standing looking at me. I said "Excuse me, I don't speak Greek. Do either of you speak English." By their response I could see they did not so I asked "ITI here?" and pointed to the boarded up building. One came over and pointed to the building next to it. I thought, that makes sense they moved. I said *efchoresto*, thank you, the only Greek word I know and went in.

It was strange. There was an elevator one call button in the center of this tiny entrance lobby and a winding staircase along its side. On the elevator's arrival, I opened the gate found it had only one button. Pushing the button, we went up slowly and then stopped. Getting out, I knocked on the unmarked wooden door one immediately in front of the elevator.

A man in a business suit opened it, and I asked, "Is this the ITI?" He looked at me strangely and indicated for me to wait. Then a man who spoke English appeared. "Who do you want?" he asked. I said, "The International Theater Institute, the ITI." He said, "Come in." Inside there stood a long table at which two men working on papers sat facing the entrance door. There were other desks with men at them scattered about the long rectangular room. On the back wall there were doors and I was taken into one of them to an office furnished with a desk and a chair at its side.

Then the questions started, "How do you know the International Theater Institute?" Another man came in so I told him about the party Actors Equity hosted and that I was an elected member of the governing body on a world tour seeing theater. "Where did I get the president's name and his secretary, do I know them, have I written to them, etc, etc." This went on for four hours. My questioners claimed to be from a branch office of the Foreign Ministry. I must have finally convinced them, for I was ushered back into the big room where one man called me over to his desk then motioned for me to sit. He said "Euripides' Medea at the Dionysus National Theater tomorrow night. They are on vacation," he said, "but I just ordered them back. Is there something else you'd like to see or do?" Once again I said *efchoresto* and wanted to get out of there as quickly as I could.

I thought, a whole company to perform for me? Well when I arrived at the theater it was true: just me plus someone from the government.

The house lights dimmed. Medea was truly a command performance. Afterwards I went on to the stage to thank them for their wonderful performances and apologized for breaking up their vacation. In talking to the actors one by one they managed to move me about to talk to me alone for a few seconds warning that there was a government spy in the company and to be very careful what I say as they can have me arrested and thrown into jail. What was most interesting was that every one I talked to said the same thing and I spoke to all the performers in the company. I guess the spy himself realized what was being said and decided to cover him or herself.

On arriving at the Athens Airport I met three men in civilian clothes who instructed the airline agent that I had to show them my passport. I walked over and handed them my passport, one man asked, "How much money are you carrying not only Greek money but in all currencies." Once again I showed how clever I am. I answered that I'd show them all my Greek money but my American Express Traveler's Checks, I was adamant, were none of their business. It got a bit uncomfortable for a moment there but they figured that this American was not only crazy but also stupid and decided to end the questions. I was off to the plane and Istanbul.

Turkey: Arriving at the airport I had no idea as to where to go, as no one was there to meet me. I phoned the ITI number in the booklet but no one answered. What to do? I went to the tourist desk at the airport and showed them the booklet. The woman tried the number herself with the same result. I asked her to recommend a hotel near that address. Fortunately it was near the business area. I took tours of the Blue Mosque and other sights and went to a Turkish bath. It had a very large half moon cement mound that was heated from beneath with a wood fire. People lay on top and on its sides. At the bath I had a massage by a man who had to be about 300 pounds. He pummeled me and twisted my arms, legs and body in positions that it was never meant to assume. I limped out of there and that limp lasted a few days. So much for Turkish Massage.

I found the old Arab market and bought a Russian Samovar and a large church candleholder, a carpet plus a few other things and had them shipped home. I was told that underneath the street level of this market was another level where slaves can be bought, this in 1967 the enlightened twentieth century. I couldn't find the entrance and didn't want to ask as I really didn't know how true it was. Finally, I gave up and went to my hotel for dinner and pack to leave Turkey for Egypt.

Egypt: I arrived in Cairo were the amount of people looking very dirty was startling. Men walked around in dirty white robes that looked like they hadn't seen soap and water in quite some time. I found a hotel that was in a business building and that surprised me, as the lower floors were offices. I settled in and went looking for a restaurant where I had couscous for the first time. It takes on the taste of the other food that you're eating. I didn't become a fan. The Cairo Museum with artifacts of their ancient culture piled one on top of the other, without descriptive or informational cards in English to inform the visitor made it trying.

On my entry into the Museum I was greeted by a uniformed guard who looked me over and said, "Jew?" not in a welcoming gesture, though not threatening. That started my visit to the museum badly and I looked around a bit and left. I went to the Giza pyramids and bought a ticket to see the light show when I returned from Luxor.

I took an overnight train to Luxor to the Valley of the Kings and saw the sarcophagus of King Tut and other tombs with lots of gold artifacts. I took one of those small open boats with two men, one steered and the other controlled the sail down the Nile. We stopped at a few tiny islands that were inhabited by flies, reeds and not much more.

On the overnight train back to Cairo, shared a sleeping car with a Captain in the Egyptian Army. He had soldier friends, seeing him off. They had sandwiches and offered me one. Not to offend I took one bite, and it tasted rancid. I kept it in my mouth until all were busy talking and not looking my way, then spit it out and placed it under the cushion. I had the lower bunk. We all went into the dinning car for tea. I began to feel ill. I couldn't keep my head up so excused myself and headed back to the compartment. Before getting there, I threw up in the passageway. Sitting on his haunches was a train employee I assumed a cleaner for the train, so apologized and gave him a dollar to clean it up. That night thought I was going to die as I was running from every orifice. The Captain was very nice and said he was being met in Cairo by his brother who is a doctor and when we arrived he'd examine me. About an hour before we got to Cairo I began to feel better but exhausted. I got a cab to my hotel and didn't go to the light show at Giza. Too ill, I went to bed and stayed there the next day also. I had room service bring me soup and toast.

Now back to me old self went sight seeing. Met a guy in front of the Hilton while I was standing looking at the Nile, he told me all the aid money given by the U.S. was not reaching the people and pointed out a brick carrier who had a triangular hod carrier on his back with a leather strap tied to his forehead. He said see that man, he makes about 50 cents a day. I don't know how he lifted it more or less carried it on his back.

He told me, "That the people were angry with Anwar Sadat as all the humanitarian money given to Egypt didn't trickle down but fattened his cronies, that under Muslim law a man can have four wives and the one we in the West knew was number two, Jihan al-Sadat, who was a very educated upper class Egyptian woman. His first wife he never took with him on his diplomatic missions for she was a dumpy peasant woman." Sadat as we all know was assassinated in 1973 for making peace with Israel.

I spent a lot of time people watching sitting in an open small coffee shop drinking Turkish coffee and smoking from a floor hookahs with four or six hoses to smoke from. One memory stands out. While I was smoking and drinking coffee in another coffee shop a young guy sat down and ordered a tea or coffee and was using the same hookah. A policeman walked over and in Arabic said something to him. He got up and since he spoke English said he was warned not to talk to foreigners and if he was seen again he would be arrested: Arab democracy at work. Next stop Israel.

In Tel Aviv, Israel, a few weeks after the Six Day War, I checked in to a bed & breakfast hotel on Hayarkan Street a few blocks to the beach and next to the American Embassy. In Israel I was on an exhilarating high. I walked over to Dizengoff Street and found a number of sidewalk cafés. Tomorrow., I thought, I will go there for people watching. That night I went to a party at the Hilton Hotel and my ITI host introduced me to the Minister of Culture. He was charming and invited me to stay in the country learn Hebrew, saying he'd get me into the Habima or Comeri theaters. He'd pay for my going to an ulpan to learn the language. Learning a foreign language is not one of my talents. When I asked why he was being so generous, he said that Israel didn't have actors my age as Hitler had murdered them and there was much need for them in Israel. He gave me his card and said, "Please call."

The next morning I went to the dining room for breakfast. I was amazed by the amount of salad, hot and cold cereals, eggs, olives, yogurt, and breads of all kinds. After a walk on the cliff overlooking the Mediterranean I found a phone and called the minister, and we arranged to meet for lunch. I enrolled in an Ulpan in Haifa and tried to learn this ancient language but finally gave up. What I did learn was my English accent was overwhelming. I was told that Anglos had a very difficult time learning Hebrew: how true at least for me. In America I was called a Jew and in Israel was called an Anglo-Saxon in the U.K. even Disraeli was "A JEW." After a few months I returned to Europe, to England, and finally home.

In New York I met Jean-Louis Barrault and his wife Madeleine Renaud. I had seen him on Broadway. I arranged a luncheon with him and his wife and brought an interpreter from Berlitz School of Languages. We had lunch in a French restaurant on 48th Street between 7th and 8th Avenues. The purpose of this meeting was to ask him to take me on as a student. I was already in my early thirties, and he felt that my body was already too mature to be able to become a mime. I said that was not my ambition but to learn enough to aid my acting career. He was especially charming. Madam Renaud sat through the lunch and said very little. I got the message when he told me he was no longer taking on new students.

In Paris, I went to see as much of French theater especially Renaissance theater as what was available plus contemporary theater.

Italy was an experience in itself. In Florence, going to dinner, saw "Restaurant Teatro" and walked in: a theater restaurant. It must have been fate. It was around seven in the evening and the place was empty. I called out 'Hello,' a man came out so I asked too early or too late? He looked at me and in passable English said, "the people come after 10 p.m. if you want food please sit." I told him yes, and a little white lie, "This is my first meal in Italy." He made food for me as if I were a close relative, I ordered a bottle of wine with two glasses and asked him to join me for at least one glass of wine, which he did after bringing out the first course. It was an epicurean delight. Florence was for me the most beautiful, though in Venice with the gondoliers touring the waterways, I felt I was in a MGM Movie.

Rome: I was in the Vatican when I heard a female voice calling, Father O'Hara over and over until this very plainly dressed woman was at my elbow. "Oh," she exclaimed, "you're not Father O'Hara from Boston, but you sure can be his double." She gave me her name but unfortunately with out my diary I no longer recall other than she was a nun. "No, sorry" I said, "I'm not Father O'Hara besides I'm Jewish." As we talked along came a man in a nondescript herringbone brown suit whom she introduced as Brother something. They asked if they could show me the Sistine Chapel and tour the Vatican with me as my guides. Who would say no to that? Not me! While this was going on I said to Brother No Name, how does one get to see the Pope? He said you want to see the Pope? With that he took a pad out of his inside pocket and wrote down an address and a message in Italian, for me to take to an office outside of St. Peter's square and show to the secretary.

After leaving them and thanking them for their wonderful tour went to that address. It was a Jesuit office. I gave the note to a young lady sitting at a desk. She immediately asked me to write my name down and wrote it on an invitation (which I had transplanted to a t-shirt which I still have, the invitation is long gone) to take in two days from then to the Swiss Guards. When the day arrived I did as instructed and was ushered into a large room with a thrown on one end. I'd say there were about 100 people in the room. Pope John Paul entered with much applause. I was in the sixth row of seats. He spoke in many languages. Knowing a bit of Spanish and English, I pretty much followed what he said. I assume he said the same thing in the other languages. He seemed a nice and very learned man. Of course I visited the Catacombs and saw the skeletons but what was most impressive there was a skeleton of a little girl that looked as if she had recently died but had been dead for many centuries, hair, skin, looked as if she was asleep. Then there was what I assumed a British officer with a curled mustache and a full head of hair. He'd also been dead for many decades if not longer though looking as he too had just died.

In Calabria, Sicily I was invited to witness a contest of student musicians from piano to violin. Lovely is not the word. I found it very exciting and exhilarating.

In London I stayed at a hotel (The Crown Royal?) in the lobby of which I ran into William Darrid, a Broadway producer who saw me shivering. It was very cold and I borrowed a sweater from him that I returned when back in New York. In London, I was on a busman's holiday. When a bus driver would go on vacation he'd drive himself where ever he was going. An actor, I went to plays. I saw two shows daily in the West End for a little over two weeks. My world tour now came to an end as I had spent all my money so back to New York with wonderful memories of The International Theater Institutes and their local offices for arranging theater tickets for what ever interested me plus dinner parties etc. Behind the Iron Curtain I was treated as a visiting American (star) actor.

The Seventies

Spain & Morocco

In 1973 I went to Spain and Morocco. I flew in to Madrid and did the sight-seeing there: the Del Prado Museum and the burial monuments of the Spanish Kings, plus a lot of Franco's fascist architecture. I rented a Morris Mini automobile and was off south, stopping at cities and towns on the way to Morocco. At Algesera, Spain I took an auto ferry to Ceuta, Spain, a six-mile wide Spanish city on the mainland of Morocco. Spain kept that enclave when Isabella the Catholic Queen chased the Arabs out of Spain and southern Europe and back into North Africa in 1492.

After crossing the Spanish border and going through Moroccan customs drove to Tangier. Arriving on the main thoroughfare there in the center of the street standing on a sort of kiosk was a policeman directing traffic. Stopping, I ask him if he knew where I could find a clean European hotel; the Middle Eastern hotels had two-foot prints and a hole in the floor for toiletry use. Sorry, not for me. He obviously understood my extremely primitive Spanish. He got off his platform and got into my car and pointing to turn right or left or straight ahead and took me to this lovely hotel. Then saluted and I assume walked back to his post. I was amazed, as that would never happen in New York City.

The hotel was nice and there met with a guide who took me sight seeing. How carpets were made and wool dyed in big vats, the women workers covering their faces not to have their photos taken as they thought, I was told by the guide, that their souls will now be in the camera. Oh well I'm sure there are just as much nonsense in our so-called enlightened Western mind. Then my guide asked if I wanted to see how hashish was made. Of course I said this was a trip for enlightenment. So into my Morris Mini which had room for me as driver and a seat for another passenger or luggage for there wasn't a trunk only a motor in back that also held a jack.

We traveled it seemed in circles as he probably did it purposely so I wouldn't be able to find it again. Totally unnecessary as my sense of direction is the worst. I once worked for MGM for six weeks and then three months later my agent called and said I had an audition at MGM and I couldn't find it. Had to go into a gas station and ask.

It was interesting as there were numerous pressings of the marijuana plant and the last pressing was Henna used to dye hair and wool red. This was a big operation as there were many people working the presses. Now over Turkish coffee and telling me how easy it was to bring it into the U.S. as they can cut a leather belt in half length wise or a valise and line it with hash and sew it up again and all different ways to smuggle the hash in. Then the reason for my visit, they wanted to know how much I wanted to buy? I was stunned as I didn't want to buy any, I could see they became quite agitated so I said ok, I'll take ten dollars worth. They looked at me incredulously as if to say we gave you coffee and this is what you want...ten dollars worth?

The big guns left the room and I was left with the guy who was sweeping the floor plus my guide. The sweeper took out a knife and cut off a piece of hash the size of the nail of my little finger, wrapped it in tin foil and passed it to me in exchange for the ten dollars. My guide was very disappointed and back at the hotel took off never to be seen by me again.

With that I decided to drive to Fez, which was two hundred miles away with no gas stations or houses or anything between Tangier and Fez. I was told to carry water and extra gas and some food in case of a breakdown. After stocking up, I started at seven a.m. It was ninety-two degrees Fahrenheit. Driving along I see three young men with backpacks walking in the direction I'm going. I stop thinking they must be American tourists and say Hi, where you heading? It turns out two are Swiss and one Moroccan. I said this auto is very small but if you'd like I'll ferry you one at a time to the nearest hamlet and come back for the next, they said no thanks but if I wanted I could take all three. It was like a clown car when the three of them got in backpacks and all. The temperature was said to go to one hundred fifteen degrees by noon.

We drove about twenty miles when we were confronted with a military roadblock. On each side of the road were soldiers with rifles and on the right off to the side was a little hut. As soon as I saw it, since I had the hash in my shirt pocket, I quickly dug it out and swallowed it tin foil and all. As I was driving up one of the soldiers said something in Arabic. At my blank expression he switched to French. I said "*Parlez-vous* English?" He put up his index finger and walked to another soldier.

Now an officer came over and said, "May I see your passport and will the passengers get out of the car and place their backpacks on the ground." In emptying their backpacks marijuana was discovered. The soldier who found it immediately beat the Moroccan guy who had it in his bag. Others came and beat him some more; the officer came to me and asked, "Do you know these men?" "No. I was just giving them a lift as it was very hot and they were walking and I thought they'd die from

142

heat exhaustion." He immediately informed me that under Moroccan Law anyone found with drugs in a car, or on a person traveling with the owner or renter in my case, the driver is held responsible.

I said, in that case please call the American ambassador and tell him that Paul Marin is being held on possible drug charges because I was a Good Samaritan in trying to help out hitch hikers so they didn't die of the heat, which as of now was one hundred fifteen degrees.

Immediately he left the car and went to speak to his Colonel who had more gold braid on his cap and shoulders plus medals enriching his left breast. I heard him say 'Consul General'. In any language I guess it's the same.

In a few minutes he returned and handed me my passport with "My colonel said, 'don't be a Good Samaritan: never pick up strangers.' You may go." I felt sorry for the guys but there was nothing I could do. As I was driving away I saw one of the soldiers hit one of the Swiss boys with the butt of his rifle. I was also beginning to feel the effects of the hash I swallowed, but drove carefully not to be stopped by anyone.

The next couple of hours was uneventful and every once in a while a few young kids would run into the road with a couple of plums or peaches in their hand trying to wave me down. Where they came from was a total mystery as there were no houses or towns that I had passed. It also made me crazy as I was driving sixty mph and they would suddenly appear. My big fear was that I would hit one of these kids.

Driving along I came across a young man who had two sticks in the ground cradling a couple of boxes of plums and peaches. I pulled over as here was an almost store keeper. "*Parle-vous Français?*" He asked. "No, *Habla Español?*" I asked. He shook his head no. "*Aravite?*" he asked. I was shaking my head "No" as a young guy on a bicycle rode up. He called out "English?" "No," I replied, "American." "I speak American," he proudly said. "Good," I answered, "tell this guy I want a half of a kilo of plums." The transaction now complete and my Moroccan money put away my translator asked me if I wanted tea. I was confused and asked "Where?" There was nothing to be seen in any direction from the road. He said, "My house," pointing in the direction of the right side of the road where in the far distance were seen a mountain range. Not too far he said, follow me. He took off on his bike and I followed in my Morris Mini.

I drove about three miles and he turned onto a dirt road and we drove on that about four more miles and then the dirt road vanished and became a dirt field that was full of rocks and boulders. How far I drove on that I really couldn't say, as I was more involved with not hitting a boulder that would disable the car. Finally there in sight was a large fence made up of branches of trees that had their leaves and twigs chopped off and dug into the ground placed one next to each other making a solid rectangular wall. This fence had a double door kind of gate made of the same branches that opened into the compound. Under the door was a tree trunk acting as a door jam.

I stopped the car and got out locking it when this young guy whose name was Abdul Khaddar said "No! Drive over the tree trunk and park, if the car is left outside when we come out it would be totally taken apart and carted away. Drive in." That's what I did.

Inside on the left side was a goat, chickens in a coop, a cow and two sleepy mangy looking dogs. On the right side was an open shed with tools and farming equipment. Straight ahead were five woman sitting on their haunches on a tile floor about six feet deep running the length of the house which had six doors that led into rooms. The woman were knitting or crocheting. As I drove in two of the younger woman got up and brought out carpets that they beat with a large flat bamboo spoon. Then cleaned brought it back into the room and Abdul ushered me in.

Inside there were no decorations, no pictures or photos, on the wall facing the entrance was a seat high and seat depth straw, covered with a cloth. On the right side wall was the same width and length. On the left wall side was more straw but this time, single bed width all covered with cloth and had a number of pillows. I was asked to sit and in came a few men. His father, (Abdul turned out to be twenty-two years old) and two of his brothers. Then a young woman came in with a folding stand of hammered aluminum set it up and left returned with a tray of the same hammered aluminum filled with fruit and some kind of bread soaked in honey.

Another young man entered and Abdul asked, "don't you recognize him, my brother in commerce," he called him. That's true; he was the guy I bought the plums from with the two sticks in the ground. Well when one sells from a store or even if only two sticks are in the ground that is "commerce."

Then in came another woman carrying another tray with glasses filled with tea and mint and a hookah (a water pipe) filled with tobacco (I think. It could have been hash.) Abdul was the translator. His father and other brothers worked on their farm, though I didn't see anything resembling plowed land or land that was cultivated.

We sat around the hookah with six attached pipes and smoked and talked. Their life was hard, up at the crack of dawn, about 4:30 a.m. There was no dawn in Africa as we know it, for the sun rose full and at night the sunset was so rapid. One moment it was light and the next it was night. There were no windows in the room I was in, so there was a Coleman lamp and that's why I hadn't noticed that it had turned dark. When I looked out the open doorway I thought, 'How am I going to find my way out of here and back to the main road'? Just as I thought that Abdul said, "My father would like to invite you to stay the night."

I told him to tell his father that I would be honored to spend the night in his home.

After a few more hits of the hookah Abdul excused himself and then returned, he said. 'Come I want to show you something'. He had a portable radio and a couple of sheepskins and we went outside the gate and walked about ten or so yards. He put down the skins and turned the radio to lovely quiet music and we lay down and he pointed at the sky. It was breathtaking. I had never seen so many stars in my life. Far from the nearest city, there were no reflections of light onto the sky. It seemed that there were thousands of stars in every square inch. We stayed there for about an hour talking and looking at the stars.

The single size straw bed was now made up with a blanket and off to sleep the next thing I knew I heard people moving about. Looking out the door it was light and the time was 4:45 a.m. It seems that the family was getting ready to go to work in the fields. Abdul came and asked if I wanted to bathe. I said "Yes, where?" 'The River,' came the reply. In the front yard I saw that I had a flat tire.

Opening the lid of the trunk where the motor was, attached was a car jack. I'd never seen one like that before but we couldn't find out how it worked. Abdul said don't worry, went to the shed in the front yard and got a pickax and started to dig under the flat tire. When the hole was deep enough he removed the flat and replaced it with the spare that was attached to the trunk lid above the motor. Very compact. Then he got a shovel and refilled the hole patted it down and off we drove.

At the bank of the river were many large black tents and lots of woman also in black robes all with veils with only both or one eye showing. We were at least one hundred yards away when Abdul said 'there's my aunt,' and shouted something in Arabic. There was a return cry and Abdul turned and said, "We're invited to breakfast but first let's go in and swim." No swimsuit required. The water was cool, not cold

146

and refreshing. I had a towel in the car and we dried and dressed and walked to the tent. Immediately after Abdul called out to her there was a mad scramble of young girls shaking out and beating of carpets for our arrival to their tent.

The entry flap faced the river and the tent was very large, I'd guess about fifty feet in circumference and at the center of the roof was a large opening that acted as a flue, when the door flap was open it brought the air from the river into the tent. It felt as if it were air-conditioned, the cool air from the river was amazing. Then there were the flies, thousands of them, settling on faces, noses, eyes, lips, when open into mouths. Now I know why the people in these very hot and desert areas carry whisks and constantly use them.

In a matter of minutes in came about half a dozen men plus Abdul and me, now all sitting in a large circle. And unless Abdul said something to them they just sat there drinking their tea eating the honeyed bread (different from what was served at Abdul's house) or eating a piece of fruit. When my eyes met one of the men he would smile and the others seeing him smile would also smile. In fact that was the dominant discourse, smiling. After a half hour Abdul made it plain that we were leaving and saying our goodbyes walked to the car.

He directed me back to the main road and I said I'd drive you back to where the dirt road ends and then I'll turn around and be on the road to Fez. He wouldn't hear of it insisting that he walked from the main road all the time. We shook hands and exchanged addresses and said goodbye. I had left money under the pillow of the straw bed I slept in, figuring when his mother or someone collecting the bed things would find it. I didn't want to insult them by offering to pay for their hospitality of staying the night. I would have had to rent a room somewhere so I felt it was only fair.

My Parents

My parents lived together in this unhappy marriage for 63 years without friends or family visiting. In the last years of her life, nine months of every year were spent in bed in deep depression. I'd feel terrible for her. The only food she ate was a glass of milk over a period of weeks, and we had to plead with her to take a sip and take a bite of an occasional piece of buttered bread. That ill and sad life of hers lasted for 84 years. As she lay in her coffin I said, "Well Momma, you prayed for death. Your wish is now answered. Unfortunately your life was hell."

When my mother died in 1973, and Mary was the first over at their apartment and went thru my mother's things like a ghoul, even taking the cultured pearl necklace that I saved up to buy for Mother's Day at the Navy PX that cost me $26 (a large amount at the time). In 1945 I was in the Navy making 21 dollars a month. Mary grabbed the pearls and more. That was one thing about her, cheap and selfish. I'm afraid the two apples that fell from that tree unfortunately stayed close to the trunk.

My Father died in 1975, after all expenses were paid (grave, rabbi, stone etc.) $1560 remained, so this money was split between the six children: $260 each, if I remember correctly. My older brother Abe, a depressive like our mother, was often fired from his work as an engineer because he was depressed and unable to get out of bed. He was married and had three children. He was very good at his work so companies were happy to hire him, but the frequent loss of employment was a hardship. I suggested that Mary give her share to Lottie who really needed it, and I would give mine to Abe. Mary who bragged about the living her husband made selling insurance said no. "It's my inheritance, it was given to me." Two hundred dollars and change…. Sad, especially since she wasn't in tough times.

A Bi-Coastal Career

Home again, I decided to become bi-coastal, working in film, TV and theater. In 1976 I was cast in a play called "The Decision" which, according to critic Jonathan Takiff of a Philadelphia newspaper, featured "the poorly timed and blocked direction by Arthur Allan Seidelman." Mr. Takiff's headline: "The Best Decision: Forget it!" The star was Hugh O'Brian, as charming and friendly an actor as one could work with. We lasted five days and closed in Philadelphia. Oh, the life of a stage actor, but that wasn't the only time a play closed before opening on Broadway.

In 1976, while in Philadelphia, Seidelman asked me and a couple of other members of the cast to view a film he made that was pro-Arab funded by Arabs. It was an anti-Israel film and I asked him how, as a Jew, he could make it? He never spoke to me again, nor, when he was working in Hollywood directing a film, would he see me for a part. I felt then that was a despicable thing to do and still feel the same. But then people like that will do anything for money or like Elia Kazan (whom I worked for on the film "Face in The Crowd") who named people he thought were Communists for the House Un-American Committee to be able to continue to work. The fact that those he named were then put on a blacklist and were no longer able to work in TV and films didn't seem to upset his sleep.

The Betty White Show

"The Betty White Show" was episodic television. I was cast to play an executive from New York who flew in to cancel the show. One of the sight gags was for two stunt people a man and a woman to fall past a window; we were supposed to be in a high-rise building. During the dress rehearsal with an audience, all went well with the first one to jump, a stuntwoman fell about 16 feet onto an air mattress. The stuntman then jumped head first from the raised platform, missed the mattress and broke his neck. I'll never forget that scream; I'd never before or since heard anything like that. It seemed to last about two minutes. An ambulance was called and he was taken to a hospital.

Georgia Engle and Betty White plus the other members of the cast were shaken and distraught. The dress rehearsal was immediately stopped and the audience was let out. We were asked to eat dinner while the powers that be decided what to do. Lynn Wood who was playing my wife, and the rest of the cast thought that the powers would cancel the taping and break for the night and tape the next day. Word came that we would continue on. The audience was brought back in and we played. When it came time for the bodies to fall this time it was a man's suit that was filled with something and a women's dress also stuffed dropped past the window. The stunt man I heard later was paralyzed; I hope that was reversible, as I never heard anything more.

In August 2008, The Academy of Television Arts and Sciences honored Betty White on her sixtieth anniversary in television. She was still working on a new show for the 2009 season. Valerie Harper took a night off from Tallulah at the Pasadena Playhouse. Georgia Engle also took a night off and flew in from San Francisco where she was playing in The Drowsy Chaperone. Mary Tyler Moore and Ed Asner, one of my sponsors for entry into the Academy of Motion Picture Arts and Sciences, were there, along with a full house of television actors, producers and writers filling the 600 seats of the Television Academy Theater. It was a wonderful night for me to see and say hello to Betty, Georgia and especially Valerie.

Checking Out

In 1981, I was cast in Checking Out at the Westwood Playhouse (now the Geffen Playhouse) across the street from UCLA. We rehearsed on Hollywood Boulevard in the Masonic Temple for four weeks before we were scheduled to move into the Westwood Playhouse. Call on the first day at Westwood was for ten a.m. I'm always early, a consequence of my theater training. If you're late the stage manager sends on your understudy you lose that day's pay. The producers don't pay you for missed performances. On my arrival waited for the stage manager who normally is there right after me. This day all the actors were assembled and no stage manager. He finally arrived at 10:30 a.m. with the news that the play had closed the night before. It seems that the producer absconded with all the monies and the sets and costumes hadn't been paid for, so were repossessed by the set builder's and the costume designer's workshop took back the costumes. Actors Equity paid us our two weeks closing pay and to the credit of the producer (who shall remain nameless) made good to Equity by sending a check a few weeks later covering what AEA spent for salaries and return fares for the actors.

Hollywood Films

In Hollywood I did a few TV shows and several films starring Goldie Hawn ("Pvt. Benjamin"), Luciano Pavarotti ("Yes, Georgio"), Peter Sellers ("Being There") and "The Greatest Story Ever Told" which starred Max von Sydow and Donald Pleasence but included every unemployed star from John Wayne to Shelly Winters.

Pavarotti was starring in the film, "Yes Giorgio," in which I had a small part. I played his director for the Puccini's opera, Turandot. This is funny in its own right, as I can't sing and in my role I instructed one of the world's greatest singers about performing. I found it hysterical.

The film was a bomb, and I understand it didn't break even here or in its World Wide distribution. Kathryn Harrold co-starred. In one scene he was dancing with her and his hand covered her entire back. Pavarotti was a big man with a very big appetite and a large frame to encompass his food and his magnificent voice. They played lovers but unfortunately there was no chemistry between them. We shot the picture at the Metropolitan Opera House in the New York City Lincoln Center. Luciano had a very big dressing room. My dressing room was right next to his and immense with a grand piano, which I don't play. Luciano's wife at that time (later divorced) was a sweet lovely lady who was there with their two daughters. They would bring all kinds of goodies to our dressing rooms. I found him charming, a great singer, but even by a stretch of the imagination, Luciano was not an actor. But it was good as it brought me to New York where members of my family came and watched the shooting.

During the filming of "Yes, Georgio" I ran into Bette Middler again. During a lunch break, coming from the commissary on my way back to the sound stage I saw Bette sitting in a half hidden staircase and crying bitter tears. As I walked over, she unfolds her agony. It seems, she said, that the film "Jinxed," was not working as she and her leading man were not getting along and the director wasn't helping. After consoling her I said she should come visit me on my set.

When the great Miss M came to the "Yes, Georgio" set and asked for Paul Marin, my stock went up a thousand percent. All of a sudden photographers descended from the front offices to take our photos, she knew that would happen though I didn't, her way of helping a fellow actor. Years later, I read that Bette Midler was to open at the Greek theater in L.A. I called the box office for tickets about four weeks before she was due. The only tickets available were on the very top balcony and to the side. I wrote a note and left it at the box office to be given to her when she arrived.

A couple of weeks later I get a phone call from her (touring?) manager, saying that Miss Midler will have two tickets for me at the box office will call window, and that I'm invited to the opening night party but the 'piece de resistance' was that she arranged for me to park my car next to hers so I wouldn't have to walk a mile from the parking lot to the theater. That's a *mensch*. The tickets and the party were something everyone would do for a fellow actor, but to arrange parking was really special.

My Unbelievable Trip to London

I received an invitation from my friend and colleague Robert Paget to come to his wedding in London. On arriving I settled in at his wonderful flat that had three floors and I was put in with his brother. That evening we went to an Indian restaurant where we were if I recall about twelve at dinner. The next day I was asked if I wanted to go to a drinks party (Londonese, for cocktail party). "Sure!" said I. Off we went to another flat, not as grand as my friend's but still upper class. When we got there, the party was in full swing. I spot this guy standing there talking to a pretty girl. With a drink in hand I stood next to them for about thirty seconds, then introduced myself. He was about 6'2" in height and I guessed about 185 lbs and standing ramrod straight.

After the pleasantries—"Oh, a Yank, visiting?" etc.—I asked, "How long have you been in the army?" A look of surprise crossed his face.

"How did you know?"

"Well," said I, "You're standing as if you have a steel rod going up from your anus to the top of your head. That'll give you away every time."

After a lot of small talk and the pretty girl got bored and decided to cast her net some place else. He asked if I had ever seen the changing of the Guard. His name was Rupert, a Lieutenant in the Queen's

Guard. The guard is split into two sections, he explained, the Blues and Royals.

We arranged to meet the next day in front of the guardhouse at the gate to Hyde Park Barracks for the Blues and Royals that bordered on Hyde Park. There he was in full dress uniform and off we went, first to the stables where the horses were being groomed all with their young soldier's who were braiding tail and neck hair, brushing and dressing the horses for their daily ritual.

I was walking through the stables watching where I put my feet when an officer, obviously in charge, walks up. My host Rupert, saluting smartly, introduced me as a visiting American whom he invited to see the changing of the guard ceremony to this colonel who was the commanding officer of both parts of the Queens Guard. We shook hands and he asked. "You're staying for lunch aren'tchu?" in typical upper class speech. Looking over at my host who had not mentioned lunch, I did not know what to say. Rupert hemmed and hawed, the look on his face told all, then replied with a clearing of his throat, "Of course, of course!" Rupert then saluted his colonel and escorted me into Hyde Park where he positioned me for the most advantage position to see the changing of the guard.

All these junior officers mounted magnificent horses, first walking then trotting sitting ramrod on their mounts. I noticed one young officer's booted foot fall out of the stirrup and he quickly glanced around to see if his commanding officer had seen that and looked relieved.

The ceremony concluded and my new friend found me outside the gate of Hyde Park Barracks for the Blues and Royals and promptly took me to the Officers Mess for lunch. The mess is not what it sounds like to an American ear. It is part barracks for the men, part living quarters for the officers, part museum, part lounge and part dining room. In the museum's glass cases, were uniforms, flags, swords, muskets, and the spoils of wars gathered since its formation in 1661 and its evolution in 1967 as The Blues and Royals, the Queen's Guard. There were large silver tea services that were taken into battle by the colonel or commanding officer. Of course they also traveled with a mobile sleeping quarters and his batman an enlisted man who was his servant. In this building was quite a thumbnail picture of their wars, campaigns, captured trophies and accomplishments.

After getting the history we went to the mess, but first for drinks in the lounge, whiskey and soda, warm (in 'Blighty' no ice was to dilute the whiskey). This lounge was connected to the dining room. It had a large window overlooking Hyde Park. There were couches and Morris chairs and when we arrived there were a number of officers already there with drinks in hand.

Rupert said that we were waiting for the Colonel to arrive before going into the dining room for lunch. One of the enlisted men came over with a silver tray in hand asking if we wanted refills. I would have loved one but thought better of it as I have a tendency to get drunk fast: two drinks and I'm flying. I mumbled, "No thanks" while Rupert just shook his head.

Just then the Colonel entered picked up a drink from a tray held for him, stopped for a few seconds on his way towards me, to say a word to one of the officers and then to the next officer in a straight line to where I was standing, shared a word and then to me.

"I'm so glad you could join us," and looking to my host, "Rupert, it was very thoughtful of you to invite our visitor. I must apologize for being a bit late, you see, I was over at the Blues' Mess as I'm also their commanding officer. I had to go there for drinks, but I most always lunch here, you see. Shall we go in?"

The dining area was something out of Gunga Din. We were about a dozen there for lunch. I was the only visitor. The table was oak, burnished with a high polish like glass. It reflected everything that was placed on it. There were champagne and wine glasses at every setting, the dishes, glasses and silver had the logo of the Royals.

One of the batmen was making the rounds, asking and pouring champagne, the Colonel singled out one of the officers with, "Derek, your foot was having its difficulty staying in the stirrup. Thank you for the champagne. Errors must be paid for" he chuckled. Then turning to me he said, "You see, any fault on parade is paid for in buying the champagne for lunch. Since Derek was the only offender he must carry the cost alone," and chuckled again.

Then pointing to a large portrait of an officer in full dress uniform with many medals and a sash of office, staring across the table perpendicular to it. "I assume your wondering what a portrait of the German Kaiser is doing here in our mess." To be truthful, I never even thought twice on it. I had assumed it was just another dead officer whose portrait was on the wall. Then the answer came.

"Besides being cousin to the Queen, he once held the position of Commander of the Blues and Royals." The conversation turned to the parade that morning and over all, for me, was quite dull. Needless to say not being a raconteur I ate silently as course after course was either served or in buffet style one got up to get seconds. Of course different wines were poured for each course. There was fish, baked and fried, sautéed, meats, a large roast, plus a ham and myriad vegetables.

For desert besides port wine, a large wheel of cheese, fruit, a gelato, and tea or coffee. I really don't know if actually so, but my impression was that these officers' young and old were of the upper ruling class. Here we were having lunch in the modern world of 1985 and I felt as if I was back in the eighteenth century at the height of the British Empire. To me it was amazing, with the British dominance gone and its power no longer, at the very least greatly diminished, in here it not only survived it flourished.

Dull though the conversation at the table was, not many American tourists can say that they had lunch with the Colonel and officers in their mess on the grounds of Hyde Park Barracks for the Blues and Royals.

After my thank you letter to Rupert, he too wrote me a note thanking me for my note and that was the last I heard from Lieutenant Rupert who by now I imagine is a colonel himself.

Now lets get back to the "Reel" world of Theater, Film and TV.

Theater

BROADWAY

Play	Year	Role	Director
Fiddler on the Roof	1965	Lazar Wolf, the Butcher	Jerome Robbins
Gideon	1961-62	Zalmunah, King of Mideon	Tyrone Guthrie
The Tenth Man	1959-61	Young Kessler C, Harris	Tyrone Guthrie
Fair Game	1957	Standby for Sam Levene	Moss Hart
What Every Woman Knows	1958	John Shand	John Stix

REGIONAL

Montserrat   Barbizon, Plaza N.Y.

Cabaret   Union Plaza, Las Vegas

Cabaret   Sacramento Music Circus

Awake and Sing   Plaza Suite

Checking Out

Glengarry Glen Ross

PRE-BROADWAY

The Decision

The Frog Pond

STOCK, DINNER THEATER, OFF-BROADWAY & L.A. 99-SEAT THEATERS

Light Up the Sky, Room Service, Paris Is Out, Don't Drink the Water, The Miser, Othello, The Sunshine Boys, Raisins and Almonds, and Red Roses For Me

L.A. WEEKLY AWARD

Best Actor in Revival of Year 1990 "Noises Off" Golden Theater, Burbank, Ca.

Television and Film

MOVIES OF THE WEEK

Title	Year	Role	Director
Face in the Crowd		Elia Kazan	
Looker		Michael Crichton	
Mommy Dearest		Frank Perry	
Pretty Boy Floyd	1960	Desk Clerk	
One Man's Way	1964	Sam Feldman	
The Greatest Story Ever Told	1965	The Crying Man	George Stevens
Doctors' Wives	1971	Dr. Deemster	
The Love Machine	1971	Dr. Lesgarn	
Punition, La...aka The Punishment	1973	Actor	
Callie & Son	1981	Judge Clairmont	
The Man Who Wasn't There	1983	Outside Attendant	
The Cartier Affair	1984	Wayne	

TELEVISION EPISODES

Program	Year	Role
The Untouchables: The Cooker in the Sky (#4.2)	1962	Will Hafnur
The Untouchables: The Man in the Cooler (#4.21)	1963	Sam Deroy
Here Come the Brides: Next Week, East Lynne (#2.4)	1969	Actor
Mannix: Merry Go Round for Murder (#2.24)	1969	Medical Examiner
Mission: Impossible: Fool's Gold (#4.5)	1969	Clerk
Mission: Impossible: Image (#6.17)	1972	Dave Scott
The Streets of San Francisco: Timelock (#1.7)	1972	Mickey McFee
The Betty White Show: The Stunt Woman (#1.14)	1978	Chase
Hart to Hart: A New Kind of High (#1.9)	1979	Dr. Wally Colby
The Rockford Files: Lions, Tigers, Monkeys and Dogs: Part 2 (#6.3)	1979	Attorney Eyler
Hart to Hart: Rhinestone Harts (#3.8)	1981	Carleton Withers
The Incredible Hulk: Patterns (#4.18)	1981	Malamud
The Phoenix: Pilot (#1.0)	1981	Anesthesiologist
Flamingo Road: Heatwave (#2.10)	1982	Actor
Three's Company: Up in the Air (#6.25)	1982	Mr. Peabody

Highway to Heaven: Ghost Rider (#3.24)	1987	Welby
Hunter: The Jade Woman (#4.3)	1987	Chemist
Moonlighting: Between a Yuk and a Hard Place (#5.2)	1988	Bald Man
Murder, She Wrote: Something Borrowed, Someone Blue (#5.9)	1989	Florist Delivery Man
Adam 12: Panic in Alverez Park (#1.17)	1991	Mr. Wilson
Ellen: The Note (#2.4)	1994	Mr. Phillips
Nowhere Man: Forever Jung (#1.15)	1996	Rudy

Also Benson, David Letterman, Max Headroom, Room 222, Studio One, Superior Court, The Judge, The White Shadow, Working, and many others.

COMMERCIALS for ARCO, Ford, California Lottery

MOTION PICTURES

Title	Year	Director	Role
Being There	1979	Hal Ashby	Other Reporter
Hardcore	1979	Paul Schrader	Joe VanDorn
Private Benjamin	1980	Howard Zieff	Leo Lemish
The Happy Hooker Goes Hollywood	1980	Alan Robbins	Tom
Yes, Giorgio	1982	Franklyn Schafner	Nello Jori
The Choice	1988	Robert Paget	Actor

"My Pretty Pony,"	2009	Mikhail Tank	For Short Film Festivals

Acknowledgement

I want to thank my daughter Tani Foger and son-in-law Soli Foger for publishing this book and for their encouragement in making this memoir possible. For my Grandchildren Ami, Ori, Elichai and Dov, and my Great Grandchildren Azaryah, Aden and Aleeza. So that they will have a keyhole peek into my life as I lived it.

To James Tartan; actor director, for the front cover photo and friendship over the last 60 or so years. To Robert Paget whose input and patience was invaluable.

To Wm. Wintersole who helped me recall "Venice by the Sea."

For the caricatures drawn by Douglas Campbell (Gideon) and Dick Gautier (Cabaret), my thanks. To Tyrone Guthrie and Moss Hart, their direction taught me about acting. Lola Fisher, the late Phil Norman, the late Critt Davis and Jimmy Firlit all wonderful friends, plus so many others too numerous to list for their encouragement and allowing me to pick their brains.

A CHANCE TO BREAK
A STORY INSPIRED BY TOP 6

MR. G. C.

iUniverse, Inc.
Bloomington

A Chance to Break
A Story Inspired by Top 6

iUniverse books may be ordered through booksellers or by contacting:

iUniverse
1663 Liberty Drive
Bloomington, IN 47403
www.iuniverse.com
1-800-Authors (1-800-288-4677)

ISBN: 978-1-4620-2229-8 (sc)
ISBN: 978-1-4620-2231-1 (hc)
ISBN: 978-1-4620-2230-4 (ebk)

Printed in the United States of America

iUniverse rev. date: 09/24/2011

DEDICATION

This urban fiction novel is dedicated to Top 6, all the fallen soldiers from the hood, and most of all, my friend since 6th grade and the only real character in the book—Marc Ariot, gunned down by Palm Spring police for nothing. You may be gone but you're living through this book!

REST IN PEACE SPOON

December 14th 1986–September 9th 2005

MORE THAN JUST TOP 6 . . .

By: MR. GC

Lake Worth, Fl.

B arack Obama made history on January 20, 2009 when he became the face of black America. This was a much needed win especially after the Bush Administration sent us flying head first into an for seen recession. Now because our President is not white, the black community has the misconception that the hard work of civil rights leaders like Dr. Martin Luther King, and Malcolm X has finally paid off, but I'm here to tell you the truth. I'm not taking away from the accomplishments that African Americans have made in the "Free World" to date, instead I'm telling you that our fight for equality is far from over. Blacks and other minorities have let down their guards and put all their hopes into one man, but this one man can't change the discrimination that goes on every day in our own neighborhoods. It's up to us as people to open our eyes and stand up against racism. This is more than just white and black. This is the rich against the poor and how the rich would do whatever it takes to stay in power, like taking away the lives of young Haitian Americans (Top 6) in the sole purpose of making money. My friends it's still far from over. We must still fight to keep our rights as human beings in honor of not only the struggles civil rights leaders have gone through, but for the sacrifices they have made as well.

When you think of Florida you automatically think of fun in the sun, beautiful beaches, Disney World and other tourist attractions. Me, I see a vast land beautifully built to hide decades upon decades of murder and discrimination, all for the love of money. In a state whose economy generates the most money from tourism, I've come to realize that politicians and money hungry tyrants while do anything to keep the wheels on the money train moving, and even if that means running over innocent people. Examples from the War of 1812 to the 2000 Bush–Gore election, which was a clear disfranchisement of not only African Americans but Latin and Haitian voters as well, is proof enough. So for me to claim that Top 6, a group of young Haitian Americans, is nothing more than victims of politics' as farfetched as it may seem? I think not!

Before the city of Lake Worth was named after General William J. Worth, the leader of U.S. forces during the last part of the Second Seminole War, it was named Jewel, by Fannie and Samuel James. In 1883 they became the first large property owners in Lake Worth. In 1889 they opened the first Post Office in Lake Worth's history. Barefoot mailmen, who delivered mail to Jewel called them "the black diamonds", which indicated that they were black. In 1903, Samuel turned all of his property over to his wife and sometime between then and 1912, Samuel died. Fannie had a desire to move back north with her family, so she sold her land to the Palm Beach Farms Co. but with one exception. In the legal documents that turned over the James' land to the company, there was a provision that a 10 foot by 10, grave site for Samuel be provided, preserving a piece of land that would still be called Jewel to this day. Records show that this provision was honored but where is this grave site today?

In the book "Jewel of the Gold Coast", which tells about the beginning of Lake Worth history, author Jonathan W. Koontz interviews Mrs. Jean Childs Addison, who was a resident of Lake Worth in the 1920's. Mrs. Addison tells about how she and her friend Dorothy use to walk past the grave site on their way to school. Mrs. Addison says there was an iron fence that went around the grave site. When asked where the grave site was, she tells about how one day, her friend Dorothy told her how she woke up in the middle of the night because of a commotion outside of her bedroom window. Peering out the window, she could see men holding lanterns and shovels. When Dorothy told her parents about the men destroying the grave site, they said there was nothing they could do about it. Mrs. Addison doesn't remember what year it was, but somebody started building a house there, and when they were going to put the sidewalk from the front door of the house out to the street, they dug up the grave.

In a city in which its state has been a tourist attraction for decades, development has to take place, spots need to be cleared. Could it be that years after Miss. Fannie moved, investors decided it would be okay to destroy the grave site? I don't know but I do know that, perhaps if the first large property owner of Lake Worth was not of color, his grave site would be a monument marking the beginnings of Lake Worth and standing tall today. One of the realest messages of this story in my opinion; is that once again in not only Florida's history, but in American history as well, money was put before the minorities of this country. The rich won again. So for me to claim that Top 6, a group of young Haitian Americans, is nothing more than victims of politics' as farfetched as it may seem? I think not!

Some people would ask well why Top 6? Why would law officials and The City of Lake Worth, indict them under the RICO act, if they are not the drug lords and gang members they are portrayed to be? I would explain this by first asking a simple question. Who is Top 6? That answer is easy. They are a group of young Haitian Americans from Lake Worth, Florida with dreams of being rap stars but instead made out to be crime bosses by the city of Lake Worth.

Being, unjustly charged with the RICO act, (racketeering) these young men are now fighting for their lives to beat a biased judicial system. Let me further explain.

The communities in Lake Worth are mostly populated by immigrants from poor countries. People in these communities most likely migrated from the same area or community in another country. Just like how a person would move from one state to another to be with friends, family, lovers etc. So basically, everyone knows or knows of each other. In these areas where these minorities now live, poverty and crime is usually high. So chances are their children will become friends, grow up and go to school with each other in these environments. So can you fault these young men for dreaming of making it out these harsh environments? Can you fault them for pursuing those dreams by starting a rap group that uses violent lyrics and a thug images to promote their album . . . a sales tactic that rappers to this very day use?

In the 1980's and 90's the downtown area of Lake Worth went through a short period of neglect and decline. After that short period, the area has seen a huge resurgence in interest and development, terrible property values soared. The city was hit hard by hurricanes Frances, Jeanne and Wilma in 2004 and 2005. The fishing pier was amongst the many properties that were damaged in the area and with the help of FEMA it was repaired, now charging $1 entry fee. Now approaching the recession, property value in Lake Worth were soon to drop again, just like the many other property values all across America. So to keep a city that contains some of the oldest commercial structures in south Florida alive, politicians would have to generate money by getting the attention of investors, tax payers and the federal government, but how would this be possible? You would need an escape route.

Targeting Top 6 would be easy. Authorities used these young men music and fame in the streets against them. Their music drew a fan base of young people from a diversity of cultures not just Haitian. Most of these minorities lived in the same poverty strict area as them, not only in Lake Worth but all over Palm Beach County. This fan base claimed and represented Top 6 just like every other famous rapper's fan base does, making them look like the gang that authorities want them to be. Next, they blame them for crimes committed by young Haitian Americans in the area where the Top 6 fan base was strong. After choosing their subjects, authorities then charged them under the RICO act, a law designed in the 1970s to take down the mafia. Hitting Lake Worth, one of the smallest cities in Palm Beach County with the RICO act would make national news, showing investors, tax payers, the federal government and the nation that The City of Lake Worth is cleaning up crime and making its streets safe. This would obviously draw in more money for development, the police department etc. Event's like the "Street Painting Festival" that happens every year has to be made sure they take place to generate money for the city. Now I ask; is it fair to hold these young men responsible for the crimes that their fans have committed? If so, then why music artists aren't held responsible when a fan say they got an idea of committing a certain crime by the lyrics in their song? Is it because they have the money to fight a biased judicial system or maybe it's just because the right to freedom of speech don't apply to Top 6. I'll let you be the judge of that, because one of the most important questions I could ask you is, is it fair to use the lives of the people in a country in which we govern as a way to get rich or in this case—richer?

When the members of Top 6 are asked is Top 6 a gang they answer no, because they are not a gang. When you think of gangs you think of the Cripps and Bloods, and other groups of individuals that act in an organized fashion. They wear the same colors have gangs signs and bandannas, all to distinguish themselves from the opposing side. When you look at Top 6 they have none of these characteristics. They live in Florida where unlike the east and west coast, gang banging is uncommon in the urban culture and authorities know this. They insinuate that black and white T–shirts are their basic color scheme but how can you prove that when people in ghettos all over the United States purchase these shirts either for fashion or just because they can't afford to go into retail stores and buy one.

The History Channel's "Gang Land" did a documentary on Lake Worth's Top 6 after the take down. This documentary painted such a bad picture of Top 6 that the citizen of not only Lake Worth but Palm Beach as well, had no choice to believe it. They used footage of violence all around Palm Beach County and displayed them on TV along with footage of Top 6 to convince the public that they were indeed tyrants. This method of controlling the public's minds is called propaganda. The Nazis used this method on the German public to further tarnish the Jews reputation as human beings. They would flash commercials on television that would belittle the Jews and keep the Germans opinion on the Jews a negative one. In this case, authorities did this with Top 6 so society could be on their side and not dispute any allegations against Top 6, which would make it that much harder for Top 6 to defend themselves in trial. What was strange to me is how shocked residents in Lake Worth were when this documentary was first aired. It was like they were unaware that such a mafia like figure lived in their city. How is that possible when this alleged gang was such a factor in the violence going on in Palm Beach County? Maybe because it's okay to believe everything you see on TV and maybe because what the police say is always true. You and I both know that's not right.

This documentary made many false accusations like claiming Top 6 had millions of dollar's worth of cocaine. If this were so, then why were these men still living in the poverty strict area where they came from? Why weren't they driving around in the flashy cars that drug lords and rappers are seen driving on television? Why weren't property or large sums of money ceased during the take down? Why can't either of these young men post a million dollar bond if they have millions worth of cocaine? These questions are yet to be answered but one of the questions I believe to be amongst the greatest, is why are these young men being trialed in state court instead of federal? People whose been indicted under the RICO act in the past, are usually trialed in Federal court so why not Top 6 if they had the millions worth of cocaine that they are accused of?

To further rid the streets of the poor, the city of Lake Worth affiliated young Haitian Americans to Top 6 because they have been in trouble with the law in the past, from the same area, and of course because they were of Haitian descent. To link someone to a gang because of their ethnicity is wrong. The city of Lake Worth is populated by a lot of Haitian Americans. Some of these Haitians Americans come from poor families, and just like any other culture, some people in poor families tend to commit crimes; that's just how it is, but here lies a serious issue. Is it fair to link them all as one because their culture is the same? Also is it fair to charge a shoplifter the same way you would a person that robs the store? Well that's what Lake Worth did.

During the Top 6 take down I was incarcerated for a 3rd degree felony no way related to Top 6 at all. While going through the legal matters and court procedures, the prosecutor offered me a plea deal which would have landed me in county jail for a year. I understood that I committed a crime and was ready to accept the state's plea deal but the day I went to sign this plea deal my prosecutor was removed from my case, and a special prosecutor was assigned. Later on I found out that this particular prosecutor was assigned to many other young Haitian Americans from Lake Worth, who law officials claimed were also affiliated with Top 6. This prosecutor removed my plea deal and offered me four years in prison for a 1st degree felony that I didn't commit. The description on this 1st degree felony didn't even match the characteristics or nature of my crime. When I inquired the reason for them up filing my felony, the special prosecutor said he had pictures of me standing on a street corner with members of Top 6. Pictures that I still haven't seen to this day. Feeling that I was being discriminated against, I took my case to trail and got the 1st degree felony down filed to my original 3rd degree, receiving 18 months in prison.

Stiffening one's punishment without concert evidence that he or she is in a gang is unjustly. Simply because I'm standing with someone doesn't mean I take part in their activities. I understand the fact that I committed a crime, but it's not fair to force me into trial for a crime that I didn't commit simply because the city of Lake Worth has an agenda of cashing in minorities.

My friends, these young men are currently still in jail and need a voice. Something has to be done! What has happened in Lake Worth is happening to minorities all over America. Lives are been destroyed simply so the rich can get richer. We must stand together and fight against this imbalance of power. The saying, "a closed mouth doesn't get fed" means a lot. If we continue to keep quiet and let these people take advantage of us, then the struggles of civil rights leaders like Dr. Martin Luther King, Malcolm X, Rosa Parks, and Fredrick Douglas meant nothing. They showed us by example so we must take heed so we can leave behind direction and guidance for future generations. *Please visit: WWW.FACEBOOK. COM/TOPSIXTHEBOOK. There you can post your comments about what you liked or disliked about the book, and how you feel about the TOP 6 situation.*

INTRODUCTION

PALM BEACH COUNTY, Florida also known as the 5 6 Ace, is about forty–five minutes north of Miami. The drug flow is rapid and niggas out here go hard to do it big in the hood. The crime rate is at its highest so naturally the police get hot like the Florida weather. At one point in time the county had the highest murder rate in the state. Police stiffened the law so tremendously, that people who came on vacation left on probation. The outlaws on the other hand live as if the law is non-existent. In Palm Beach County you either play ball, you're a dope boy, a jack boy or a rapper. The wetter your paint job is the wetter these hoes get, but most importantly in the 5 6 Ace money is the issue and you aint shit without it! In a county where the cities are filled with minorities living in harsh environments, people can only dream of making it out. We often forget that Blacks and Haitians are one. We are African people, and the core of our beliefs and religion is music. My purpose in writing this novel is to show how powerful music is and when you add this element to an already bad situation, anything is bound to happen. Check me out . . . .

CHAPTER 1

" J amal Pierre pack it up A.T.W (all the way)!" A deputy shouted at the top of his lungs, so the inmate could hear him over the noise in the crowded dorm.

"It's about time!" Jamal shouted back, while finishing his last set of pushups.

"Yo old school these crackas finally setting a nigga free man!" He then said to the inmate who bunked in the bed above his. "I'm out of here!"

"Yeah they set ya free," said the inmate who was awoken from his catnap, due to the shouting. "But do you plan on staying free?"

"What you mean Brooklyn?" Jamal questioned his Bunkie. "These crackas got to kill me fo' I comeback to this shit!"

"And that they will do baby boy," Brooklyn interrupted in a calm but serious tone.

1

"Listen to me Jay," the older man continued. "You can't go back in them streets again with your eyes closed son, I've been telling you that for the entire year you been down," he said. "Ya either gonna end up dead or locked up again son"

"Yeah okay, your hot shot lawyer helped you dodge prison this time but what about next time huh?" Brooklyn asked. "Your 21 and they tried to give you more years then that as a so-called plea deal," Brooklyn continued. "Nigga that alone should be enough to tell you them crackas downtown ain't playing with yo black ass!"

"Shit, don't get me wrong now," he told Jamal after hopping off his top bunk. "I ain't knocking your hustle . . . get money and provide, *but you got to be on point son!*" He said poking Jamal in the chest with his finger to emphasize his words. "You can't sell dope forever," he reminded him. "I'm telling you this because I believe in you and it seems like no one else has. Just remember this if nothing else: take heed." Brooklyn said looking Jamal in the eyes. "Take advantage of this chance God has given you, because it could be your last."

In the back of his mind, Jamal knew Brooklyn was right. Shit, ninety-nine percent of the time he was always right. Brooklyn was a forty-year-old African–American, and from the constant serious look in his eyes, you could tell he's been through a lot in his lifetime. The multiple gun shot wounds to his body were enough to credit one assumption. Not to mention he had the rap sheet to prove it. He talked with a heavy, up north accent, and represented his hood to the fullest, that's why every one in the open bay dorm, called him Brooklyn. Spending most of his life in and out the system since a youth, kept Brooklyn in good shape. He was very tall and two hundred and fifty pounds of solid muscle, and could handle him self very well. He had pearly white teeth, wavy hair, and his dark chocolate skin was free of tattoos. He was a quiet person, and only spoke to a selected few. He came to Florida on a business trip, and got jammed up in a drug transaction gone wrong, when some locals tried to rob him. That landed him in county jail, facing a life sentence for murder.

Jamal was one of the selected few Brooklyn spoke to. Brooklyn often felt it was necessary to give Jamal a few words of wisdom, to prevent the youngster from ending up like him. He also admired Jamal's "get money" attitude and cool head. I guess you could say he kind of reminded Brooklyn of himself when he was younger.

"Don't worry B.K. I ain't slipping this time man g shit," Jamal said as he gave Brooklyn the rest of his canteen. "This food here should last you a couple of weeks"

"Good looking out baby boy," Brooklyn said giving Jamal dap. "That's some real shit son"

"You already no I got you," said Jamal. "You just keep ya head up in here"

"Don't worry bout me Jay, I've been doing time since before you were born son," Brooklyn chuckled. "Now get out of here fo' these crackas change they mind"

"Pierre!" The impatient deputy shouted, "You leaving or staying?"

"Hold on dep.!" Jamal shouted as he gave dap to some of the inmates he shared the open bay dorm with. "I'm coming"

As the deputy shut the heavy medal door that enclosed the freedom hungry inmates inside the dorm, Jamal made eye contact with Brooklyn. His facial expression would forever be sketched in his mind. If looks were words Brooklyn's expression would say, "Remember baby boy . . . take heed!" so Jamal nodded at him as if to say "I will". The only problem was Jamal wondered if he could.

Mr. G. C.

After an hour of waiting to be released from a year long bid in the Palm Beach County Jail, AKA "Gun Club Hotel", for three sell of cocaine charges (within a thousand feet of a church zone), and possession of a fire arm, Jamal was finally a free man thanks to God and his expensive hot shot lawyer. It was Thursday July 25, 2007, 9:00 a.m. and freedom never smelled better. He took a deep breath then started to smile. All thirty two of his gold teeth shined in the sun light as he looked at his hands, and the rest of his body. Not begin exposed to sunlight for a year caused his brown skin to get lighter in complexion. Even the few tattoos he had, like the Lake on his right forearm and the Worth on the other, seemed to have gotten darker. Standing at an even six feet, and wearing a fresh white T, and Polo jeans he claimed from the property room, Jamal walked down the steps in his white socks and jail slides, thanking God that it was finally over. He was a free man. His self-esteem was high, and he was anxious to get his life back in order, but at this point in time, Jamal wanted some pussy and he knew his baby mama would get wet instantly. Not because he cut his dreads a few days prior to his release, but because he'd been working out his whole bid, and wanted to let her examine his hundred and eighty pound physique.

"Damn man!" Jamal said while waiting to be picked up by his best friend Spoon. "This nigga ain't neva on time"

While walking over to ask a taxi diver in the parking lot to use his phone, Jamal heard a loud thumping sound that made a few car alarms go off, in the parking lot. Stopping in his tracks, he turned around and saw Spoon's candy red, 2006 Monte Carlo, on twenty four inch rims, pulling up.

"What's up jailbird?" Spoon shouted over his loud system. "You gon' stand there or hop in nigga?"

Marc was Jamal's ace boon-coon. He named himself Spoon, because if you let him tell it, he wasn't too much or too little. He

4

was just enough or a teaspoon . . . whatever that meant. He and Jamal have been the best of friends since the sixth grade. In fact, the first time Jamal skipped class it was under Spoon's influence. People often thought they were brothers, because they hang around each other so much. When it came to beef, they had each other's backs to the fullest.

Spoon had dreads to his mid-back and was slim, only weighting a hundred and forty pounds. He had a dark brown complexion and brown eyes. Unlike Jamal, who had a smooth baby face, Spoon wore a full beard, which made him look sinister. Especially, when he let down his dreads, and grilled you with his mouth full of gold teeth, like he was doing now. Spoon, was always hyper. He was the shoot first ask questions later type. Jamal on the other hand, was more calm and collected. Together the two made one hell of a combination. Not to mention lethal.

Spoon was always a sharp dresser. Today he decided to go with the dope boy look, wearing an Enyce outfit. His grey shirt went perfectly with his stone washed grey and white jeans, and the all white number thirteen Jordans on his feet. To top it off, his Cuban link necklace hung down to his dick. It was anchored down by a huge chunk that read "South Side Boy". The damn thing could blind you if you stared too long.

Jamal was happy too see his childhood friend. He threw up his hands and yelled, "Wassup bro?" before approaching the car. As soon as Jamal hopped inside the whip, he could smell the wonderful aroma of weed coming from Spoon's joint. The smell alone made Jamal cough, on the count of him having virgin lungs after a whole year. He wanted Spoon to pass that shit ASAP!

"Damn Jamal!" Spoon started after turning down the volume on his CD player. "It's good to have you back on these streets nigga . . . know what I'm saying!"

"Man it feels good to be free," Jamal said with a smile as he eyed the joint in Spoon's hands. "Man pass that shit nigga!"

Jamal hit the joint once and instantly went to coughing up a storm, as if it was the first time he'd ever smoked weed. "This some fi ass shit", he thought to him self as his eyes began to water. Being locked up for a year or any amount of time would make the dullest weed seem potent.

"Damn ease up!" Spoon said laughing at the look on his friend's face. "That's that kush nigga!"

"I needed to smoke one bad," Jamal said wiping the tears from his eyes. "Ima hit the rest of this shit"

"Go ahead nigga," Spoon said as he pulled off. "I got plenty more"

"Ight then," Jamal said as he leaned back in the passenger chair. "So wassup with these streets bro?" He asked. "I mean what they lookin' like?"

"Man, These streets on fi, and these crackas playing for keeps out chea," Spoon began. "Jump out boys be riding heavy twenty-four seven, so a nigga can't even stand on the block like that no more," he told him. "I really just hustle off my phone now . . . know what I'm saying?"

"Damn my nigga," said Jamal. "I heard them crackas had shit on lock out cha too, *but* not *that* bad"

"Man you have no idea," Spoon informed him. "You already know them crackas don't like us Haitians"

"G shit bro," said Jamal. "You ain't even got to remind me"

"But that aint even it," said Spoon. "Them North Side Niggas still be with that fuck shit too . . . beefing with us and shit so you know I stay strapped," he said motioning towards his glock .40 underneath his seat. "But at the end of the day uh nigga still gettin' it out chea . . . dope boy or jack boy . . . know what I'm saying?"

"Yeah I feel ya bro, but hear me out," Jamal said before taking another puff. "While I was locked up I was doing a lot of thinking"

"I bet," Spoon interrupted. "Uh nigga like me uh be thinking bout hitting a bank or something," Spoon laughed while reaching out for some dap. "Know what I'm saying?"

"Bro?" Jamal said failing to dap his friend. "Can I finish please?"

"Oh my bad nigga," said Spoon. "Shit, I thought it was funny"

"Anyway," Jamal continued while shaking his head. "You see I got a plan that'll put a stop to all that jack boy shit, and put us on our feet for good," Jamal claimed. "You know I'm cool with Chico, so I was thinking if I could talk him into frontin' me some bricks, then showing him I could move it fast enough, we could start an on going business deal with buddy," he said before taking another puff. "I'm telling you Spoon, if I could pull this one off we set for good," Jamal assured him. "These streets ours for the taking, and this my last chance, so I got to take advantage of it."

"Damn bro what's up with this last chance shit?" Spoon asked staring at his friend as if he didn't recognize him. "Who you been talking to in there?"

"Nobody man," Jamal lied, thinking about Brooklyn's words of wisdom.

"Well, I'm down with that taking over shit," Spoon said while using his knees to control the steering wheel to light another joint he had previously rolled." Just remember tho mo money mo problems . . . know what I'm saying?"

"You ain't got to remind me nigga," Jamal said throwing his roach out the window. "I've been off the porch"

"That's wassup," Spoon said after exhaling the weed smoke. "Now where we headed, to the hood right?"

"Naw bro take me to my baby mama's crib," Jamal declined. "I'll hit Lake Worth up later"

"Okay I got ya," Spoon said while reaching for the volume on his pioneer. "Hey you know Top 6 got a new album out?"

"Naw I didn't," said Jamal. "I was in jail remember"

"Well you gotta hear it bro," said Spoon before turning up the volume. "I love this shit"

As Spoon bumped Top 6's new album, Tearin' Da House Up, Jamal was thinking about ending his savage life. All his friends wanted to do was sell drugs all day and fuck hoes. When they weren't doing that, they were in the studio trying to be rappers like Top 6, a rap group from their hood on the fast track of making it big. Jamal on the other hand was different. He wanted to get a job, but that thought went out the window with the roach he tossed out minutes earlier. The white man was not going to hire no one with the felonies he had. In addition to the time it would take him to get a job, how would he pay his bills and feed his child in the mean time? After taking a fifteen thousand dollar hit to pay his hotshot lawyer and his year long canteen bill, Jamal was dead broke. He had to come up fast, but he would worry about that later, because at the top of his to do list right now was Kim.

"Here we go . . . home sweet home," said Spoon as they pulled up to Jamal's baby mama's house. "Here's some weed and a few hundred to hold you down, call me tomorrow so we could hit up the mall," said Spoon as he handed the jailbird the items. "I got to get you back looking right bro; after all you did it for me when I came home from my lil bid"

"Thanks man," Jamal said sincerely. "I appreciate it"

"Naw bro," said Spoon waving both his hands. "We like brothers' man . . . you ain't got to thank me"

As Jamal went to step out the car, Spoon stopped him and jokingly asked, "What if Kim got a nigga in there?"

"She ain't stupid!" Jamal said with a smile on his face. "Besides that nigga better kick rocks or get hit up," he jokingly said while forming a gun sign with his fingers. "You ain't heard when Juvi said, **uh nigga bust ya head if ya bang his hoe**?" Jamal asked, causing them both to laugh, while he stepped out the car and then shut the door.

"Ima fuck witcha bro," Spoon yelled before he disappeared behind his dark tinted window and turned up the bass in his trunk.

While walking up the pathway to Kim's house, Jamal wondered if she did have a friend in his absence. Shit, Jamal was happy he was home, the big smile on his face made it evident, but he still had his doubts. The thought of her cheating, crossed his mind many of nights as he lay on his bunk in jail. He'd been gone a whole year and knows a woman needs attention. Shit, if the tables were turned, he would probably dog Kim out. Through their five year on and off rollercoaster like relationship, Jamal's dope boy lifestyle gave him the opportunity to fuck plenty of hoes, in which he did. In fact, they were on bad terms when he went in because of them scandalous hoes calling his phone, so he knew there was a possibility of infidelity, but it didn't really matter now. What mattered was that, he was out of jail now, and if Kim was fuckin' someone else, Jamal hoped they both knew the lyrics to Juvenile's song . . . **Knock Knock.**

"Who is it?"

"It's me Jay," he said. "Open up!"

"Oh my goodness!"

When the door opened, Jamal's eyes widened to the sight of a beautiful queen in green hospital scrubs. Kim stood 5'8 with legs of a track star. Her sandy brown shoulder length hair and gold streaks went perfect with her coco butter like skin. Her baby face and dimples made her look young but the curves on her body made one realize that she was far from a child. Weighting a hundred and thirty pounds, c cupped, with an ass like Buffy, she was truly a stallion and Jamal knew it oh so well. Her brown eyes were those of a caring person and her big heart proved it. She was one of those people that loved helping others. Personality wise, she was funny and always wore a smile, but get her wrong and Ms. Ghetto fabulous would come out in a split second.

"Baby, Baby!" Kim said in excitement as she jumped into Jamal arms, wrapping both legs around his waist and planting a long kiss on his lips. "I missed you so much!"

"I missed you to baby" Jamal said carrying his overly excited girlfriend into the house then placing her down.

"Baby I thought you said you were getting out next week." Kim questioned while hitting his arm.

"I thought so too," Jamal lied knowing he planed to sneak up on Kim, to see how she really was living. "I guess you never know with these crackas huh?"

"Yea whateva boy," Kim responded, seeing right through his lie. "You just don't trust anybody"

"So *anyways*, what's to eat?" Jamal said quickly changing the subject. "I'm hungry."

"Don't worry baby Ima make you some breakfast," said Kim standing up. "I know you miss my cooking."

"That's not all I miss," Jamal said while flirtatiously slapping her on the ass.

"Stop it boy," said Kim hitting his hand away. "You can't handle this"

"We'll see about that," Jamal said as he got up and walked down the hallway towards the bedroom.

When he entered the bedroom it stilled looked the same. It smelled like roses which was Kim's favorite scent and it was clean and neat as usual. The furniture arrangement was just like he remembered and his 60' flat screen TV was still in good working condition. Looking around the room, he walked over to the nightstand on Kim's side of the bed and grabbed a picture frame. Inside it was a family portrait he took a while back with Kim and their three year old daughter Kayla. He missed her dearly and couldn't wait to pick Kayla up and hold her. He couldn't believe how long he was gone, and how miserable he was with out them.

Still thinking about the length of the bid, Jamal grabbed his towel out the closet, then went into the bathroom and ran the water. Before getting in, Jamal through his clothing to the floor. The water was so hot and steamy that it was relaxing. ***Hell is over,*** Jamal thought to himself, referring to what the white man called jail, as he watched the water fall off his body. The feel of serenity made his mind wonder about his upcoming plans with Chico and Spoon. He wondered if he could really talk Chico into giving him that big boy weight that he so desperately needed.

The drama he could be exposed to crossed his mind, but didn't worry him. He's been a target before because of money. Shit like that was just protocol, but this time it would be drastic, sense his product would be going for the low, instead of every body else prices. In actuality, he would be taking food out of other dope boy's mouths, and that could be detrimental. "Oh well fuck it," Jamal thought aloud. See he knew the game was a dirty game, so dirty is how he would have to play it, if he wanted a chance to break out of it.

Brooklyn's words of wisdom kept ringing in his head. Jamal planed on getting enough money to move him and his family to Haiti; there he would go legit for good. See, everybody makes plans, but they don't always go as planned, was what Jamal was soon to find out.

Immediately after stepping out of the tub, Jamal smelled the aroma of morning breakfast through the bathroom door. The smell of eggs, bacon, and sausage took over his stomach, causing him to quickly dry off. Opening the door, his eyes widened to the seductive sight of Kim, standing in the hallway with nothing on, but a red see through thong, and matching stilettos. His towel unfastened and fell to the floor, due to his erection. "Follow me," Kim said softly as she turned her back and walked towards the bedroom, signaling Jamal to follow with her finger.

Hypnotized by the jiggling of Kim's ass, Jamal took no time to do as he was ordered. Walking into the room, he watched as Kim sat on the corner of the bed and spread her legs. She then began to rub her clitoris with two fingers while sucking on another finger in her mouth. Jamal took a second to observe as he gently stroked himself.

"Bae I've been playing with my self like this for a whole year, thinking about this moment," Kim confessed as her lips quivered and hips rotated to her own touch. "Come here"

"Oh you were thinking about me huh?" Jamal sarcastically asked as he walked over to the sex driven female.

"Uh huh," Kim hummed as she grabbing a hold of his dick, still pleasing herself.

Bobbing and weaving just the way he liked it, Kim could feel Jamal's heart beating in her mouth, through his manhood. Her mouth was as wet as her, making Jamal sigh in ecstasy with a hand behind Kim's head. His toes curled and knees buckled each time Kim deep throated his 8 inch dick; making Jamal became weaker and weaker. After five minutes of fingering herself, and humming in satisfaction, Kim caused herself to have an orgasm. Leaving Jamal's dick-dripping wet with saliva, Kim crawled on all fours like a cat to the middle of her bed. "Taste me bae," She said in a soft tone, as she looked over her shoulder, and curved her back, further exposing her swollen clit.

Jamal pulled her back to the corner of the bed then ripped Kim's thong into two. He could tell that really turned her on by the way she softly squealed. Jamal took one knee and began to eat her luscious fruit from behind. He could taste the hot juices that flowed from her steaming body. After a few minutes, Kim turned around and enjoyed his tongue while lying on her back.

"Oh my goodness bae . . . your tongue . . . it feels so . . . so good . . . . don't stop please!" Kim screamed as she rubbed and squeezed her breast together. "Damn bae," she continued now gripping both his ears as if she was driving. "Oowww it feels good"

After being pleasured by the rapid movements of Jamal's talented tongue, Kim's body was shaking like she was standing outside in zero degree weather. Jamal watched as she lay in a fetal position with both hands cupped over her vagina. "Baby I'm still coming," she said as Jamal smiled and licked his lips, tasting her juices. Watching her laying there made Jamal want her so bad. He'd been gone so long, and just wanted to be inside her. He turned Kim on her stomach then pulled her back up into doggy style position. Next, he inserted himself into her hot and wet womb. She was tight like a virgin it seemed, causing him to stroke her slowly. After a few slow strokes, he then began to pound Kim from behind, spreading her butt cheeks to further his self inside her. Kim's face was buried deep into the pillow as she screamed in a mixture of pain and pleasure. Her pussy began to leak due to multiple orgasms. "That's right bae take it!" Jamal ordered. "That's what I like!"

While enduring every powerful stroke from the back, Kim began to get tired. She fell to her stomach pulling Jamal down with her. Lying on her back still inserted deep, Jamal could feel the affects of her tight pussy taking its toll. Wanting the feeling to last forever, Jamal slowly stroked his queen and sucked on her ear. Their bodies were like conductors of passion, as electricity flowed wildly between them.

"Shit baby . . . . I missed you," Kim began to cry, feeling him about to come. "Don't leave me again"

"I won't," he whispered in her ear. "I promise"

"Ooow . . . get it bae," she moaned as she rotated her hips and pumped the muscles in her pussy. "Nut for me"

Not being able to hold out any longer Jamal came inside his queen. They both sighed in passion as Jamal lay dead on her back, still deep inside her. "I love you Jamal," Kim said noticing that her heavy breathing patterned matched his.

"I love you too bae," Jamal ended.

CHAPTER 2

Hours of lovemaking made the two tired and very hungry. The breakfast that Kim made was left untouched, so their stomachs drove them out of bed and into the shower, so they could drop in on Jamal's mother's house for dinner. The two lovebirds left the house at around 6 o'clock. Jamal took a second to reminisce on how happy Kim was when he brought her the black 2006, Nissan Altima, on twenty-two inch rims, that they were riding in.

Jamal missed his mother and his little girl Kayla so much. Kim, who called off work for the day, would leave their three year old daughter at Jamal's mom's house, since she often worked doubles, and would come home the next morning. Kim stayed in Boynton, only a couple cities south of Lake Worth. Finally entering the city, Jamal examined his surroundings as they made way through the hood. It was hot as hell outside, but that didn't stop the locals from going about their everyday activities. He saw fiends or "buddies" as the dope boys called them, fighting in the streets. He also noticed police officers harassing their victims, and some new faces serving on the block where he hustled when he was younger. Bums were still roaming the streets, and Chico's were still walking around drunk. Jamal immediately started laughing when Kim almost hit one walking in the middle of the street.

Lake Worth was a city filled with minorities; a lot of them were illegal immigrants from Haiti and Hispanic countries. When these immigrants migrated, they also brought their way of life with them, and that was evident in the city streets. Yard sales were like every other block and roosters roamed the streets like cats and dogs. Crime and poverty was high through out the south and north side. As Jamal continued to look out the window, he noticed that fiends and the police weren't the only things hard at work. A lot of construction was going on around the city as well. The roads were being redone and graffiti left by Hispanic gangs, were being painted over. New houses were being built like every other block; so literally there were old houses form the 1970's that were in terrible condition, standing next to a modern day house. Houses for rehabilitated junkies called halfway houses were being restored, and empty fields were now occupied buy fancy apartment buildings. Even the park where Jamal played at when he was little was now brand new. Everything from the monkey bars to the bleachers on the basketball court was renovated. It was like the city was trying to save its self.

"Damn wassup up with all this construction going on?" Jamal asked Kim. "The hood is starting to look different"

"I know baby . . . it's been like this for a few months now," said Kim. "I remember watching the news last week, and they said something about bringing Lake Worth back to its full value and stopping the violence"

"It's full value?" Jamal asked as they pulled up in front of his mother's house. "Good luck with that one"

"What you mean bae?" Kim asked as they stepped out the car.

Mr. G. C.

"How they plan on stopping crime with all these junkies and drugs out here?" Jamal asked. "I mean look at all these half way houses," he said as he glanced at the old white, two story apartment building, down the street. "They care about the value alright but it ain't the city's value they interested in"

Palm Beach County was like rehab capital, so halfway houses and drug clinics were everywhere. Jamal remembered getting serious beatings by his mother, when he was younger for getting caught coming out of that apartment building, down the street. For her it was trouble, but for Jamal it was a gold mine. Twenty rehabilitated junkies, living together all in one building, in a neighborhood, were there is a nearby park and an elementary school? Children were subject to fall victims to either selling drugs, or becoming users themselves.

The house that Jamal grew up in, and then got kicked out of when he was seventeen for dealing drugs, still looked the same but at the same time was very different. The green paint on the house was still there, but it looked freshly painted. The black metal bars on the windows didn't even look rusty anymore. What use to be a semi large lawn, looked huge and his mother's garden seem brighter. Even the gate that they opened to walk down the path didn't squeak as loud as he remembered it use to. He was anxious to see his little girl again but not as excited to see his mother. He'd missed his mother dearly, but knew she was disappointed in him for getting arrested again; so he was kind of scared to see her. His mother had a temper of a bull sometimes and Jamal knew that all to well. By the time they reached the front door, Jamal was filled with a mixture of feelings, mainly fear.

"Yeah who is it?" A voice asked in respond to a knock at the door.

"It's me Jay"

"Damn nigga!" Jamal's younger brother Junior said as he opened the door to hug him. "When you jumped?"

"Early this morning," said Jamal. "Wassup with ya?"

Junior was a younger version of Jamal. They looked alike walked alike and both were laid back individuals. The only difference was their opposite lifestyles, and Junior's long braids and pimpled face. Jamal often teased him about the acne on his face and he hated it. He was sixteen and a sophomore in high school. He was very intelligent, and had all honor classes. Jamal often kept an eye on him, and brought him whatever he wanted, so he would have no reason to want to pursue the lifestyle he was living. Junior was also very athletic. He was the star point guard on his JV team, at the local high school, and scouts were watching him closely. He was bound for a scholarship, which would make him the first in the family to go on to college.

"What's up big head?" Junior asked Kim.

"The only thing big is your nose lil' ugly," Kim snapped as she moved her neck in an s motion.

"Ya'll tighten up," Jamal intervened. "Can't ya'll ever get along?"

"That be his lil' ugly ass!" Kim said in a ghetto like attitude.

"Whateva nigga," said Junior. "I aint ugly"

Just as round 2 was about to begin, Jamal heard a small stampede coming down the hallway full speed. He quickly turned his head and drew a Kodak smile when seeing his little girl. It was like a piece of his heart was being put back. He took one knee and opened both his arms wide.

"Daddy, Daddy, Daddy!" The little girl said a hundred times as she jumped into her father's arms.

"Kayla" Jamal said embracing his child not wanting to let go. "I missed you so much"

"I missed you too daddy"

Kayla was Jamal's pride and joy. Jamal bent over backwards to make sure his little girl was spoiled. Kayla was half-Haitian and half African American. She favored both her parents who loved her dearly. She had her mother's coco butter like skin, her long hair, and Jamal's smile, nose and eyes. Kayla had no front teeth and looked adorable in her favorite sunflower dress that she was wearing.

"Oh Kayla," Kim said in a jealous tone. "You don't know mommy no more?"

"Come on now Kim, don't act like that, she just happy to see me," Jamal said noticing the jealous look in her eyes. "Besides, you should be happy she all on me anyways, since you being tired and all from this morning." Jamal chuckled, referring to their lovemaking, as he handed Kayla to her.

"Whateva boy don't start with me," Kim blushed. "And it wasn't all that either, minute man"

"Damn big bro," Junior laughed. "I ain't know you was a minute man"

"Oh so that's funny?" Jamal asked feeling insulted.

"No you straight baby," Kim said as Junior and her giggled, while giving each other dap.

"Oh so you guys got jokes now?" Jamal asked feeling his temper raising. "Okay I got ya'll . . . see what happens when uh nigga—"

WACK! Right when Jamal was about to finish his sentence, his words were cut short by an all too familiar slap to the back of the head, which made him bite his tongue. "What the hell!" Jamal exclaimed before receiving another slap to his mouth for his foul language. He quickly held his mouth as he covered his face with his free hand, just incase more punishment was on its way.

"Damn!" Jamal yelled in anger. "Stop mommy!"

"Boy what's wrong with you," Mama Pierre said as she raised her hand to show him she wasn't playing. "You better stop using foul language in my house"

"I'm sorry mommy but I'm twenty-one now," Jamal said rubbing his jaw as Kim, Junior and Kayla laughed. "You can't keep hitting me"

"What's so damn funny?" Mama Pierre asked the trio who quickly shut up. "I got plenty more to go around"

"Yeah!" Jamal interrupted. "Ya'll need to shut up"

"Boy I don't need your help!" Mama Pierre said, positioning her hand to slap her son again. "If you wanna help someone then help your self get a job somewhere!"

"Tell him again mama" Kim encouraged.

"Thank you Kim," Jamal said unable to believe his ears. "She don't need your help"

"I surly do need it," said Mama Pierre. "Right about now I need all the help I could get dealing with your ass"

Mama Pierre was a heavy set woman in her late fifties. She always wore her hair in corn rolls, and always wore her blue robe around the house. She loved her three boys dearly. Her tuff love methods kept them in check, but not as well as she hoped for Jamal and her oldest son Kenny. *"Sometimes it just takes a man to raise a boy,"* is what she often thought. Their father was deported back to Haiti for dealing drugs, when the two brothers were toddlers. A few years later he died of a real high fever. Not having a father figure around, the two fell victims to the streets. Not being able to deal with them Mama Pierre put them out of the house, Ken first then Jamal. She swore to herself that Junior, her youngest son, would go to college and stay off the streets. She still had hope that one day her oldest sons would see the light and make something of themselves, but that day has yet to come to past.

"So," Mama Pierre began as she looked at Jamal's graduation picture, when he was in elementary school, on her dresser. "They finally let you go huh?"

"Yeah mama," he responded in a nervous tone, while starring at her back. "I'm a free man now"

"What you going to do now?" She asked turning around. "Sell drugs again like your father?"

"Naw mama I got a plan this time," he lied as he stared at the floor. "I don't want to tell you what it is, because you just gon' tell me I can't do it," He continued. "Don't worry tho, Ima tighten up"

"Just make sure you do," she said lifting up his face with her hand to look him in the eyes. "Kayla needs a father not a daddy"

Mama Pierre gave her son a kiss on the forehead then a big hug. She'd missed him so much. While his incarceration, she spent many long nights praying for his release. She also prayed for change, and now that Jamal was finally free, she hoped that he would do just that.

After their long talk, the mother and son joined the rest of the family in the living room. They were watching television quietly when Mama Pierre told them it was time for dinner. She had made Jamal's favorite, Haitian rice and griot (fried pork). They laughed at each other's jokes as they enjoyed their food. Kayla through most of her food on the floor as her uncle cleaned it up.

Mama Pierre told most of the jokes. She was always fun to be around. She often asked the couple when she was going to get another grandchild, and when they planned on getting married. The couple just laughed and tried to ignore the uncomfortable questions. They did want to get married, but felt they weren't finically stable enough. Really, Jamal felt more that way. Nevertheless, their stability would have to strengthen soon enough, due to their passionate, not to mention unprotected, sex life with each other. After dinner the couple got ready to leave.

"Mommy the food was wonderful," Kim said gratefully. "You have to give the recipe one day"

"Thank you baby," Mama Pierre said as she walked the couple to the door. "I did put my foot in it huh?"

"Yeah mama you did the thing like always," said Jamal before kissing her on the cheek. "I didn't realize I missed your cooking so much"

"Ya'll bums can eat here anytime," Junior teased. "Are doors are always open to the poor"

"Shut up acne face," Jamal teased him as Kim sucked her teeth in disgust. "Don't make me hurt you"

"Whateva," Junior responded, "You can't whoop me bro"

"Ya'll stop all that arguing," Mama interrupted. "Junior gone and clean them dishes boy"

"Aw man," Junior said in anger as Kim laughed and pointed at him. "That's too many dishes"

Whack! Junior caught one to the back of the head. "Boy what I told you bout talking back?" Mama asked as Kim and Jamal laughed harder. "Go clean those dishes before I slap you again"

"Mommy, daddy can I come too?" Kayla asked as her mother picked her up. "I want to come home"

"Mommy got to work bookie," Kim explained to her teary-eyed daughter. "But daddy coming to see you tomorrow"

"Why can't you watch her?" Mama asked her son. "You just got out of jail boy"

"I can't mommy I got stuff to handle tomorrow," Jamal said grabbing Kayla from Kim. "Plus when I'm done Ima stop by anyway"

"Uh huh," Mama said putting her hands on her hips. "Already back to that fast life I see."

"Come on mommy," Jamal pleaded. "It ain't even like that"

"Yeah tell the old lady anything," she said. "What you think I was born yesterday?"

"Come on now mommy," Jamal continued to plea. "I told you I got something to handle"

"All I can do is pray for you and your brother," she stated as she shook her head in disappointment. "Have you even seen Ken yet?"

"Naw mommy Kim had me held up all morning," he explained causing Kim to hit him on the arm in embarrassment. "This the first place I came to"

"Well that's information I didn't need to hear boy," Mama explained. "If you see your brother tell him to stop by . . . his mama misses him"

"Fo'sho mommy I got ya," Jamal said as he kissed his mother on the cheek. "Be easy now"

"Be easy?" She chuckled. "I should be telling you that"

"Don't worry mommy," Jamal said. "I got a plan remember"

Kim and Jamal said their final good byes then headed home. Reaching their destination at around midnight, the tried couple snuggled up in their bed. Jamal was in deep thought. Feeling that her man was deeply thinking, Kim broke the silence.

"Baby what you thinking about?" She asked while rubbing his chest.

"Life," he simply stated. "I just got to make things happen so I could leave this lifestyle alone"

"Don't worry baby you're a smart man . . . that's one of the qualities I like most about you," She said snuggling closer to him. "I know your gon' make something out of yourself but I'm just scared I'm going to loose you again"

"Loose me?" Jamal asked in a voice of concern as she began to cry. "Why you thinking like that bae?"

"Jamal look how you were living before you went to jail," she said with tears streaming down her cheek. "Shooting at people, dealing drugs, robbing and God knows what else . . . baby I think jail saved your life," she continued. "And when you were gone Jay, I almost lost it. If you were to die or go back to jail again, I don't know what I'll do"

"Don't worry baby you ain't gon' loose me," Jamal said as he kissed her on the forehead. "I ain't going anywhere I promise"

CHAPTER 3

That morning Jamal had the house to himself, due to Kim having to go to work early. Waking up at around 7 am, he sat up and stretched his arms as he yawed. He looked around the room and smiled. It felt good not waking up to a bitch ass dep, yelling chow time. After throwing on his favorite blue basketball shorts, he turned on the TV then went into the bathroom. As he brushed his gold teeth while looking in the mirror, he could hear the news anchor lady talking. The words stop the violence drew Jamal's attention, causing him to stop brushing and walk toward the room. As he stood in the doorway, he watched as the anchor lady explained how the on going violence in Palm Beach County was bringing down the property value. One old lady, who was accompanied by many more protesters at city hall, blamed it on the music. She said the rap music was corrupting the minds of the youth and something had to be done. The next news segment explained how the country was on the verge of a recession, and how it would affect the economy. Jamal shook his head then walked back into the bathroom. An approaching recession was news he didn't want to hear. This meant he had to hurry up and get right before prices started going up. Especially dope prices. After finishing up in the bathroom, he grabbed his weed and a Dutch from a drawer in the kitchen, and went outside to smoke a joint. Kim would have a fit if he smoked in the house. After rolling a perfect joint, that looked as if it was made in a factory, he sparked it up and replaced the morning air in his lungs with weed smoke.

The THC didn't take long to have Jamal air bound with the birds. Soaring through the clouds, he could see Brooklyn preaching to him. The word chance was spelled out with clouds, in big uppercase letters. His mind made loops and circles around each letter. While still on board the "Refer Express", he also realized he was still broke. *Chico would sure come in handy right now,* he thought to himself. Right then he made a mental note to call Chico, after hitting the mall up with Spoon today.

Jamal took a few more puffs of that sticky stuff then went back to the clouds. He thought about the tears that Kim shaded last night. His heart ach because he knew the painful words she spoke were true. The lifestyle that he was living was detrimental to their relationship. Though he knew Kim loved him with all she could, he also knew there was only so much she could withstand. Jamal wanted the "American Dream" or a piece of that "Apple Pie" so to say. He wanted his own business the home with the picket fence and the dog running around in the front yard, but he hated living in the states, so Haiti was the next best thing. There he could achieve his dreams, not only for him but also for his family.

While still in a trance like state of mind, Jamal didn't notice a shadow sneaking up from the side of him. The silent footsteps of a person with a glock .40 pointed straight at Jamal's head were getting closer. The culprit clearly had devilish intentions in mind.

"Fuck nigga!" The culprit yelled with his glock now touching Jamal's temple. "What's up now huh?"

Jamal was speechless. His mouth fell open, as the half-smoked joint in his hand, fell to the floor. His heart skipped a beat and he had a dumbfounded look on his face. At the same time, his stomach knotted up like shoelaces. A split second of not knowing what to expect next went by, before his encounter with death was cut short by laughter.

"You slipping boy!" Spoon said as he broke down in laughter. "You slipping big time!"

"Fuck you Spoon!" Jamal said furiously, as he slapped the gun away from his face. "You need to chill out with that bull shit man!"

"Bro you should have seen the look on your face," Spoon informed him, now on the floor holding his side in pain. "You bitched up like a lil' hoe"

"What if you fucking shot me by mistake?" Jamal asked. "Then what?"

"Don't worry man," Spoon assured him while still on the ground, pointing to the switch on his weapon. "It's on safety"

"That don't mean shit!" Jamal warned him as he snatched his joint from the ground. "It could have still gone off!"

"Calm down bro . . . I just couldn't resist," Spoon said as he dusted himself off. "Besides better me then somebody else," he joked. "But on the real tho you got to tighten up man . . . you slipping bad outchea," He continued. "I think jail got your street senses fucked up a little"

"Whateva nigga," Jamal said ignoring his last comment. "How you knew I was back here anyways?"

"That shit stink bro . . . I smelled it from the front," he joked. "I bet the whole neighborhood knows you back here"

"You dumb," Jamal chuckled. "Come inside man"

After taking a seat in the living room, Spoon asked, "Where ya fi at anyways bro?"

"It's in the attic," Jamal informed him. "I put it up there before I got locked up . . . you know . . . so Kayla wouldn't find it"

"Oh I feel ya," Spoon said eagerly. "Shit, go get that bih . . . I wanna see it"

Spoon went rummaging trough the refrigerator, while Jamal went to the attic to rummage through junk. After climbing up the latter and turning on the light, Jamal just remembered he hated going up to the attic. It's was dusty as hell, had cobwebs everywhere and worst of all it was small. The compacted area reminded Jamal of jail. While in his search, Jamal came across some high school pictures of him and Kim. The pictures brought a sudden smile to his face as he reminisced about the past. After a few minutes, he came back to the present and found his black .45 and the box of bullets he had put away in hiding with it. "That's wassup," he said aloud after cocking the gun back then pulling the trigger to hear the clicking sound.

Coming back down form the attic, Jamal spotted his friend in the kitchen downing the last of the orange juice, neglecting to use a cup. With his back turned and head tilted back to down the rest of the juice; Spoon didn't realize Jamal was standing directly behind him. At that very moment Jamal shoved the barrel of his gun to the back of Spoon's head, causing him to take in to much, and spilling the rush of juice on his fresh white–T.

"What the fuck man!" Spoon said coughing repeatedly as if he was just rescued from drowning in a pool. "You play too much bro"

"Who's slipping now . . . bitch?" Jamal asked, exploding out in laughter. "Catch ya breath"

"Whateva nigga," Spoon said. "I just brought this shirt this morning man"

"Wow five bucks . . . you a dope boy nigga . . . go get another one," Jamal teased. "And this ain't ya house either; use a cup next time bro"

"Yeah yeah," said Spoon after taking off his shirt and throwing it away, revealing his .40 at his waistline. "Let me see the fucking fi bro"

After Jamal handed him the gun, Spoon cocked it back then pulled the trigger as he aimed in space. "I'll buy it from you," He offered. "What you want for it?"

"Naw man that's the only fi I got," Jamal explained. "I sold my other guns to help pay for the lawyer . . . I even sold the SK"

"Damn not the SK. . . . I loved that gun," Spoon said in disbelief. "If we gon' be moving all this work, we gon' need more guns incase of war, and you know war is bound to happen with them North Side Niggas, once we set up shop," he warned him. "Them niggas gon be hatin' . . . know what I'm saying"

"I know bro I know," Jamal said as he hoped on the counter to sit down. "Ima talk to Chico about that shit since he sells guns too," Jamal continued. "Ima call him when we come back from the mall"

"You do that bro," Spoon said still admiring the gun. "A nigga ready to get paid . . . know what I'm saying?"

"Yeah, you and me both bro," Jamal agreed as he hoped off the counter to grab a cloth by the sink. "Here use this to load it up so you don't leave any finger prints on the bullets, Ima gon' hit the shower," Jamal ordered as he threw Spoon the box of bullets. "Oh yeah, and try not to shoot ya' self"

"Whateva man . . . I got this," said Spoon. "Hey you heard Top 6 performing tonight at the Heat Box?"

"You foreal?" Jamal asked walking down the hallway. "I guess that's where we at tonight then huh?"

"You damn right, you know I love them boy's music," Spoon said as his phone began to ring. "But hurry up tho, money calling"

"What buddy that is?" Jamal wondered.

"Judy"

"You still fuck with her?" Jamal asked now yelling from the bathroom.

"Damn right, that baser brings in a lot of cash . . . she steady blowin' a nigga phone up," Spoon said as he pressed the ignore button on his phone. "I think she wants a hundo"

After a quick shower, Jamal through on his clothing and was ready for the day. He had on some black dickeys shorts, with red and black Jordan's on, and matching NBA socks. His only flaw was he needed a fresh t-shirt from the store. Spoon handed him his gun, then the two left the house and entered Spoon's Monte Carlo. Their destination was Lake Worth.

On their journey to the hood, the two made plans to stop at the 12th Ave. store to buy more Dutch's, and fresh white-Ts. They also planed to stop by the block to cop some weed, and say what's up to some of the boys, but money came first, so Judy was the primary target.

Spoon handed Jamal the last of his weed and final Dutch master. Jamal quickly rolled it up. He was always a better roller then his best friend. Couple of seconds later, the vehicle was fogged up as its trunk rattled to the sounds of Top 6's album. Spoon sung along to the rap lyrics as if he wrote them. Rap music was a big part of the young generation's life in the hood. It's either you played ball, sold drugs or rapped. It was like another way of making it out the hood. After making it to the city limits, Jamal noticed a lot of houses had for sale signs in their front yards. Some blocks literally had three to five houses next to each other, all for sale. Before he went to jail, he remembered most of the houses being occupied, he even know some of the home owners. It was like the neighborhoods were turning into ghost towns.

"Damn Spoon," said Jamal after turning down the volume on the CD player. "You don't see all these houses up for sale?"

"Yeah so what about em man?" Spoon asked in an annoyed tone. "I'm trying to listen to this Top 6 shit"

"What you mean, what about em?" Jamal asked as Spoon passed him the joint. "It's a recession coming nigga . . . shit about to get serious outchea"

"Man as far as I'm concerned shit been serious," said Spoon. "I aint worried about no fuckin recession . . . I gets money"

"Bro all that shit ties into this," Jamal informed him as he shook his head. "A recession means people gon' be out of jobs, everything gon' cost more, and police gon' be even hotter!"

"Man fuck the police . . . I ain't worried bout them man . . . you need to stop smoking," said Spoon before answering his phone. "This Judy calling me man . . . you bug"

"Okay nigga," said Jamal as he leaned back in his chair. "You gone see"

Judy was one of Spoon's and Jamal's many buddies. She only stayed a couple of blocks away, in a halfway house, from the street corner they sometimes hustled. She was one of them buddies that goes straight for a month or two, then goes right back to it. She had just gotten out of jail and swore she was rehabilitated for good this time, but soon fell victim to temptation, again. Spoon wasn't able to reach his maxim high, because Judy's constant calling disabled him to. Ten calls later, they finally arrived to the fiend's house. As the two pulled up, they spotted Judy standing outside with an angry look on her face that caused Jamal to laugh.

"That shit ain't funny man," An angry Spoon said as the lady knocked on his window. "If this lady wasn't spending so much I wouldn't even fuck with her ass"

"My bad bro but the lady is crazy . . . I mean look how she acting," Jamal chuckled, referring to her fidgeting. "She needs a hit bad"

Judy had been a costumer of the two for a while now. She knew them as Jackie and Tito because that's the names Spoon and Jamal gave her. Judy was around thirty but because of the crack she was smoking, she looked as if she was in her fifties. She had long black hair, pale white skin and only weighted 100 pounds. She smelled as if she hadn't showered in days. You could tell she was missing two front teeth because she would get so stuck sometimes, her mouth just hang wide open, and this was one of those times. Her braless breast sagged to her belly button, and you could see them through the holey white tank top she had on, even though no one wanted too. Judy's blue jeans were also dirty, her nails were filthy but worse of all, the crack Spoon gave here before going to Jamal's house, had her fending for more, so the only thing on her mind was getting another hit.

"What the fuck lady, why you keep banging on my window?" Spoon shouted in a tone that clearly showed he was irritated. "Don't you think I see you standing there?

"Come on Jackie . . . I've been calling you for like two hours man," the lady complained to Spoon while scratching her neck. "Fucks up with that?"

"Look Lady," said Spoon. "I said I was coming right?"

"Uh huh"

"Then why the fuck you keep blowin' up my phone?" He asked.

"Because I need it man," she said as she handed the money to Spoon. "I got eighty . . . hook it up"

"You blowing my phone up and you don't even have the whole hundo!" Spoon complained as he pulled out a plastic sandwich bag, full of fat yellowish chunks of crack.

"I needed a cigarette," she explained. "And I got hungry waiting on you"

"Whateva Judy," he said as he gave her five pieces of crack. "Huh man"

"Awww come on Jackie," Judy complained. "Hook it up man!"

"Hell naw," Spoon stated. "I can't do it"

"Well I ain't calling you no more," she said. "You don't treat me right"

"Guess what, I don't care . . . you always say that shit Judy," he said as he shifted the car into reverse. "I gotta go, call me later"

"Fuck you Jackie you never hook it up like Tito!" She yelled. "Is he out of jail yet?"

"Yeah I'm right here Judy," Jamal said as he revealed his face from the darkness in the car, due to the limo tinted windows and the hail of refer smoke. "Wassup?"

"Hey Tito!" She said now lowering her face to see the passenger. "When did you get out?"

"Last week," Jamal lied.

"Oooohhhh," said Judy, not really caring. "Well front me a piece"

"Damn Judy," said Jamal. "I just got out man I ain't got shit"

"Come on Tito," she begged. "Hook it up man"

"Man we got to go!" Said a fed up Spoon, before reversing out the drive way. "Bye Judy!"

"Fuck you guys!" Judy yelled jumping up and down with her fist in the air. "Fucking assholes"

"Same ol' Judy," Jamal chuckled. "She ain't never gonna change"

"Yeah I know but I need her," Spoon explained. "She getting me a rental car tomorrow"

"Oh I was wondering why we wasn't in one now," said Jamal. "We can't be dirty and riding clean at the same time bro"

"I know man," Spoon said sounding irritated. "You know Judy be working on her own time"

"Yeah cause she be too busy getting high," said Jamal. "*Come on Jackie hook it up man*," he mimicked Judy in a white girl like voice, causing them to both laugh. "That lady crazy"

Pulling into the 12th Ave. store's front parking lot, which was crowded as usual, Spoon handed Jamal fifteen bucks. Ten was for the T-shirts and the remaining five dollars were for Dutch Masters. Stepping out the car he noticed a Top 6 poster taped to the store wall. It read **Top 6 live in concert at the Heat Box.** This group really came a long way Jamal thought to him self. He remembered watching them when he was a little kid on his bike, doing music videos around the hood; now they're on the fast track to blowing up big and had the entire hood hooked on their music. Little kids represented music groups like this simply because they came from nothing and the music was all they had or the closest thing to doing it "big". Jamal was happy someone from the hood was making it out even though it wasn't him. As he continued to read the poster, a loud screeching sound drew Jamal's attention. When he turned around he saw a black later year Mercury, Grand Marquis speeding down the road with no regard for the law or other vehicles as it cut between slow moving cars. Staring for a few seconds, Jamal then proceeded to enter the store.

"Aaahhh Jay my friend, long time no see," said Abar the Arabic owner of the store, working at the cash register. "Where you been hiding?"

"Locked up my friend but I'm free now," Jamal said handing him the money. "Let me get two 2x white Ts and 5 Dutch Masters . . . Cognac"

"Free yes this is very good," Abar said handing Jamal the items. "Stay free . . . no trouble my friend"

"I got you Abar," Jamal said as he took the items and started to leave. "Be easy man"

"Yes yes," said Abar. "Easy is good"

While putting on his white T, Jamal noticed the same black Mercury speeding down the road again, but this time going in the opposite direction then before, as if it made a u turn. Not taking the particular vehicle as a threat, he entered Spoon's car and handed him the white T and placed the Dutch Masters in the cup holder at the center console. Their next destination was the block where they hustled, a couple streets down.

Arriving at the block, the two saw a group of familiar faces with concerned looks, all huddled up like football players, in the yard of a big white house that was up for sale. Instead of a fence, the house was surrounded by small bushes that you could easily step over. Sensing something was wrong the two grabbed their guns from under their seats, then concealed it in their waist lines and exited the car. While crossing the street to approach the huddle, Spoon put on his shirt, not caring if anyone saw his gun. Jamal could smell ribs being cooked by the lady next door to the empty house. He could see the smoke coming from the back of the old lady's yellow house, where she had a huge grill set up. A bunch of people were in back of the house trying to buy some food. She loved cooking for people so much that she turned her passion into a business, and the Haitian boys where some of her best customers, so she didn't mind them standing in front of her house, especially on a hot ass Saturdays like this one when her business was more lucrative. She figured the Zoes were there to draw in more customers, since they were popular in the hood.

"Wassup ya'll," said a concerned Jamal. "What the play is?"

"What the fuck!" Yelled Fat Zoe whose questions were followed by many more. "When you jumped *bitch*?"

"I got out yesterday *bitch*," said Jamal as he gave everyone dap. "And a nigga ain't going back either"

"I hear that," said Ronny. "They can't hold a Zoe down forever"

"I'm saying tho," said a jealous Spoon. "Ya'll act like ya'll don't see a nigga standing here"

"Man who you is," Troy joked. "Kick rocks my nigga we don't know you"

"I bet ya mama know a nigga very well tho," Spoon replied as everyone laughed at his usual wise cracks. "As a matter of fact take yo as home and tell her Ima be there later"

"Fuck you bitch," Troy shot back with a mean mug. "You gon' stop talking bout a nigga mama like that man"

"Man fuck all that," Jamal interrupted before the situation escalated. "When we pulled up it looked liked ya'll boys was trippin' about something . . . wassup?"

"A black Merc keep riding by speeding and shit," said Ronny. "We think its jack boys or something"

"No lie bro," Jamal said. "I seen that same car speeding down the street while we was at the store"

"I know one thing tho," Fat Zoe declared after grabbing his AK-47 from some nearby bushes. "They come through here again Ima wet that shit up . . . straight like that"

Fat Zoe, Ronny, Troy and Jamal's older brother Ken, were home boys to the death. Jamal and Spoon were apart of the circle as well, since even before they were teenagers. Ever since they were off the porch, Jamal and Spoon use to try and keep up with the older ones. Jamal's older brother Ken, and the others, tried to guide them the right way, but Jamal and Spoon were just too damn hardheaded. They wanted to get money like the big boys, so the others decided to show them the ropes, since they wouldn't listen. After a while, Jamal and Spoon started getting money and block hustling just as good as the others, which made the three to four year age difference easily forgotten. They all loved to rap and practiced their skills in Ken's studio. One day when they were younger, Spoon was free styling in the booth and accidentally came up with the name South Side Boys. The men liked the idea since they lived on the South Side of Lake Worth so they decided to keep it. Four years later, they still called themselves the South Side Boys and created a nice buzz for themselves. They had it in their minds that they were going to be the next hottest thing out of Lake Worth, just like Top 6.

Fatsen was also known as Fat Zoe because of him being over weight, or damn near obese, he was like the back bone out of the group. He was usually the first person to fight making the others sure to follow. He had ten big, fat, ugly, dookie dreads that hung down to his mid back, and he wore a fully, grown bread and had a mouth full of gold teeth. His dark skin was covered in tattoos and he always wore a fresh black wife beater to show them off. Today he had on long blue jeans and black Jordan's. His "South Side Boy" chain glistened in the light as he held his AK in his hand, making sure it was off safety. Ronny and Troy were cousins and could always be caught chilling with each other when they weren't with the others. Ronny had long dreads that hung to his waist and this high yellow skin was inked up. His most prized tattoos were his brother's portrait with the words rest in peace under it tattooed on his forearm, and the tear drop underneath his right eye. Ronny's older brother was killed last year in a robbery and every since then Ronny wasn't his same cheery self. He was more quite and hardly smiled. Today he wore a black shirt with his brother picture on it, some tan cargo paints, and black Jordan's. He had a mouth full of gold like the others and was a ladies man, his hassle eyes and 6"3 stature drove the ladies wild and he knew it. Troy also had dreads but his were only shoulders length. He had dark skin but wasn't fully tatted like the others. His only tattoo was the word South on the back of his right arm and the word Side on his other arm, both in fully colored bubble letters. He was one of them niggas that was bout whatever and always down for the cause. He joked around a lot but getting him mad wasn't in your best interest. He had on a white T shirt and short blue jeans with all white Jordan's on. He was dark skinned, 5'5 and very muscular. He was the athletic type, and was always on the basketball team since middle school. Troy had the potential to be a point guard in the NBA one day, but the street's influence took a hold of him. He dropped out of high school like the others and became a full time dope boy.

"Where your brother at?" Troy asked after coming back from near by bushes with his and Ronny's tech-9s. "I ain't seen that nigga since the day fo' yesterday"

"I ain't seen him either," Jamal answered as he looked down the street for the black Mercury. "I don't even think he knows I'm out," Jamal added. "He probably at the studio . . . you know how he do it"

"Hell yeah," Troy confirmed. "That bih loves that music shit"

"Hey Fat Zoe let me get some bo-zac," Spoon ordered as he pulled out twenty bucks from his pocket and handed it to Spoon. "Five fo the dub right?"

"I got you lil' bro . . . ya'll boys keep your eyes open," said Fat Zoe walking back to his stash spot. "You see them niggas again wet they shit up"

As Jamal stood in middle on the yard with the others, he kept looking down both ends of the street making sure he was on point, just incase the Mercury came back. Shit like this was protocol in the hood, that's way Jamal was ready to go. He did not want to start off his second day home getting shot at.

"Yo Spoon," Jamal said in an irritated voice. "Go tell that nigga Fat to hurry up"

"The man said he was coming," Spoon told him with his gun in hand. "What's wrong with you?"

"Nothing man," said Jamal. "I'm just ready to go fo shit get crazy"

"You been acting strange since you got out bro," Spoon joked as Fat Zoe came from around the back with his weed. "There go Fat now"

"Whateva man," said Jamal. "Just hurry up"

Spoon walked towards Fat to get his weed. Just as soon as Fat Zoe handed Spoon his order, the notorious black Mercury came speeding around the corner with its tires screeching. Fire was blazing out of its backseat window from a high powered assault rifle; with a trash bag around its center to catch the many bullet shells flying out of it. Everybody was caught of guard by the attack. Spoon dropped his bag of weed and fell to his stomach before letting off a few shots. Fat Zoe instantly returned fire, hitting the car a couple of times. Customers who were buying food next door screamed and began to run for their lives. Some jumped over Spoon as if he were a hurdle. Jamal ran to a near by parked car, returning fire as Troy and Ronny threw themselves to the ground. As the car sped by, Ronny quickly stood up and ran into the middle of the street to return fire but failing to hit the vehicle. Luckily no one was injured.

"Pussy ass niggas!" Fat Zoe yelled as he ran to the middle of the street too. "I got something fo'ya!"

"Hey lets go fo' troll come!" Troy said as he jogged for his car causing Fat and Ronny to follow.

"Yeah let's ride my nigga," Spoon said to Jamal before they ran to his car. "100% and them other crackas gon' be on fi fo' real"

Fleeing from the block like thieves in the night, both the best friends hearts were racing and their adrenalines were pumping. Spoon, who was trying not to exceed the speed limit by too much, had it in mind to get out of the city ASAP. Jamal kept his eyes open for the black Mercury and the authorities. Finally making it to I-95, their hearts settled back in their chest.

"We straight now bro," said Spoon. "Troll ain't fucking with us"

"Damn man," Jamal complained. "Not even forty eight hours out of jail and I'm getting bust at"

"I told you its ratchet out chea bro!" Spoon explained. "Niggas playing foul"

"I see that," Jamal said leaning back into his chair. "You saw Fat gettin' off with the K back there man?"

"Fuck that . . . did you see how I was dodging bullets while I was dumpin," Spoon lied. "I mean I was doing some movie type shit"

"Naw bro I ain't see that part," Jamal chuckled. "But I did see ya scary ass on the floor"

"Whateva my nigga I know what I was doing," said Spoon. "Besides them niggas had uh big boy choppa"

"*Did they* . . . bro what the fuck was them niggas shooting?" Jamal asked. "That wasn't no jack boys . . . them niggas was trying to kill something"

"Hell yeah you right," said Spoon as he checked his phone. "Ronny said they gon' hide out at Ken's until shit cool down and he suggests we do the same"

"Hell yeah cause the city to hot rite now," said Jamal. "We might as well shoot to the mall like planed"

"Might as well," Spoon agreed as he handed Jamal some weed. "Here roll up . . . I got to calm my nerves"

Fifteen minutes or so of sliding and burning went by before they finally made it to the West Palm Beach Mall. Just like every weekend the mall was crowded. It took them approximately ten minutes to find a parking spot. Spoon parked in backwards just incase something popped off.

"Damn bro!" Spoon said as he observed the many vehicles in the parking lot. "It's thick ass fuck out chea!"

"Thick ain't the word," Jamal responded as he stepped out the car. "This bitch swoll"

"I bet them hoes live and affect," Spoon stated as they both made way towards the mall entrance. "And just waiting fo' a nigga like me"

"You crazy bro," said Jamal as he chuckled "I don't even know why I chill with you"

"Cause I'm that nigga," Spoon stated. "Plus you don't have any friends"

After entering the mall, both the young men eyes widened when realizing that Spoon's predictions were right. The "hoes" indeed were live and affect. Beautiful women swarmed the mall from front to back.

"Damn look at that baby!" Spoon said loud enough so the high yellow female could hear him. She had an ass that jiggled as if it wasn't tamed by draws. "Hey girl, come here"

"Calm down bro," said Jamal trying to control his hormone driven friend. "You gon' run the hoes off"

"Oh yeah I forgot," Spoon chuckled. "You on lock down"

"Whateva dawg," said Jamal. "Call it what ya won't"

"Yeah, yeah, yeah . . . lets get down to business man," Spoon said before pulling out 5 stacks from his pocket to give Jamal 3. "I'm glad you out of jail bro and like I promised I was gon' return the favor so, let's do what it do . . . . the mall is ours"

"That's why I love ya bro," Jamal said hugging his best friend. "You my nigga fo' life"

"Man tighten up with all that sentimental shit bro," Spoon said as he pushed away from Jamal's bear hug. "I told ya I don't need no thanks . . . you like a brother to me . . . know what I'm saying"

The two hit up almost every store in the mall. Spoon mainly brought Jordans and air forces. Jamal leaned towards buying a variety of outfits designed by Encye, Akademiks, Coogie and Parish. He balanced his new wardrobe with only a few selections of shoes with basic color scheme. He also brought a cell phone. Not being selfish

Jamal got a few things for Kim and Kayla as well. He thought if he was to look fresh his family would have to be fresh as well. Making their way out the mall the two were being eyed by people because of the many bags they were carrying. The two clearly looked like dope boys and the strong aroma of weed that came from their clothing assured the old white people that stereotyped them.

During their walk of fame, Spoon's stomach stopped him in his tracks. Reminding Jamal that they haven't eaten all day, he suggested that they lunch at the food court. Jamal's stomach didn't let him decline. On the way to the food court they decided to eat Chinese food. After ordering the two sat at the table where they had sat their bags down in advance. Waiting until Jamal prayed over his food, Spoon gave him a Cuban link necklace equipped with a "South Side Boy" charm that was exactly like the one hanging around his neck.

"Damn bro I respect you for this my nigga . . . I was wondering how I was gon' finish paying fo' it," Jamal said in appreciation. "How you knew I had money down on it?"

"Remember I was at the flea market with you when you put the 3 stacks down on it?" Spoon explained. "You only had five hundred left to pay on it, so I took care of it fo you while you were down"

"I don't know what to say," said Jamal. "A nigga speechless bro"

"You straight man," said Spoon "I got ya fo' life"

"That's wassup bro," Jamal said as he put the necklace around his neck. "This some real nigga shit"

"You my brother from another mother," Spoon stated as he put his fist out to receive dap. "That ain't neva gon' change you feel me"

"I fell ya," Jamal answered as he dapped Spoon's fist to sign off the bond between them. "We brothers fo' life"

As they finished off their meals, Spoon sensed someone's eyes burning a hole through the side of his face. Taking his eyes away from his plate he saw four guys with dreads, dressed in black T shirts, blue jeans and black Reeboks, looking hard in his direction. Being that he was near sighted, Spoon had to squint to make out their individual faces.

"Bro there go them niggas right there," said Spoon in an almost wispier like tone. "Don't turn around tho"

"Who man?" Jamal asked trying to resist the urge to look. "Who you talkin' bout?"

"Them north side niggas man!" Spoon said feeling for his gun at his waist. "I think that's Travis and them"

"Man fuck them niggas," Jamal said as he turned around to mean mug the individuals now walking towards their table. "Them niggas ain't shit"

"Well they on us," Spoon said cocking his gun back under the table before concealing it. "You got your strap on ya?"

"I stay strapped," Jamal declared as they both stood up and grabbed their bags before making way towards the young men walking in their direction.

Travis, Buck, Man Man and Ray Ray were North Side Boys till they die as they would tell you and they were on the fast track to doing just that. The name "North Side Boys", originated from them living on the other side of the city from the Haitian community. When they were younger they use to fight Haitian kids everyday after school, just because. You see, African Americans and Haitians have always bumped heads since Haitians started migrating to this country. From generation to generation, Haitians and Black Americans often feuded in school. The Americans bulled them just because of what they wore or how they talked. The Haitians were different so they often had to fight for their respect. Fat Zoe, Troy and Ken weren't on that getting bulled shit either. Ever since middle school, the south side beefed with the north side and went to war whenever they crossed paths.

Ever since Travis was little he had a short fuse. He wasn't much of a talker but when he did, his deep voice made people listen. He dropped out of school in the 8th grade and started selling drugs. His sister's boy friend named Bird, thought him everything he new about the dope game. His mother died giving birth to him and his father was severing life in prison. Travis and his older sister Shay; lived with his cousin Ray Ray and Aunty until Shay moved out to live with her drug dealing boyfriend. Travis got kicked out when he was fifteen for selling drugs. He was 5'8, weighted 180 pounds and was very muscular. His brown skin had no tattoos. The only permanent mark on his face was a scare across his left check he got from a drunken chico with a knife; he tried to rob when he was younger. Like all of the N.S.B, he had long dreads and gold teeth. His eyes were always bloodshot even when he wasn't smoking. He was known in the hood to put in work and had a couple of bodies' under his belt. His motto was M.O.E all the way; money over everything. Buck was very light skinned like his mother who he lived with, he was the tallest out of the bunch and was very slim. He had brown eyes and his many dreads were long and thin. His lips were black from smoking so much and his body was covered in tattoos. Ever since they were little he tried to talk the others out of doing wrong but ended doing the deed along with them. He was one of those guys that didn't like letting their friends down, so he would ride for you until the wheels fell off. Man Man was your definition of grimy. He would do whatever to get money. Anything from selling dope to robbing you, he was willing to do it to get paid. He dropped out of middle school with the others and hit the block strong. He and Travis were always arguing about something and Buck would be the one to break it up. He never knew his father and lived with his mother across the street from Buck. He was 5'5 very dark skinned, slim but very toned. He always wore a black bandanna around his neck and liked to let his dreads hang down his face. He was a hot head and very trigger happy. He was one of them niggas that always had a chip on his shoulder for no reason. Ray Ray was the youngest and the smallest one amongst the others. He stood 5'3 and weighted 120 pounds, so he was pretty much the butt of all jokes and the other's punishing bag. Although Travis put him through hell, Ray still looked up to his older cousin. The guys sold dope and hung out on his front porch with or without his permission. Ray was pretty much the team lackey or water boy so to say. Like the others he fit today's description of a "thug". His long dreads touch his shoulder and his 8 on 8 gold grills shined like a light. His dark skin was inked with hood hieroglyphics and he wore them proudly . . . from the North Side Boy in old English letters on his back, to his "Lake Worth" tattoo on his back arms.

Jamal and Spoon had their eyes dead locked on the pack of men lead by Travis. Still walking in the same direction like two trains on the same track about to crash, the two groups of men had no intentions of making way for each other to pass by. A few long seconds of walking and mean mugging finally ended by them colliding and bumping shoulders. The odds two to four put no fear in Spoon's and Jamal's hearts as they quickly dropped their bags and pushed two of the members. They then stepped back both with their hands on their weapons concealed underneath their shirts, being careful not to reveal them in the mall as shoppers stopped to look.

"Nigga wassup?" Spoon yelled as he taped his gun to show the men he was armed. "Ya'll boys ain't see us walking?"

"What you mean fuck nigga?" Man Man shouted as he slightly lifted up his shirt to show that he too was also carrying a gun. "Ya'll bumped into us"

"What that mean bro?" Jamal asked after seeing Man Man's gun. "Use that shit!"

"Whoa, whoa, whoa . . . . ya'll boys calm down," Travis said as he put a hand on his trigger happy friend's shoulder to compose him. "What ya'll gon' shoot up the mall?" He chuckled. "Them boys should be tired of dodging bullets anyways the way we wet they block up earlier"

"Oh that's funny huh?" Jamal asked not seeing any humor in his joke. "How bout I wet yo ass up now?"

"Naw I don't think so lil' nigga," Travis sarcastically said. "Maybe when we cross paths again you could try me"

"Hey what's going on?" A West Palm Beach officer followed by five security guards all armed with tasers yelled before Jamal had a chance to answer. "You guys break it up!"

"Ain't no problem officer," Travis lied. "We were just leaving"

"Well make it fast boy!" The officer ordered. "You two stay here and wait until they leave!"

Jamal and Spoon were questioned by the officer for a few minutes before he escorted them to the parking lot. The police officer was a skinny white man that looked like he was in his thirties. Spoon felt like giving the officer lip, but didn't want to get him mad since he was strapped. Following them all the way to their car, he stood watch as Spoon pretended to struggle with unlocking the trunk so that he could stall. He was dirty and the car smelled like weed. Observing Spoon's unusual behavior, Jamal tried to distract the officer by telling him they were okay now. While doing so Spoon quickly unlocked the driver door and entered the vehicle.

Agreeing that everything was okay, the officer walked off. Just as soon as Jamal, who was standing in front of the car, took his eyes away from the officer and fixed them down the parking lot road, he saw the same black mercury that shot up the block earlier, racing at him. Man Man with the black bandanna now around his lower face, was hanging out the window firing a high powered weapon.

"Spoon watch out!" Jamal yelled as he ran behind Spoon's car while dodging bullets at the same time.

"Fuck!" Spoon yelled as he flew out the car onto his stomach and rolled under it and continuing on to the other cars parked next to his. "My car man"

"Pussy ass Haitians!" Man Man shouted before ducking back into the car. "This The North bitch!"

"Fuck niggas!" Jamal shouted as he ran to the middle of the road letting off a few shots at the vehicle that was already in the far distance. "Spoon where you at bro?"

"I'm right here man," said Spoon appearing three cars away from his. "Damn look at my fucking windshield man . . . them pussy ass niggas gon' die!"

"I know I know bro," said Jamal who was alerted by the sounds of sirens in the distant. "But we gotta go"

As they sped off in the car, Jamal spotted the police officer face down on the ground with his back filled with bullets. Shaking his head at the sight of the dead, Jamal knew he had to take advantage of his chance to break loose from the game, or that dead man could be him.

CHAPTER 4

Yo onetime for them Top 6 niggas . . .
yall boys doing it big out chea man
check me out . . . .

This cocaine could be yours fo the right price
24-7 grind got my niggas rocking big ice
The only one that I fear is J Christ
So when that fi in ya face it's nothing nice
South Side, South Side yeah we raise hell
That choppa ripping through niggas,
Their go them hot shells . . .

"**O**kay I got that," Ken said after Troy finished his verse in the booth.

"What that shit sound like bro?" Troy questioned, stepping out the heat box that served as a recording booth, dripping in sweat.

"That shit was fi," said Ken turning from his mother board in his roller chair to face Fat and Ronny sitting on the couch. "But if we wanna get some real exposure like them Top 6 niggas we need to do better," he informed them. "Calling out they name on some songs ain't gon get us nowhere . . . now who's next?"

"Ima go next," said Fat as he stood up to walk inside the booth.

"Then let's get it nigga!" Ken ordered as he turned to his computer. "Time is money"

The heavy set rapper studied his lyrics while standing in the booth. After a few minutes of looking over his musical poetry, he was ready to begin. "I'm ready," he shouted into the microphone so the impatient producer could start the beat. As Ken reached to hit a button on his mother board, his arm was stopped in mid reach by a loud knocking at his studio door; that sounded as if it was the police. Everyone quickly grabbed their guns. Ken grabbed his pistol from a nearby drawer as Troy and Ronny grabbed there techs from underneath the couch.

"Who that is?" Ronny whispered as he tightly griped his tech and looked at the others.

"I don't know let me check," Ken whispered as he walked towards the door with his gun drawn. "Man it ain't nobody but Spoon ass," said Ken looking in the peephole. "Nigga why the fuck is you banging on my door like you the police?" He questioned a furious Spoon who was followed by Jamal as he let them in.

"Maybe cause we were almost killed!" Spoon shouted before lighting a joint to try and calm his nerves. "Man . . . watch, just watch . . . every single one of 'em gon' die!" He went on in a rage. "They mamas, daddies, baby mamas naw fuck it, they whole family gon feel me . . . know what I'm saying!"

"Man slow down Spoon and tell me what happened," said Ken.

"Man them muthafuckas shot up my car!" Spoon continued ignoring Ken's questions. "They put holes all in my windshield!"

"Who man?" Ken shouted clearly sounding irritated. "You ain't telling me shit bro!"

"Man I'm too mad to talk," Spoon said plopping down on the couch. "Ask Jay to tell ya,"

"Bro please tell me what happen," Ken said shaking his head at Spoon's difficultness. "Cause this fool here crazy"

"After we left the block we went to the mall and got into it with Travis and them," Jamal explained. "Them niggas tried to murk us in the parking lot but fucked around and killed troll and shit"

"What!" Fat Zoe yelled throwing down his lyrics after over hearing the conversation through his headphones. "Please tell me you lying"

"Wish I was bro," Jamal said wondering why Fat was in the booth for that long. "As a matter of fact they the ones that shot up the block"

"Them fuck niggas sizing us bro!" Troy said as he paced in circles. "Shit I want blood now . . . I'm talkin' ASAP!"

"That's real talk bro!" Ken added. "G shit"

"Don't worry them niggas gon' get it," Fat assured them. "Top 6 performing tonight so they gon' be at the "Heat Box" fo' sho . . . we'll take care of them then . . . straight like that," said Fat. "You niggas in or what?"

"My nigga you know I'm in all the way!" Spoon stated. "Them boys' gon' pay for what they did to my car"

"Well Jay?" Fat questioned Jamal after the others confirmed they were in. "You gon' ride or what?"

"Uh . . . yeah Ima ride," Jamal hesitated. "It's whateva"

"Okay then its official," said Fat as he gave Jamal dap, unable to detect the uneasiness in his voice.

"Hey man lets finish this track fo' it get too late," Ken advised. "Ronny record Fat while Jamal and I talk outside"

The brothers walked outside to talk. Ken heard from Fat and the others that his little brother was a free man. Even though he was happy his brother was out of jail, he was still mad that he was the last one to hear about it. He was the tallest one out the bunch standing at 6'7. Besides his height he looked like a typical dope boy. His gold grill, long dreads and "South Side Boy" chunk was all intact. Ken was quick to fight like the others but like Jamal, he was a laid back kind of guy, calm cool and collective. He had a long gold tea, brown eye and also was quit the ladies man. He had no tattoos and his skin was light brown. He had a strong passion for music, so when he wasn't on the streets you could catch him in the studio he built in his garage. There the South Side Boys recorded all their music and Ken even recorded people to make some money on the side. He was like the smart guy of the group.

"So that's how we do things now?" He asked. "You jump and I'm the last one to hear bout it huh?"

"Naw man," said Jamal. "When I got out I was trapped up with Kim and shit then we went to go see mommy and you know how that goes"

"Yeah I feel ya lil' bro," he lied. "How is mommy doing anyway?"

"*I don't know bro,*" said Jamal in a sarcastic tone. "Maybe if you go see her you'll find out"

"Man you know how mommy is," Ken said as he waved the idea away with his hands. "I don't be tryna hear that shit she be talking"

"Ken you know mommy don't mean no harm," Jamal explained. "She just wants the best fo' us bro"

"I know man," said Ken. "She just be talking too much tho"

"That she does but I'm going to see her and Kay after this," said Jamal. "You might as well come too since its been a few months . . . since you seen mom"

"Yeah you right Ima be there," said Ken. "We might as well ride out together"

"That's a bet cause I ain't riding in Spoon's shit," said Jamal. "That bih too hot"

"Yeah troll gon' be lookin fo' it," Ken agreed as he walked closer to take a better look at the damages to the car. "Them North Side Niggas wild'n," he chuckled. "It's cool tho they gone get it"

"Real talk," Jamal agreed as Ken examined a bullet hole in the diver seat with his finger. "They gotta get it fo' real"

"Look Jay you ain't gotta go tonight," Ken told him. "I mean I seen you hesitate when Fat asked you to ride"

"Man whateva bro," Jamal said defensively. "I ain't that lil' nigga ya'll use to beat up . . . I could hold my own"

"Aight bro I'm just looking out fo' ya," said Ken. "Do what you do man . . . just be easy"

Before Jamal could further the conversation, Spoon and the others walked outside. Spoon walked to his car then gazed at it in silence for a few seconds. The others watched as he balled his fist tightly in anger. Looking like Lucifer himself he then kicked the vehicle as he cursed.

"Man chill bro," Ronny told him. "What the fuck you kicking your car fo'?"

"Them fuck niggas sized my shit!" Spoon exclaimed. "If we don't handle em' tonight Ima handle em' myself . . . know what I'm saying!"

"Boy I already told you the plan?" Fat said. "Stop acting like a hot boy for once cause that shit uh get all us jammed up fo' real"

"Man miss me with that fuck shit bro," said Spoon as he waved Fat Zoe off. "I could handle me"

"That's what your mouth say," said Fat. "You too hot bro straight up . . . It ain't just about you dawg it's about us"

Remembering that he needed to call Chico, Jamal walked off towards the street as Spoon and Fat Zoe bickered. He went to his contact list in his phone and strolled for Chico's name. Chico's phone rung for a few seconds then went to the answer machine, sort of like someone pressed the ignore button on him. Not wanting to call again in fear of looking desperate, Jamal just left a message informing Chico to call him back. As he started to walk back his phone rang. Not recognizing the number Jamal still picked up.

"Hello," he answered. "Who's this?"

"A car will pick you up tomorrow," said an unfamiliar voice. "We will find you please do not call again"

Jamal wasn't surprised because Chico took know risk what so ever. So a phone call like that was expected. Walking back he noticed Fat and Spoon were still arguing. Them two could argue from sun up to sun down, but it was always out of love. Jamal interrupted their bickering by asking Spoon what the agenda would be for the night. Spoon told him Ronny was taking him to Enterprise to meet Judy, so he would pick him up at the house tonight. After agreeing everyone said their goodbyes and was all ready to touchdown at the Heat Box later that night to cause hell.

ⴲ　　ⴲ　　ⴲ

Back in the hood Travis, Buck, Man Man and Ray were lounging on Ray's front porch. They were reminiscing and cracking jokes about the day's passed events as they drunk and got high as usual. Travis being the more serious of the bunch wasn't laughing. Instead he was worried about covering his tracks.

"So Buck," he said in a serious tone that caused everyone to shut up. "Did you burn the Mercury like I told you to or what?"

"Of course I did man," Buck replied. "I took it to the woods and set that bitch on fire"

"That's good," said Travis. "So what your buddy say about his car?"

"Shit really," Buck chuckled. "He was mad when I told em' it got stolen then forgot all about it when I gave him some dope"

"Good work homie," said Travis. "But I don't want you fucking with em' anymore ya hear me?"

"Why not man?" Buck complained. "Them crackas spend a lot of money with uh nigga!"

"I know but I don't want no connections to this murder," Travis explained. "Blame this none aiming nigga over here"

"Man whatever," said Man Man. "That cracka shouldn't have got in the way"

"See I don't think you understand the seriousness of this situation," said Travis in a calm but serious demeanor. "Nigga you just killed a cop . . . which means 100% gon' be looking fo' answers," he continued. "And since we be round here thuggin' and shit he gon' come asking us and them Haitians first"

"I'm saying tho Travis," Ray interrupted. "You think Jay and Spoon gon' snitch on us?"

"Naw they ain't gon' snitch," said Travis. "That's one thing I could say bout them Haitians"

"Yeah I was thinking that too cuz," said Ray. "Them Zoe's bout that shit"

"What you said nigga?" Travis asked feeling offended. "Repeat that shit again"

"Ummmm," said Ray staring at the floor. "I was just saying—"

"You was just saying what!" Travis yelled. "Them south side niggas more bout this shit then us?"

"Naw Trav . . . I . . . I," Ray stuttered still eyeing the floor. "I ain't say that"

"Yeah, that's what I thought!" Travis said as he through a bag of weed onto his cousin's lap. "Don't say shit nigga . . . just sit there and roll!"

When Ray Ray started rolling the joint, a pearl white, 2008 Titian truck, with jet black windows pulled up. "Hey grab ya fi!" Man Man said causing the others to do so. "I think that's them Haitians!"

"Man ya'll some scary ass niggas!" Travis said after receiving a text message seconds before the car's arrival. "That's my sister!"

"Oh yeah?" Man Man questioned as he tried to get a glimpse of her through the tinted windows. "That's Shay sexy ass?"

"Hey watch ya mouth nigga," Travis said in a chilling tone with his gun pointed in Man's face. "You know I don't play bout my sister"

"I suggest you take that gun out my face nigga," Man said in a tone equivalent to Travis'. "I don't play that shit"

Before Travis could say another word he was interrupted by the sound of Shay's horn. Taking his attention away from Man Man, he walked over to the passenger side door and entered the car. Man himself was fuming in anger. He sat down in his seat and placed his gun in his lap. Ray told him to calm down as he passed him the joint. Man was a hot head but he knew Travis was like a loose cannon, so he decided to let the situation slide but he surely wasn't going to forget about it.

On a scale of one through ten, Shay was a dime on her worst day. With the skin color of J–Lo and the body of Lisa Ray, people would often mistake her for Hispanic heritage. Her green eyes and long hair did nothing to solve the confusion, so evidently Travis had his hands full. Although she dropped out of high school, Shay still maintained a high classy life. Learning how to hustle from her boyfriend Bird who currently was doing ten years fed time, Shay defined herself as an independent woman.

"What they do sis?" Travis asked.

"What they do?" Shay questioned as she put on a fresh coat of lip gloss in the visor's mirror. "I don't care what they do . . . I just care bout my money you owe me nigga"

"Come on sis don't even come at me like that," Travis said before handing her the money. "You know I got ya"

"Boy you 500 short!" She said after taking a few seconds to count the money. "I know you my brother and everything but I told you I ain't with that shit," she continued. "Just cause Bird gone don't mean I ain't handling business so don't try me," she said as Travis stared out the window in silence. "Listen Travis I'll cut you off seriously man you bad business"

"I know Shay . . . that's my bad," He said remorsefully. "I got you next time"

"You know what ya problem is Travis?" She asked showing off her perfectly manicured nail as she pointed at him. "You can't stay out of trouble," she told him. "I saw the news this morning about some cop getting killed at the mall, and if I know you and your clown ass friends, I would bet all my money ya'll had sum' to do with it cause ya'll be at that mall"

"What!" He shouted. "We ain't have shit to do with that!"

"Uh huh . . . well Ima tell ya like this," Shay said seeing through his bad acting. "You ain't gon' be bringING heat down on me . . . like them niggas did Bird," She explained. "Brother or not Travis I will cut you off," She warned him. "You need to stop fuckin with them Haitians and get money!"

"First off . . . fuck them Haitians," he said glancing at Man Man as he concealed his gun back in waist line. "Secondly I wouldn't snitch on anyone!"

"Maybe so but this game dirty baby brother," she said. "I bet Bird ain't think his brother would snitch on him huh?" She asked causing Travis to finally look her in the eyes. "Plus you out here waving guns in ya homebody face . . . you can't get loyalty like that"

"Man fuck those niggas," he calmly said. "I run them"

"Whateva don't say I ain't try to tell you boy," she warned him before throwing a large Gucci bag in his lap. "Here I need seven back plus the five hundo you owe me"

"Damn sis you taxing uh nigga" he complained. "What's up with that?"

"Shit them Papis taxin' me twenty a key now," she explained. "You lucky I ain't tax ya nine an ounce instead of eight like I do everybody else"

"Whateva man I got ya," Travis said as he halfway stepped out the vehicle. "Who truck this is anyway?"

"See now you asking too many questions boy," Shay informed him. "Get out my car"

"You betta not be fucking with these busta ass niggas round here," Travis warned her. "I'm dead ass serious"

"Boy you cant tell me what to do," she said. "I'm two years older then you and most of all you ain't my daddy" Shay continued. "But anyways what ya'll doing tonight?"

"You already know," said Travis. "We at the Heat Box live in affect every Friday"

"I don't know shit bout ya'll lil' kitty club," said Shay. "But me and my home girl might hit it up since Top 6 gone be out there"

"Shay you know I don't like you in the hood like that," he said. "So you betta stay ya ass home"

"Yeah and you betta have my money!" She said with a ghetto like attitude before skirting off. "Bye!"

CHAPTER 5

Lead by a beautiful full moon, the night over came the day. Regardless of the night still being fairly young, the chaos was very old. It made its presence felt through the distant gun shots and sirens that flowed through the night air. The birds of the night (police helicopters) ruled the skies. The main event for the night on everyone's agenda was indeed the "Heat Box". Lame or not, that was the place to be. The club was nicknamed "The Heat Box" on the count of it being so packed inside that it was just that; A heat box, and since Top 6 was performing tonight the temperature level was sure to reach drastic highs.

The Zoes made plans to meet at Ken's studio after getting ready and handling their own affairs. Spoon him self was in search of a vehicle since his was out of commission. The two brothers made way to their mother's house.

"Damn where you been at bro?" Junior questioned Ken after opening the door to let them in. "I haven't seen you in months"

"I've been chillin," Ken said while giving his brother dap. "How you been?"

"You know bro same ol' shit," said Junior. "Fucking hoes, and going to school"

"Bitch you ain't fucking no hoes," Jamal said as he carried the bags from the mall, causing Ken to laugh. "Man tell me where Kayla at cause I can't hear that shit you be talking"

"Whateva nigga she in mommy room sleeping," said Junior. "I see you went on a shopping spree . . . you on the grind again?"

"Something like that nigga," Jamal answered as he made way to his sleeping beauty, barring gifts. "You just need to mind ya business"

"Come in," Mama said in response to the soft knock at her bedroom door. "It's open"

"Hey mommy," Jamal said to his half asleep mother. "How are you?"

"I'm fine baby," said mama as she rubbed sleeping beauties back next to her. "She been up all day waiting for you"

"Yeah mommy," he began to explain. "I was really busy today"

"Doing what?" She questioned in a firm whisper. "Running around with your friends?"

"Come on mommy don't start," said Jamal. "I had important things to handle"

"Anyways boy," she changed the subject upon noticing the bags in Jamal's hands. "What's in the bags?"

"Some gifts for Kayla," he said in a proud tone. "I copped em' at the mall"

"Oh you coped em' at the mall huh?" She said in a tone dripping with sarcasm. "Boy I told you she don't need a daddy she needs a father and gifts ain't gon' change that"

"Please mommy man," he begged. "Tighten up"

"Tighten up?" Mama said in a voice now showing she was clearly irritated. "Boy don't make me get up and—" Mama said before she was interrupted by a knock at the door. "Lord Jesus has my eyes deceived me?"

"What's up Mommy?" Kenny asked. "How you been?"

"I've been fine and in great health thanks to Jesus," said Mama. "And you?"

"I'm good," Ken replied. "Living one day at a time"

"I'm glad to hear that baby," she said. "You two look like ya'll up to no good tonight"

"Naw," the two brothers denied. "Why would you say that?"

"Well Jamal," said Mama. "Just call it mother's intuition"

"Naw you got it wrong mommy," Ken lied. "We just going out to enjoy ourselves"

"Uh huh tell mommy anything just know she ain't stupid," Mama warned them. "I try telling you boys to stop this foolishness and get ya'll self's together," she continued. "This world is harsh and the paths ya'll on will lead to nothing but—," Mama's preaching was interrupted by Ken's cell phone.

"Excuse me Mommy I got to pick this up," He said before answering his phone.

"You see that's what I'm talking bout right there," said Mama now sitting up in bed looking up at the ceiling. "Lord please help these lost souls"

"Yeah I'm on my way," said Ken. "Hey mommy I got to go back to the studio and record someone," he said before kissing his mother on the cheek. "Ima come by tomorrow"

"Ya'll boys just don't know," Mama said as she watched Ken head for the room door. "Ya'll just don't know"

"Jay meet us at the club tonight," Ken said. "Aight?"

"Fo' sho'," Jamal said noticing his mother's facial expression. "Stop worrying mommy," he said trying to comfort her with a kiss on the check. "We just chillin"

Once again a hot steamy shower brought Jamal into deep thought. He was still in disbelief that he'd escaped death twice in one day. Death was surly lurking and Jamal knew that it would make its presence felt at the Heat Box tonight. He wonted to stay home but if Spoon was to get killed in his absence, he wouldn't be able to live with him self. Spoon was also a key part of his planes to break . . . so he had to protect his investments.

Jamal's thoughts were interrupted as well as his shower by a pounding on the bathroom door. His mother was ranting and raving about her water bill, so Jamal left the bathroom and entered his childhood room. It was just like he left it, from the smell to the curtains and pictures on the wall.

He dressed himself up in straight Polo. His white and blue platted collar shirt went perfect with his creased linen shorts and Polo deck shoes. To top it off the chain around his neck made him look like a million bucks. While making sure he was on point in the mirror, Spoon texted him that he'll be outside in five minutes. After kissing Kayla on the forehead as she slept, Jamal waited outside. Waiting fifteen minutes more than he was told he would have to; Jamal was relieved when Spoon finally pulled up in a silver, 2008 all factory Chrysler 300.

"What the fuck bro?" He angrily asked Spoon. "What I've told you bout having me waiting on ya like that?"

"My bad pretty boy," said Spoon noticing Jamal's outfit. "Me and Judy was at the car lot tryna rent this shit"

"Whateva nigga you always late," said Jamal. "That's what you rocking bro . . . You had that shit on all day"

"Fuck it," Spoon said as he passed an already lit joint he was smoking. "I ain't have time to change and besides I'm tryna murk me uh nigga tonight . . . know what I'm saying?"

"Spoon man . . . when we get in there please keep a cool head," said a concerned Jamal. "You know how you get"

"Don't worry bout it Jay," said Spoon. "I got this bro"

"Uh huh," Jamal agreed knowing better. "That's what I'm afraid of"

"Whateva bro," said Spoon. "Fat and them said they'll meet us inside the club"

"Okay . . . but what about our guns?" Jamal asked. "Them bouncers' gon' let us in with them?"

"Hell yeah we just gotta pay extra," he explained. "You know how it goes"

"Fo' sho," said Jamal as he passed the joint. "Everything set then"

CHAPTER 6

T he parking lot was filled. Even VIP parking was over crowed. Spoon had to park his car behind other cars. The club was live and affect and people all over Palm Beach County came to party with Top 6. There were women of all sorts wearing outfits that strippers would wear. The die hard fans wore Top 6 promotional shirts and brought the groups album along with them to get signed. The drugs were evident and the cups were over flowing with liquor. Some club hoppers were already wasted before stepping foot inside the club and the evidence were on their faces and in their body language. Just like the club the police were on fire too. Ultimately "The Heat Box" was the place to be.

"Damn my nigga," Spoon said after popping three beans at once. "You ain't gon' pop off?"

"Yeah let me get some," said Jamal before popping two of his own.

"Yeah that's what I'm talking bout!" Spoon shouted feeling the effects of the beans he popped earlier before picking up Jamal. "Beast mode nigga!"

As the two made way towards the club everyone eyed them as if they were superstars. The little rep. they had in the hood made lots of people notice them. Their large medallions around their necks that read "South Side Boy" had a lot to do with it as well. People knew that name meant business and no chumps could rock it. As they walked past the long line towards V.I.P, females stared in lust as guys stared in jealousy. Jamal stopped a few times to greet associates that acknowledged him to mainly ask the same old question, "When you jumped?"

Finally arriving at the V.I.P entrance the men gave the large bouncer a hundred dollar bill each. Fifty to get in and fifty to get there guns in. After pocketing the large tip the bouncer gave them both a quick pat down then let them in.

As soon as they entered the half lit club they were overwhelmed by the sweltering heat. The feeling made Jamal glad he wore shorts. Females were grinding and shaking ass everywhere. Some were on men some were grinding on the wall, floor and even on each other. The bass that came from the large speakers rumbled through the club as everyone sung along to Fabo's and Jeezy's hit song "Geeked Up". Making way to the bar, Spoon shouted in Jamal's ear. "This bitch jumpin'!"

Pushing and shoving their way through the crowd they finally made it to the bar. Jamal ordered two cups of Hennessy on the rocks for them, as Spoon grabbed a hand full of every thick ass female that passed him. One female stopped and whispered in his ear as she gently squeezed his dick, "is this for me?" Before Spoon could respond, her friend pulled her away by the wrist leaving Spoon with a devilish smile on his face.

"Damn Jay you seen that shit?" Spoon asked as he eyed the female's thickness. "I gotta have her dawg"

"Slow down bro," Jamal warned him. "Don't forget why we here"

"Just cause I'm fucked up doesn't mean I ain't on point," Spoon said as he directed Jamal's attention across the room. "Them niggas don't even know we in here"

"Them niggas slippin' bro," said Jamal. "Big time"

"Yes sir," said Spoon. "I should go over there and slap fi from em' for what they did to my car"

"Naw bro just chill," Jamal ordered. "Lay low for now until Fat and em' come"

Shay and her home girl were the "baddest bitches" in the club that night. They heard every pick up line in the book. Shay was approached the most being that she was a little thicker then her friend. Her sexy sky blue open back dress, with a v cut down to the tip of her crack did nothing to conceal her figure either. Her feet were throbbing from walking in her matching high heels so she and her girl decided to go stand by her brother and his home boys.

"Didn't I tell you to stay home Shay?" Travis asked after hitting his joint. "That's what I be talking bout"

"Boy please, I'm here to see Top 6 perform!" Shay snapped. "Pass that joint or something nigga"

"Whateva Shay," he said. "But since you here put me down with that bitch you with"

"Uh uh boy you must have lost your mind!" Shay's home girl snapped as her neck moved in an s motion. "Who you calling a bitch?"

"Chill out girl he don't know no better," said Shay as she grabbed her friend's wrist to calm her down. "That's why he ain't got a girlfriend now"

"Don't want a girlfriend sis?" Travis said as he pulled out a wad of money from his pocket. "I'm married to this money baby"

"Well since you got it like that you can buy me a drink," Shay said snatching a hundred dollar bill. "Thank you"

"Shit I should be asking you to buy me a drink," said Travis. "You the ree up lady"

"Whateva boy," Shay said as she made her way to the bar. "Just don't be sizing my girl while I'm gone"

The club was getting packed by the second. Everyone was waiting for the arrival of Top 6. The music and drugs caused fights to break out every other minute, but they were quickly controlled by the bouncers. It seemed as if the bouncers where the ones doing most of the fighting the way they knocked out club goers. Looking at the way a bouncer man handled a guy by the bar, Spoon imagined shooting the bouncer if it were him. Now on his third drink, Jamal was tipsy and felt good thanks to the beans. Spoon on the other hand felt like superman and was itching to use his gun. While buying another drink, Jamal eyes widened to the sight of the finest bitch he'd seen in a long time. She was standing right next to him trying to buy a drink as well.

"Let me get two Incredible Hulks," The woman shouted to the bartender.

"Damn you shouldn't have," said Jamal. "I mean usually the guy offers to buy the drink"

"Boy I don't even know you," The woman replied as she received her drinks.

"So you saying I ain't worth a drink?" Jamal asked flashing his million dollar smile.

"What makes you so special?" She questioned him with a smile. "Why are you worth me buying you a drink?"

"Cause baby . . ." Jamal began. "If I ain't worth it, then who is?"

"Is that so?" She asked. "You that confident huh?"

"Straight up baby," he said. "But what's your name?"

"If you really must know my name is Shay," she said as she admired Jamal's chain. "And what's yours?"

"Well, *If you really must know*," he chuckled while mocking her. "My name is Jay"

"And what does that stand for?" She wondered. "Cause I'm sure yo mama ain't name you Jay"

"Damn baby," said Jamal. "Who you work for?"

"Who I work for?" Shay thought for a second before playfully hitting him on the arm. "Boy don't play with me"

"I'm just fucking with ya baby . . . my name Jamal," he told her. "But what you doing after this?"

"Going home," said Shay before giving off a giggle. "You got a lil' accent?"

"Oh you think so?" he asked.

"Yeah I do . . . I think it's kind of sexy too," she told him with a smile. "I heard ya'll Zoes good in bed . . . is that true?"

"Shit you could find out tonight if you curious," Jamal offered.

"Naw I don't think so," She declined.

"Naw?" Jamal said in confusion. "Then let uh nigga get your number or something"

"I can't give my number out like that," she stated. "But I'll take yours"

"That's cool," Jamal said before putting his number in her phone. "Fuck with uh nigga now"

"I'll think about it," Shay teased as she walked away. "Bye Jamal"

Spoon who observed most of Jamal's conversation with Shay from a far, rushed over to his friend for details. "I seen ya with that bitch," he slurred. By now Spoon was clearly more then tipsy and his body language showed it. "Real talk bro she was bad," he said as he leaned against Jamal with his arm around him. That was more for support to stand then to get in closer to be heard. Before Jamal could respond, Spoon interrupted him when he saw Fat Zoe and the others making way towards them. "There them niggas go right there"

Fat Zoe, Troy, Ronny and Ken made it to the club fashionably late. They were dressed to impress and their chunks shined and swung left to right almost in sync as they flocked their dreads to the music. The crowd quickly made way for the group of men trying to avoid any confutation. The appearance of straight money that they portrayed drew the lustful eyes of women. The entire club knew the South Side Boys were in the building except the NSB.

"What's up ya'll boys?" Asked Fat as him and the others ordered drinks. "Ya'll ready to do this?"

"You already know," Spoon said touching his gun at his waist line. "So what you won't me to shoot them now?"

"Naw stupid don't shoot them now theirs too many eyes," Fat said trying not to slap Spoon for asking such a dumb question. "When they come outside I got something for em"

"Okay then cool . . . that means I get to see Top 6 perform," said Spoon with a smile on his face. "I'm telling you guys we need to get where they at with that music shit . . . know what I'm saying?"

"What's up lil' bro?" Ken asked Jay leaning in closer to be heard. "You okay?"

"Yeah I'm straight," said Jamal before the DJ cut the music. "I'm just ready to do this"

At this point, all that could be heard was the crowd talking amongst themselves. The lights in the building keep flickering and the word for the feeling in the air was anxiousness. The intensity in the club was high but just not over the edge yet. The club wanted to explode and you could feel it. "Are you ready to see Top 6?" The DJ yelled into the mic. The crowd roared yes in response. "I can't hear ya. Are you ready to see Top 6?" He asked again toying with the crowd. This time the reaction was even louder. Satisfied by the crowd's response, the DJ then decided to give the people what they came to see. "Then give it up for them niggas straight from the hood . . . . TOP SSSIIIIXXX!!!!" When the group hit the stage all hell broke lose. The crowd rushed to the edge of the stage. The females started to scream as a couple of the rappers reached out to grab their hands. The thugs in the crowd started to get rowdy to Top 6's hit song, "Leave us Alone" as they threw up their hoods.

Fat Zoe and the others flocked their dreads and threw up their hood as well as they bopped to the music. Jamal watched as Top 6's music took a hold of the club. Young men that represented hope to a better life, struggle and pain was on the stage "given it to em" and the crowd couldn't get enough.

"Man them niggas on fire!" Spoon screamed in Jamal's ear. "These hoes going crazy!"

As Top 6 continued to perform, Fat Zoe singled the others to follow him. They got behind each other in a train like fashion and headed for the North Side Boys. Travis, Buck, Man Man and Ray was now aware that the Haitians were in the club. None of them were in full control of their minds. The beans and powder in their systems made them unpredictable and very dangerous due to the fact they were all strapped. The North Side Boys knew that pay back was trying to pay its debt plus interest. Shay and her home girl headed for the door when seeing the South Side Boys coming.

"Them Zoe's on us," Ray said as the Haitians made way towards them. "What the plan is?"

"Man fuck them niggas!" Travis shouted. "They ain't bout shit!"

"Shit I'm ready to bust me a nigga!" Man Man declared as he made a gun sign aimed at the on coming train, clear enough so everyone onboard could see. "Anybody could get it"

"Oh that nigga think this shit sweet," Spoon shouted in Jamal's ear in front of him. "Ima show his ass!"

After bopping, bumping and pushing their way through the crowd the Haitians stopped directly in front of the North Side Boys mean mugging and pointing in their faces. NSB mean mugged and flocked their dreads to show they weren't intimidated. Both sides had mouths full of gold teeth and didn't hesitate to grill the apposing side. A crowd started to form around them sensing that it was about to go down. When Top 6 started performing their hit single, "Tear it up", tension in the club reached a drastic high. Everyone through up middle fingers along side Haitian flags, bandanas and Top 6 shirts. The two groups of men moved around each other as if they weren't there. As Travis flocked his long dreads one of them slapped Spoon across the face. At that point all hell broke loose, beginning with a direct punch from Spoon to Travis' chin. The sucker punch immediately knocked Travis off of his feet. At that very moment fights exploded inside the club in every corner.

Heineken bottles and barstools could be seen flying across the room. Fat and Spoon were stomping a mud hole into Travis, while Ken, Ronny and Troy were throwing down with Buck and Man Man, who put up a good fight. Jamal had Ray beat as he worked him with a barstool. Top 6 had to stop performing and leave the stage. You could hear the DJ on the microphone trying to stop the fighting but it was useless.

During the commotion the bouncers' rushed the floor tasing and knocking out as many people as possible. Some clubbers turned their aggression towards the bouncers by fighting and hitting them with bottles. Two bouncers grabbed a hold of Spoon and slammed him on his shit. While staggering and trying to gather his composer, Spoon pulled out his .40 and let shots off at the ceiling. The shots caused everyone including the bouncers to flood the exit. During the stampede people were falling and tripping over each other in fear of getting hit by a stray bullet. Jamal quickly grabbed the gun from Spoon's hand and pulled him towards the back exit, following Fat and the others.

Outside there was an equal amount of ciaos. Police were throwing tear gas and shooting paintball guns in failed efforts to control the crowd. People ran to their cars and some were even hit by other cars during the drama. Coincidently Fat and the others parked next to Spoon and Jamal. They all meet up at their cars breathing hard and their Adrenalin's pumping.

"There them niggas go right there!" Troy yelled pointing at the North Side Boys running to their cars.

"I got em' dawg!" Fat said as he popped the trunk and pulled out an AK–47. "I got em"

Fat pointed the gun at them as they ran to their car for safety. They were about ten yards away as he let his high powered weapon ring out in the night. Blllaaakakakaka . . . He had no regard for the law or Buck letting of a shot as he ran. Officers were scared for their lives as they hid behind vehicles for safety. Ray Ray who stopped to shoot, took three hot ones to the chest and died before his body hit the ground. "Fat get in the car!" Troy yelled before Fat Zoe finally jumped in the vehicle that sped off behind Spoon's car. Travis walked over to his fallen cousin and fell to his knees before giving off a loud cry. While Travis was holding Ray Ray in his arms, Buck who kept running to the car came back with the others.

"Ray wake up man!" Travis cried while covered in his cousin's blood. "Get up dawg"

"Trav man he dead!" Buck shouted from the driver seat. "Lets go fo' troll come!"

"Let's go Trav!" Man said as he tried to wrestle Travis inside the car. "Let's go!"

"Ray get up!" Travis yelled repeatedly before he was finally forced into the car. "Get up man!"

CHAPTER 7

J amal was home sound asleep in the same clothing from that night. The drinks and beans he consumed took a toll on his body. Events from the club flashed through his dreams. He could see Fat Zoe shooting up the parking lot, him and the others fighting, and people running for their lives. He also saw Ray Ray's lifeless body falling to the ground over and over again. As the slide show like dream went on, he could see his self in the backseat of a police car handcuffed. At this point in the dream, the ciaos was gone and left dead bodies and ambulances in its aftermath. Next, Brooklyn who was dressed in a police uniform dragged Jamal from the backseat to a body covered with a white sheet. "This is what you do with your chance?" Brooklyn asked him as he threw Jamal to his knees. When Brooklyn lifted up the sheet, the sight of Jamal's own lifeless body caused him to sit up out of his sleep, dripping in sweat and gasping for air.

"What's wrong bae," Kim asked after being startled out her sleep by the man next to her. "You okay"

"Huh . . . yeah . . . yeah I'm okay bae," Jamal said as he felt for his gun at his waist line. "I just had a bad dream"

"Bad dream?" She questioned whipping the sweat from his forehead. "What about?"

"Nothing baby," he said hoping he didn't leave his gun in the parking lot. "Where my gun at?"

"I put it in the drawer," Kim informed him not knowing she just prevent him from having a heart attack. "You fell asleep with it . . . I figured you were drunk or something"

"Oh thank God," he said in relief. "So when you got home bae?"

"A few hours ago," she replied. "I got you some breakfast if you hungry"

"Thanks bae but I think Ima just throw it up," he said feeling the effects of his hangover as he rubbed his head. "Damn I don't remember falling asleep in my boxers," he continued after realizing his pants were gone and boxers were wet and sticky.

"You were sleep baby," She explained as she lay back down and snuggled underneath the covers smiling. "So I decided to take me some"

"Take you some?" He asked now looking at her back which was turned towards him. "Girl you crazy"

"Not crazy baby," she corrected him. "Just horny"

"Well take your horny ass a cold shower next time," he said grabbing his phone before making way towards the bathroom as Kim giggled louder.

Face down in the toilet, Jamal threw up his insides as his phone began to ring. Not looking at the caller ID he ignored it. It was 9 in the morning and he did not feel like being bothered. When he was done washing his face he looked in the mirror at his own reflection. He thought about how Spoon lost it in the club. He told Spoon to keep a good head before they even stepped foot in the club but did he listen? No. Spoon's actions could really get them jammed up. While still staring at the half dead man in the mirror; Jamal's phone rang again. *Aww Man,* he though to him self as he looked at the caller ID.

"Wassup hot boy?" Jamal said in a sarcastic tone.

"Okay okay," said Spoon. "I deserved that"

"That's not all you deserve nigga"

"Whatever man I ain't tryna talk about that shit on the phone," said Spoon. "So get ready I'm on ya in like thirty"

"Damn bro," Jamal complained. "Don't you ever sleep?"

"Not when money calls," Spoon informed him. "You gotta get money too dawg"

"I know man I know," said Jamal. "Just hit me up when you outside"

"Fo' sho," Spoon ended.

After hanging up the phone Jamal stormed into the kitchen. The sight of a sausage egg McMuffin brought a sickness to his stomach. He quickly put it back in the take out bag and then looked inside the cabinet and grabbed a can of chicken noodle soup. Being a victim of plenty hangovers in the past, Jamal found that soup and Gatorade always did the trick of bring him back to health. Also popping a couple of aspirins didn't hurt either.

The sound of the microwave bell meant that his soup was done. He quickly filled his belly and then took a shower. He dressed himself in gray dickeys from top to bottom, a fresh white t underneath and gray Jordans. As soon as he kissed a sound asleep Kim on the forehead, Spoon texted him that he was outside. A blue 2005 Doge Magnum pulled up. Not knowing what to expect, Jamal pulled his gun from his waist line.

"What the fuck Jay? Spoon said after putting down the tinted windows to let the trigger man no it was him. "What's wrong with you?"

"Shit what you mean bih?" Jamal shouted in relief as he walked towards the car. "I ain't know what car you were in"

"What you was gon' shoot me dawg?" Spoon chuckled as Jamal entered the car. "I texted you I was outside . . . you must still be rolling or something?"

"Shut up man . . . I ain't know it was you," said Jamal. "Plus after last night I ain't taking any chances"

"Whatever nigga," Spoon said not trying to hear his explanation. "You just scary"

"Scary?" Jamal asked as if he was insulted. "If you say so hot boy . . . when you got this car?"

"This morning bro . . . I had to switch up cause them crackas could be looking for the Chrysler," said Spoon. "And stop calling me that!"

"Why nigga?" Jamal asked. "After what you did last night I thought you would like your new nickname"

"Man I was on beans bro and the Top 6 performance got me hype," he tried to explain. "Then when them pussy ass bouncers slammed me on my shit . . . I just lost it"

"That's yo problem . . . you always losing it," Jamal began to preach. "You a hot head bro, you got to think fo' you do shit," he continued. "I mean what if someone told troll Marc shot up the club . . . then what?"

"Yeah you right bro," Spoon said remorsefully. "My bad"

"I know it's your bad," said Jamal. "But as usual . . . you know Ima ride for ya"

"I know bro," said Spoon as they dapped up. "Oh yeah I saw the news this morning man we made top story"

"What?" Jamal asked him. "Man troll gon' be on fi today boy"

"I know bro," Spoon assured him. "The news said an unknown man with a high powered assault weapon killed two people, wounded three, including a police officer but they have no leads"

"Fuck," Jamal said shaking his head in amazement. "That nigga Fat got off decent last night"

"I know man," said Spoon. "They named the victims who died and Ray Ray was one of em"

"I know," he said now thinking about his dream. "I seen em' get shot"

"Well fuck him and them pussy ass North Side niggas!" Spoon shouted. "They got what they had coming!" He continued. "I hope that nigga Ray burns in hell!"

"Damn my nigga," Jamal said looking at his demented friend as if he was a stranger. *"You hope he burns in hell?"*

"Damn right," Spoon said. "They should of never tried us . . . you feel me?"

"Uh, yeah I feel ya," he lied. "So where them boys at?"

"They at your brother's shit," Spoon informed him. "That's where we going now"

Jamal's mind was over flowing with thoughts. Unlike the egotistic Spoon, Jamal wasn't proud in taking a part in last night's events. His dream kept flashing in his head. Brooklyn pointing at his lifeless body, asking him about his last chance had Jamal baffled. What did it all mean? Did it mean he was going to die or maybe someone close to him? Maybe God was sending him a sign? All Jamal knew was that he was going down the wrong path and needed to get his cash up before it was too late to get out.

ॐ   ॐ   ॐ

After the club, Fat Zoe and the others went to the studio to lay low. Young Jeezy's song "Get Ya Mind Right" was blasting out of Ken's speakers as they sung along. *"A big shootout on the highway, Jeezy hanging out the coup letting ride sideways"* That was Fat Zoe's favorite line. "Yo Ima do that one day watch ya'll boys" he claimed as he hit his joint. The others just shook their heads and doubted him as they hit their solo joints. The studio was so thick with smoke; it was like a camp fire was burning inside. Jamal and Spoon were knocking on the door nearly five minutes before Ken finally answered it.

"Mr. Hot boy," Ken said referring to Spoon as they walked in. "Wassup man?"

"Man go head on with that shit," Spoon said as he plopped down on the couch next to Fat. "Pass that shit nigga"

"Now will someone please tell me," said Fat as he passed the joint while everyone started to laugh. "Did I or did I not tell this dummy not to shoot inside the club"

"Man what I was supposed to do dawg?" Spoon tried to explain as he rubbed his sore chin. "The fucking bouncers slammed me on my shit!"

"Yeah I had seen them boys take yo ass to sky!" Troy joked. "How's your face?"

"Fuck you dawg," said Spoon as the others laughed harder. "That shit ain't funny"

"But all jokes aside," Ken said bringing silence to the room. "That shit you pulled Spoon could've gotten us jammed up fo' real and still can"

"I was just telling him that shit in the car," Jamal informed them.

"And like I told you my bad okay," Spoon said in a fed up tone. "My bad ya'll"

"Well my niggas besides that we got off last night real talk," Fat said changing the subject. "But be on point tho cause if I know Travis . . . this shit here is far from over"

"Shit I'm always on point," Ronny said showing off his chrome 9mm.

The men joked around and recorded music for a few hours. Jamal him self was in another world. The more he observed the others, the more he felt distant. He felt as if he was an outsider now. He's killed before and thought nothing of it, but this time it made him feel sick to his stomach, and he wasn't even the trigger man. Ken shut down the little get together and opened the studio up for businesses, since he had a customer coming in early to record. The rest of the men decided to hit the block up to make some fast money. On their way out the door Jamal's phone rang. A smile appeared on his face when realizing Chico was calling. After a few seconds of small talk, Chico informed him that he would send a car to the block for him later.

ꙮ   ꙮ   ꙮ

It was around one in the afternoon and the sun was on its job. The men were posted on the block smoking weed and cracking jokes while waiting for buddies to come through. Every so often troll would ride by but the men weren't worried since there drugs were hidden in nearby bushes. Things were quiet and Jamal didn't like it. Besides the couple of police cars he saw, troll was quiet and that was unusual. Plus after an "eventful" night at the Heat Box, troll usually stormed the block looking for answers. Feeling uneasy Jamal decided to call Chico and find out the status of his ride. Just as soon as he reached for his phone, two white Suburbans and a patrol car rushed the block.

"Oh shit!" Ronny yelled as he tossed his blunt in the bushes. "Jump out!"

"Hey don't run don't run!" Fat Zoe said wanting to run himself. "We ain't got shit to hide!"

Five police officers jumped out of both SUVs dressed liked SWAT team and armed with semi automatics. The officer in the patrol car had a K-9 by the leash barking at the top of his lungs and ready to sink its teeth into someone. The men quickly threw their hands in the air to show they had no intensions of resisting.

"Get the fuck down!" The officers yelled as the men complied.

"I said get the fuck down!" An officer yelled as he struck the slow moving Spoon in the stomach with the butt of his gun.

"Damn man!" Jamal yelled in concern for his friend as Spoon gasped for air on one knee. "Be easy"

"Shut the fuck up!" The officer said kicking Jamal in the rib. "Fucking Haitian"

The officers searched the men and their nearby surroundings after placing them each in handcuffs. In their search and seize they found two Garcia Vega bottles filled with crack hidden in some bushes. The discovery of the narcotics caused further harassment by the muscle bound officers. Ten to fifteen minutes of police brutality passed before a black Ford Taurus pulled up. Stepping out was a white detective dressed in formal clothing with his shiny golden shield attached to his belt, the opposite side of his gun. His black tie matched his black pants and blue button down shirt.

Detective Stacks was not only Lake Worth PD's top detective, he was also one of the most racist. He had no wife or children. He just dedicated his self to his career. Like many other notorious cops on the force, the streets gave him a nickname. His was 100%. The name struck fear in the streets. He earned his name by doing his job to the fullest or a 100% and by being an asshole in the processes. His any means necessary attitude meant he was dirty. A few months back, he planted two ounces of weed on a guy who was on probation. Basically 100% was a cracka not to be fucked with.

"Well well well," 100% said as he walked up then squatted next to the young men who were now seating on the curb handcuffed. "What do we have here?"

"Sir we found these bottles filled with dope," said one of the officers pouring out the dope in his palm. "Over there in the bushes"

"Wow I wonder which one of you punks I could pin this one on," said 100%. "That much dope looks like fed time to me"

"Come on 100% man," said Fat Zoe. "That shit ain't ours"

"Okay there we go," said 100% walking over to Fat. "I see we have a volunteer"

"You got me fucked up cracka!" Fat shouted. "That shit can't stick"

"Says who?" He asked. "You or my police report that states I found it in your possession"

"Why you always fucking with us for man!" Jamal asked. "We ain't do shit"

"What a minute, is that Mr. Pierre the rapper slash gang member slash drug dealer?" 100% asked as he walked over to Jamal. "Boy I heard them stupid fucks down town let you go after I put in all my hard work into locking you up" he continued. "Tell me something, how much did you pay that lawyer of yours? Because he's good"

"I don't know what you talkin' bout"

"Yeah yeah yeah . . . no one ever seems to know what I'm talkin' bout," said 100% while shaking his head. "Look boys I don't care about this stupid dope shit today," he went on pacing back and forth. "I'm pretty sure you immigrants know something about that shooting last night . . . I just want some answers"

"We don't know nothing about no shootin' man . . . straight like that," said Fat. "And if we did we wouldn't tell you"

"Is that right?" The detective asked. "Then why does the North Side Boys tell me different?"

"I don't know," said Fat. "Maybe you should ask them that"

"Well I see I have no love amongst the Haitians huh?" The detective asked sarcastically. "Well before I leave let me tell you boys this," he said before walking to his car. "I know you boys killed Ray Stubbs and I will prove it," he said. "Oh yeah bring Mr. Fat Ass in for more questioning"

"Man what the fuck!" Fat Zoe shouted as he struggled with the officer taking him to car that just arrived. "I said I ain't know shit!"

The officer put Fat Zoe into the backseat, as the other officers poured their drugs down the sewer, before removing the handcuffs off the other young men. The sight of their money being destroyed made them mad but it beat going to jail any day. Fat's heart was pounding in fear as he sat in the backseat. "You straight my nigga!" Troy yelled as the patrol car rode off.

"Damn you think them crakas got something on us man?" Spoon asked in a concerned tone. "This shit serious"

"Hell naw!" Troy said. "If they did we all would be going in right now"

"You think Fat gon' say anything man?" Spoon asked. "You never know"

"Naw man Fat ain't no rookie at this shit . . . he knows the game," said Ronny. "All he got do to is don't say shit"

"Yeah you right man," said Spoon trying to reassure himself. "I'm just trippin' right now"

As the men stood there talking, a black 2008 ford Crown Victoria with limo tints pulled up. As the men wondered who was in the mysterious car, the window came down and a cocky Hispanic man asked for Jamal. Realizing that it was the car Chico sent for him, Jamal walked toward it as the others looked on in confusion.

"Damn Jay," said Spoon. "Where you going?"

"Chill bro its business," Jamal said before getting into the backseat. "Ima call you later"

❧   ❧   ❧

On the north side of town, there was much mourning and grief in the Stubbs household. Family and friends gathered to console Ms. Stubbs in her time of need. Ray Stubbs was her only child and naturally like any mother would, she took the loss of her son hard. After coming from the horrific journey of identifying Ray's body at the morgue, she sat on the living room couch slouching against the armrest as if the energy was sucked out of her. Tears flowed down her cheeks as she stared at a picture of Ray on the coffee table. Her quietness was interrupted by her occasional sniffles and sighs. Friends and relatives efforts to comfort the grieving mother were outweighed by her lost.

Shay who was also shaken by the loss of her younger cousin, fought back tears as she held her aunt's hand and listened to the preacher read scriptures from the bible. Travis walked in the house while Buck and Man stood outside. After making way through the crowded room, he greeted his sister with a kiss on the cheek. As he went to greet his aunt she snapped out of her zombie like state of mind and slapped Travis dead in the face.

"You . . . it's your fault!" She yelled as she tried to slap him again. "It's your fault!"

"Stop aunty!" Shay shouted as she tried to hold back her enraged aunt. "Stop please!"

"NO NO NO . . . it's his fault my baby dead!" Ms. Stubbs shouted as everyone looked on in disbelief. "I told Ray not to hang with you!" She told Travis as Shay and the preacher restrained her. "You killed him . . . it was you!"

"Me aunty me?" Travis asked pointing at his self. "I killed him?"

"Yes you killed my baby!" She shouted. "Get out of my house you bastard . . . get out!"

"Just go Travis!" Shay said as she strained to control her aunt. "Please!"

The weight of Travis's words disabled him to speak. His aunt's accusations broke his heart causing tears to roll down his cheeks. He removed the rubber band that held his long dreads in a pony tail to cover the pain that was written on his face; as he made way towards the door, pushing people out the way. The words of his aunt were like fuel being added to the fire that was already burning inside him.

"You okay?" Buck asked over hearing the loud confutation.

"Man fuck her!" Travis said. "She don't know shit . . . I always tried to protect Ray . . . I loved him too!"

"I know dawg," said Buck feeling his friend's pain. "It's gon' be okay"

"No the fuck it ain't gon' be okay!" Travis shouted. "Not until we get them Haitians back!"

"Shit it ain't nothing to me," said Man Man. "I was thinking the same thing"

"On everything I love man!" Travis said. "They gon' pay for this shit"

Shay was in the door way listening to the whole conversation. She was mad at the fact that after one death, Travis and his friends wanted more, but she wasn't surprised. She knew her brother was a loose cannon and could predict his next move before he even did it. Shay was always against killing. The loss of her cousin hurt her but the loss of her brother would surly kill her.

"You stupid motherfuckas," she said. "After what happened last night you guys still want to continue killing?"

"Shay man listen," Travis said turning his back. "Just stay out of this"

"No you need to listen to me and stop this shit!" She said turning him around by the shoulder. "Who's gon' be next huh . . . you, Buck, or Man Man?"

"Naw you got it fucked up sis!" He said with an evil smile. "Them Haitians gon' get it next and that's on Ray Ray"

"You ain't never gon' learn Travis," Shay said before going back inside the house. "Just remember this . . . I will cut you off if you don't tighten up," she reminded him. "And don't try me"

CHAPTER 8

C hico lived in a rich community that was separated from the rest of the city by a bridge that leads to the beach. The area had its own police station as well. When finally arriving to their destination, Jamal was applauded at how beautiful Chico's pearl white mansion was. The golden gates that were guarded by two guards with automatic weapons, opened up to a large front yard, inhabited by five savage pit bulls and video cameras. The long path they drove down, led them to a large golden water fountain with the world spinning on it axis, in the middle of it. The words "The World is Yours" was literally in orbit around it. Stepping out of the vehicle, Jamal was greeted by steps that led to the three story mansion's solid gold double doors. Inside the tightly secured house resembled a palace. Expensive paintings hung on spotless white walls and the solid gold ceiling, were decorated by crystal chandeliers. The two body guards led Jamal to the living room where he waited for Chico.

Jamal and Chico went way back. They were from the same hood and went to the same middle school. Chico who was of Columbian decent, kept many Haitian friends so he picked up the majority of their language. Losing her husband to cancer when Chico was fourteen, his mother moved them back to Columbia where her brother was a big time drug supplier. There Chico with the guidance of his uncle; became the drug lord that he is today.

"Jamal Sake pase (What's up)?" Chico asked, drawing Jamal's attention towards the stairs. When Jamal looked up he saw Chico being escorted by three beautiful exotic women. The twenty three year old Columbian was wearing a black Armani suite with matching gators. His fifty thousand dollar Bvlgari watch complemented the diamond ring on his pinky. He wasn't a very large man weighting only 125 pounds. His skin was a vanilla color and his long black hair was slick back into a pony tail. He sported a clean shave and had a million dollar smile. His whole oar let you know that he was about business.

"I'm happy to see you're free," he continued as he shook Jamal's hand then singled the women to leave.

"Thanks man," said Jamal as they sat down. "I'm happy to be free"

"That's good old friend," said Chico while turning on the TV with his remote. "So how's life?"

"You know how it is man," said Jamal searching for words. "Uh nigga just out chea tryna get it"

"There's nothing wrong with that," Chico told him.

"I know," said Jamal. "But there's better ways of going about it"

"Wow you've spoken like a wise man," Chico informed him. "If I had more business partners with your mindset I would make a lot more money"

"I feel ya," said Jamal.

"Looks like there was another exciting night at the Heat box huh?" Chico said referring to the news.

"Huh?" Jamal said caught off guard. "Oh yeah . . . It goes down out there"

"That type of attention I don't need,' said Chico. "You understand?"

"Yeah I understand," Jamal said still feeling guilty about the night before. "I feel you"

"That kind of shit is bad for busniess," Chico informed him. "If it makes no money then what good is it huh?" Chico asked laughing at his own joke.

"Yeah you right," Jamal said trying to hide his guiltiness with a fake laugh. "It ain't good at all"

"That's right," said Chico. "So what can I do for you?"

"Well a nigga tryna eat big time Chico," Jamal begun. "I'm tryna get out the game but I'm broke so I need bricks man and notice I put an S behind that"

"Okay you do understand that I am a business man?" Chico asked. "Right or Wrong"

"Right"

"Then you would understand when I ask what would I gain in doing this?" Chico said. "This is a very large favor"

"Money man," said Jamal. "I'm your connection to the hood"

"You seen what happens in the hood," Chico reminded him. "I'm not sure I like that type of attention"

"Listen Chico I need a chance to break out this shit," Jamal said now on his last leg. "And right now you're my only way out," he continued. "Yeah you getting cash but I can get you more . . . Palm Beach County has a lot to offer trust me"

"Trust, that's a strong word in this business," he said as one of the exotic women come back with a folder. "I'll tell you what, do me a favor and I'll do you one"

"Anything," said Jamal.

"This is Mr. Washington, he likes to calls himself J Dub," said Chico handing him a picture. "Mr. Washington stole five keys of heroin from one of my warehouses and I don't want my dope back I just want his life," he stated. "My sources tell me he is a jack boy and hangs out on a street corner on Tamarind in West Palm Beach . . ." he continued. "If you take care of this for me I would be willing to start you off with five bricks my friend ten a piece"

"Ten a piece?" Jamal said unable to believe his ears. "Man consider this chump dead"

The two friends spent a few hours catching up while smoking some of Columbia's finest weed. Jamal was a dope boy but nothing compared to the drug lord that was Chico. The lifestyle Chico lived Jamal wanted a part of. He felt like he didn't only deserved it but Kim and Kayla did as well. The favor that was asked of him was a big one since he was done with the killing, but if that's what Chico needed in order for his plan to succeed then so be it; and besides he had just the perfect man to help him with the job.

"Ten a key!" Spoon shouted. "Are you sure?"

"Man why you so loud?" Jamal asked while a few of the other customers dinning in the Haitian restaurant glanced their way. "Keep your voice down"

"My bad bro but damn that's good," said Spoon. "Chico got it man we should rob his ass"

"Shut up stupid," he said forgetting his friend often spoke before thinking. "Why the fuck would we rob our connect?"

"Okay yeah you right," Spoon said coming to his senses. "So when we get our first load?"

"After we do him a favor"

"What favor man?" Spoon asked. "I knew there was a catch"

"We got to get it bro," Jamal reminded him. "Don't shit come easy"

"Tell me about it," Spoon said with a sigh. "So who we got to kill?"

"Some nigga from Down Town"

"Then we gotta be easy," Spoon informed him. "Them niggas from up that way ratchet as fuck"

As they ate their meals, Jay filled Spoon in on the beef Chico had with Jimmy Washington AKA J Dub. From the picture Chico gave Jamal, Spoon didn't recognize their target which made it much easier to kill him. Spoon's theory was, "If I don't know him I won't hesitate to kill him". Jamal shook his head at his ignorant friend's comment. They planned to wait until night fall, kill J–Dub then make it back to the hood smoothly. Little did they know their mission would be everything but smooth.

Q   Q   Q

The young men made their way to one of the most violent areas in Palm Beach County, Down Town West Palm Beach, and Tamarind Avenue. A person dies every day in that area and the two young men were there to keep up with tradition. The Palm Beach County court house and police station was just a few streets over. So literally people were getting shot just a few blocks away from where justice was being served. So the balls of these locals were like those of an elephant. Unlike Lake Worth, everything in this hood was sort of congested. All the buildings were built closely together down the entire Tamarind strip. The adjacent street led to some of the wildest neighborhoods in the county. As they drove through the area, the boys on the block mean mugged their strange car as it drove by. Both Jamal and Spoon had their guns and ski mask ready. Chico informed Jamal that J-Dub ran a big money dope hole, some where in the area and was usually there. After stopping to get directions from a local buddy (crack head), they found themselves parked down the street from J-Dub's dope hole.

There were a bunch of men standing outside an abandon house serving each buddy that came through. The two scoped the area with a pair of binoculars that Judy sold to Spoon a while back for a hit. He knew one day they would come in handy. Comparing each face with the picture, the two men found their target. J–Dub fit the description of a typical Palm Beach County Dope Boy: Gold teeth, long dreads, black T and a big ass chain. The two smoked weed to calm their nerves as they waited for their target to make a move. A drive by was out of the question since they were in a rental, and Spoon didn't want to take the chance on Judy snitching if someone got the plate number.

A half an hour went by before a car full of females pulled up where the men were standing. Stepping out was a dark skinned female with an ass that made Spoon say, "Damn!" while staring through his binoculars. Finally the chance to get him came when J Dub took the dark skinned female inside the abandon house, while the other men flirted with the rest of the females outside.

Not wanting to be seen, the men drove around the block with intensions to enter the house from the backyard. After creeping down an alleyway and jumping the house's back gate, the young men broke into the two story house through the back door. The house looked abandoned, but the black leather couch and TV with an X Box 360 game console, showed otherwise. The two gun men attentions were stolen by a loud moaning sound that led them up stairs. As they looked through a door slightly cracked open, they saw J–Dub pounding the female from the back on a dirty mattress. After watching for a few seconds, the men rushed the room, startling the couple.

"Don't nobody fucking move," said Jamal in a firm inside voice as Spoon snatched up the girl by her hair and placed his hand over her mouth. "Or I'll put one in your head right now"

"Whoa hold up man," said a naked J Dub. "I ain't got no money or dope"

"We ain't come here for that lover boy," said Jamal before shooting the man in the head with his silencer equipped gun as Spoon muffled the girl's screams with his hand. "Let's peal dawg"

"What about her?" Spoon asked causing the girl to look Jamal in the eye for mercy. "We just gon' leave her?"

"Fuck her she straight man," said Jamal. "We got mask on"

After Spoon threw the girl to the floor, he followed Jamal towards the door. Just when Spoon was about to make it out the room, the naked female grabbed a gun that J Dub place on the floor next to the mattress, and let off two shots barley missing him.

Spoon quickly fired back and hit her twice in the chest. Hearing the gun shots the men outside rushed in the house with their guns drawn. As Jamal and Spoon tried to rush down the stairs, they were stopped midway by gun fire. The two ran back up the steps as they dodged bullets. They ran into the room where they left the dead bodies and locked the door behind them.

"What now man?" Spoon panicked. "I knew we should of killed her too man fuck!"

"Man shut up," said Jamal as he opened up a window. "We just gotta jump"

"Man you crazy!" Spoon told him. "I ain't jumping out no window!"

"That's okay with me," said Jamal as he got ready to jump. "Stay here and got shot then"

"Well since you put it like that" said Spoon coming to his senses when the men started shooting at the door.

The men filled the door with bullet holes before kicking it in. Realizing that the intruders jumped out the window they made their way back down stairs to the back door. Jamal and Spoon jumped the back gate before making way up the alleyway. When Spoon looked back he saw the men closing in on them as they let of shots but that was the least of their problems. At the top of the alleyway a police car could be seen just pulling up. Not giving the officer a chance to get out, Jamal shot at the patrol's car windshield repeatedly as they ran. The over weight officer ducked down in his car for cover. Both Jamal and Spoon cleared the front end of the cop car before getting into their car across the street and speeding off.

CHAPTER 9

The church was filled with people wearing black clothing. Kim and Mama Pierre were in the front row crying as they held each other. Jamal's brother Ken and the others were at the front of the church in all black staring at a gold casket. Brooklyn who was dressed in a preacher's attire, was at the podium preaching to his large audience. Jamal, who just arrived at the church, entered the building wearing all black and had a Haitian flag hanging out his back pocket. He had a strange look on his face as he made his way down the isle.

"Mommy, Kim . . . . what's wrong?" He asked the two weeping ladies who failed to answer him. "Who died?"

"Young man," Brooklyn addressed Jamal with his finger pointed at him. "What happens when you take life for granted?"

"What you talkin' bout?" Jamal asked. "What's going on?"

"What happens when you take life for granted?" Brooklyn asked now pointing towards the casket. "Take a look my friend"

Jamal looked at Kim and his mother who were still crying before slowly walking towards the casket and his friends. "Don't be afraid son, face the truth," said Brooklyn still pointing at the casket. The others moved aside so he could have a look. Before he could react to the sight of Spoon's dead body dressed in a black suit, it opened its eyes and grabbed him as Ken and the others tried to push him in.

3 "Let me go!" He yelled as he quickly sat up on the couch. "Let me go!"

"Man what's wrong with you?" Spoon asked him after running in the living room with his boxers on and gun in hand. "I thought it was going down in here"

"Naw man it aint nothing . . . I was just dreaming," said Jamal. "Where we at?"

"At my house nigga," said Spoon. "You sure you okay?"

"Yea bro I'm straight," he said. "What time is it?"

"8a.m. nigga rise and shine," said Spoon. "Ima hit the shower before we peal"

"Irite"

As Jamal laid back down on the couch he wondered why the hell he was having nightmares. What did they mean? He was starting to think he was going crazy. Once again he saw Brooklyn and another dead body but this time it was Spoon's. Still staring at the ceiling in deep thoughts, his cell phone rang. Mario's "How Do I Breath" ring tone meant that Kim was calling.

"Wassup bae?" Jamal answered.

"Jamal baby you okay?" Kim asked. "Where you at?"

"I'm at Spoon's crib," he answered. "I got fucked up and fell asleep"

"Oh well I just got home from work," she said. "When you coming home"

"I'm waiting for Spoon to get out the shower now," he informed her. "I'll be there in like an hour"

"Well I'm missing you baby," she said. "Try to hurry please"

"I'm coming bae," said Jamal. "Just chill"

After hanging up the phone, Jamal sat back up and turned on the TV. When switching channels to the news, he found out that once again he'd made headlines. The anchor man explained how two masked man entered an abounded building and killed a Jimmy Washington and his girlfriend Tameka Johnson. Jamal shook his head and said a quick prayer, hoping God would have mercy on his soul. The next top story was about more protesters in front of City Hall complaining about the ongoing violence in the streets. **Save are streets** they chanted while holding their signs and police stood watch. When the reports interviewed an old man, he said he blamed the violence on lack of police work. He also blamed it on the clubs and the music. Another news segment started talking about the oncoming recession. They explained how the gas prices were expected to soar and how people across America were already losing their homes. Shit was getting serious and Jamal knew it, he had to start stacking up as soon as possible.

Jamal's train of thoughts were interrupted when Spoon walked in the living room yelling at Judy on the phone. She wanted two hundred dollars worth of dope and kept calling him about it, so the first stop was Judy's house. They lit a joint to calm their nerves since last night's episode had them a little paranoid. Their guns had one in the head and off safety just incase pay back was on its way.

Of course they had on mask but anything was possible in Palm Beach County. On their way to Judy's house, they decided to drive through the block. As they bent the corner, they spotted Fat Zoe "busting down" a buddy.

"What's up early bird?" Spoon asked looking out the passenger window from the diver seat.

"Shit you tell me," Fat answered. "Ya'll the ones in the big boy Magnum"

"You know how we do things my nigga," said Spoon. "So what happened with 100%?"

"Man he asked me a bunch of questions about the club thing then let me go," Fat explained. "I told him and the rest of them pussies to kiss my ass," he continued. "But ya'll be easy man cause he looking for answers"

"Fa'sho," said Spoon. "So that cracka ain't got shit on us huh?"

"Not a clue," Fat assured him. "So ya'll going to the studio?"

"Yeah nigga but I got to holla at Judy," said Spoon. "Then take Jay home"

"Shit Ima slide with ya'll then," said Fat. "Aint no money out chea anyway"

Jamal watched Spoon argue with Judy for about ten minutes before finally getting dropped off. He entered the house and placed his gun on the kitchen counter. When walking into the room, he was greeted by a half asleep Kim, snuggled underneath the covers watching TV. He walked over to his side of the bed and placed his phone on the charger before lying down.

"Why you ain't sleep yet bae?" He asked.

"Was just waiting for you to get home," Kim said before turning around and laying on his chest. "Ummm . . . can I ask you a question Jamal?"

"What's on yo mind?"

"Why are you dressed in all black?"

"Ummmm," Jamal said searching for words. "I had too . . . ummm"

"Don't lie to me Jay" she said sitting up to look him in the eyes.

"Okay man I just had to handle something," he said. "Nothing major"

"I hope you not getting into trouble again Jamal," she said as she started to cry. "You just got out of jail"

"Naw bae it ain't nothing like that . . . I just had to do something important," he lied as he whipped a tear from her cheek. "Come on now you know I hate when you cry"

"Well what am I suppose to do Jamal?" She asked. "I just worry about you so much"

"Everything gon' be straight bae," he said before kissing her. "Just trust me"

The two fell asleep in each others arms for a few hours before the ringing of Jamal's phone woke him up. Top 6's ring tone "Picture This" meant that Chico was calling him. He slowly reached over to grab his phone off the nightstand, careful not to wake Kim, resting on his chest. During their quick conversation Chico informed him that he was coming to pick him up in thirty minutes. Hanging up the phone, Jamal quickly showered and got dressed. Before leaving he kissed Kim good bye.

A few seconds after stepping outside, a stretched 2008 black Mercedes limo pulled up. The chauffer wearing a black suite, open the door for Jamal. He looked more like a body guard Jamal thought to him self, since the chauffer was muscular and armed with a gun at his side. Stepping inside, Jamal was greeted by Chico and two of his many bodyguards.

"Jamal my friend," said Chico as he smoked a Cuban cigar. "How you been?"

"I'm okay man," said Jamal. "Just tryna live"

"That's good," he said. "Would you like a cigar?"

"Naw I'm okay"

"Oh I know what you want," said Chico before reaching for a wooden box full of joints. "How about some of Columbia's finest weed"

"Shit I can't say no to that," said Jamal before grabbing a joint and lighting it.

"Good man," said Chico before introducing his body guards. "This is Hector and Pablo they are both head of my security"

"Wassup?" said Jamal to the men who just nodded in response.

"They're not exactly people friendly," Chico informed him. "Now my sources tell me that Mr. Washington is know longer with us and I believe I have you to thank for that"

"You ain't got to thank me," said Jamal. "I always keep my side of the deal"

"And so do I"

"That's good to hear," said Jamal. "So where we going?"

"Out west Boynton," said Chico. "I have many town houses for rent out there"

"Hold up," said Jamal. "You own town houses too?"

"Do I own town houses too," Chico chuckled causing the body guards to laugh as if Jamal just told a joke. "Good one"

"What's so funny?" Jamal asked failing to see the humor.

"Jamal you have to learn that the "Dope game" is not the only game," Chico explained. "I not only deal in real estate . . . I deal in stocks, I own night clubs, restaurants, hotels, dealer ships and a few more investments all over Florida," he informed him. "Basically I like anything that makes money"

"I see that," said Jamal as he ashes out his joint. "So why are we going to your town houses?"

"I just want to show you my gratitude for taking care of my dirty work," said Chico before reaching for the refrigerator. "Please have a drink"

The limo pulled up to a rich gated community owned by Chico called "Chico's Trail". The few times Jamal driven by it, he'd seen the name "Chico's Trail" on the huge sign facing the highway, but never figured it was the Chico he knew. The guard at the entrance didn't bother stopping the car since he already recognized it. As the limo drove through the community the sight of the beautiful white two story town houses and marvelous landscaping captured Jamal's eyes. It was far different from the usually scenery he was used to.

The limo pulled into the drive way of a two car garage townhouse. The chauffer opened the door to let the four men out. The two bodyguards entered the house, scanned the area then allowed Chico and Jamal to enter. The house was decked out. In the living room was a big screen plasma TV, an expensive surround sound system with speakers through out the house, two red leather couches that matched the linen curtains and area rug. Also a large aquarium filled with exotic fish took up most of the wall next to the couches.

"This bitch decked out," said Jamal as he looked around. "I thought you said this house was for rent"

"It was for rent," said Chico before tossing him a set of keys. "Until you rented it"

"What you talking bout?" Jamal asked. "This wasn't apart of the deal"

"I think you should go look up stairs," said Chico. "First room on your right"

Jamal went up the steps then entered the room. It was also decked out. It had a Plasma TV and a very expensive bedroom set. Noticing some items on the king size bed in the room, Jamal walked over to it. On one side of the bed lined up neatly were two .223 automatic weapons, four AK 47s, three Mac 90s, and two duffle bags filled with ammunition and extra clips. On the other side of the bed were two more black duffle bags. Opening one of the duffle bags he found ten pounds of weed. From the strong smell it gave off he could tell it was the same Columbian weed he was smoking earlier. Opening the second bag, Jamal's face lit up when he saw what was inside it.

"Ten kilos of cocaine," said Chico walking into the room. "Just like we agreed"

"Yeah but you didn't have to do all this extra stuff," said Jamal. "I mean I cant except this house"

"Come on Jamal where you going to hide all that cocaine . . . *in the hood?*" Chico asked as he lit a cigar. "I feel better knowing my product is safe," said Chico. "And I'm not giving you this house, your going to be renting it from me"

"Huh?" said Jamal. "I'm lost"

"Here's the deal I need 50,000, bi weekly . . . the faster you move it the more quantity you get," Chico explained. "Also I will need an additional 2,000 a month for the rent," he continued. "This is not a hang out spot for you and your friends. This is simply a storage place and drop off point," he said. "You and your friend Spoon I think his name is . . . are the only ones allowed here understand?"

"Yeah I got ya," said Jamal. "What about the weed and guns?"

"Oh yeah the weed is on the house," Chico informed him. "The guns are for your protection not only from others but from me if you cross me" he said pausing to take a puff of his cigar, so his last statement could sink in Jamal's mind. "Please understand your friendship is valuable but not more then my money," said Chico. "No hard feelings huh?"

"Naw we cool man," said Jamal shaking Chico's hand. "Business is business"

"Very good," said Chico as they headed down the steps. "I'm running late for my flight to Columbia but I will be back in time for your first payment," he said. "Now Jamal please be careful this game is dirty"

"I already know Chico," said Jamal as Chico entered the limo. "But thanks for reminding me"

"Big money means you a big target now," he said before shutting the door not bothering to let Jamal in. "Remember that"

"I go you but ummm," said Jamal scratching his head. "How I'm suppose to make it home"

"Oh yeah I almost forgot," said Chico before reaching out the window to hand Jamal a pair of keys. "Here you go"

"What's this?"

"Your ride home my friend," said Chico before the limo pulled off. "Look in the garage and call me if you have any problems"

Jamal quickly walked over to the garage door. The red 2008 Porsche almost gave him a heart attack when he saw it. Quickly getting inside the car, Jamal started it up and listened to the engine purr as he smiled like a kid with an ice pop. Finally, the first part of his plan was complete, now it was time for the next step.

CHAPTER 10

"Tunk out double!" Fat yelled as he slammed his cards on the table. "Ya'll niggas owe me a hundo each man pay up!"

"Man how the fuck?" Spoon said as he pealed a hundred dollar bill from his wad then throwing it on the table. "You a lucky ass Haitian,"

"Damn Fat," said Ken. "You got a nigga for like five hundo already"

"I know bro," said Ronny as he threw his hundred on the table, "This nigga on a roll"

"Naw ya'll just some sweet ass Haitians," Fat chuckled as he collected his money. "Fuckin' with ya'll I might take the day off"

"Hold up man," said Troy. "Run that shit back"

"Yeah nigga it's either I win it all or go home broke . . . know what I'm saying?" Spoon agreed as he slammed a fifty dollar bill on the table. "Hold up ya'll I got a text"

Spoon went into his pocket for his phone. Jamal sent him a text message that read **"These niggas chasing me come outside!"** When Spoon read the text aloud him and the others grabbed their guns and ran outside. Seeing Jamal leaning against his new Porsche with his arms crossed, made the guys instantly forget they were victims of a joke.

"Damn who ya'll bout to shoot man?" Jamal asked as he laughed at the puzzled looks on their faces. "Where them niggas at?"

"Ha Ha Ha . . . fuck you," said Spoon failing to see the humor in Jamal's joke. "But damn all that . . . where you stole this car from bro?"

"Come on man why I had to seal it?" Jamal asked as they shook hands and hugged. "How you know I ain't buy it or something?"

"Yeah right my nigga," Spoon answered as the others checked out the inside of the car. "You must have robbed a bank without me or something?"

"This shit here hard!" Troy said from the diver seat. "What you got a power house (buddy with lots of money) or something?"

"Something like that," Jamal said modestly. "But don't worry we all gon' be riding like this"

"You must be back on your feet bro," said Ken. "That's what it do."

"Ken man you have no idea," said Jamal. "Starting tomorrow Ima have the streets on lock"

"*Oh really?*" Fat asked in a jealous like tone. "Just make sure we eatin' too"

"I ain't got to make sure nothing my nigga," said Jamal in a serious tone. "But like I said we all gon' be straight," he informed them as he turned his back on Fat and walked towards his vehicle. "Spoon let's peal"

"Hey Fat, you with the bullshit man," Spoon chuckled as he walked towards the car. "Stop Hating"

"Whateva nigga" said Fat.

"Hey Spoon let me hold the Magnum fo' you go," said Ronny. "I gotta handle something right quick"

"Yeah go head bro," said Spoon before tossing him the key. "Just make sure you fill her up"

"Damn this shit hard," said Spoon checking out the interior on the car as they drove off. "How the fuck you got it?"

"Chico gave it to me," said Jamal with a huge grin on his face. "We on bro!"

"Fo' real dawg?" Spoon asked as he turned around in his seat to face Jamal. "You mean Chico came through?"

"You have no idea bro!" He said in excitement. *No fucking idea!*

"Oh shit dawg I can't believe it!" Spoon shouted. "Hey you think Chico can get me a Porsche too?"

"Shit in about a month you could get your own," said Jamal. "G shit"

As Jamal drove back to the townhouse, he told Spoon about everything that Chico did for him. He also filled him in on how the transactions with the money and dope would take place every two weeks. They were excited because they never had that amount of cocaine at one time, so they had to capitalize on their opportunity. They planned to wholesale each brick for 17 and breaking them down one kilo at a time, letting the ounces go for five hundred. The key to the plan was Spoon's talent in cooking dope. If you asked the hood, they would tell you he was a "chef" in the kitchen. Spoon could turn one brick into two, which would almost triple their profits. Calculating the numbers they figured they could make up to $130,000 Bi weekly after Chico's cut.

"Damn that's the house bro?" Spoon yelled as they pulled into the driveway.

"Yeah that bitch right ain't it?" Jamal answered as they exited the car.

"Hell yeah!" Spoon shouted. "Let's go inside!"

Spoon was more amazed at the inside of the house then the outside. He ran around the living room like a child then ran upstairs to check out the rooms. Looking at the exotic fishes in the aquarium, Jamal laughed at his insane friend. Hearing Spoon's foot steps coming back down the steps, Jamal turned around and saw Spoon holding one of the .223 automatics that Chico provided them with.

"Check me out bro," said Spoon with a grin on is face. "I'm taking this home with me"

"You stupid bro," said Jamal. "Put that shit back and stop playing"

"Why you ain't tell me Chico left us guns too?" Spoon asked as he placed the weapon on the couch. "You know I love guns man"

"Because I knew you would act like your acting now," said Jamal. "Like a little ass kid"

"Whatever man," said Spoon. "But I'm sayin' tho Chico must know how ratchet the hood is huh?"

"Yeah he do but them guns ain't just fo' our protection from others," Jamal informed him. "They to protect us from him if we try him bout his money"

"Man fuck that gwat," said Spoon. "I ain't neva been scared"

"Man fo' real Spoon we can't fuck this shit up," said Jamal in a serious tone. "We gotta be strictly bout money," he told him. "I ain't tryna go through it with Chico . . . he on another level bro," Jamal continued. "We the only ones allowed here . . . that means no hoes either got it"

"I got you man money first, no hoes, so like you always say . . . just chill," said Spoon as he placed the gun on the couch then walked toward the kitchen. "Now let's stop all this rappin' and get to whippin' me up a Porsche," Spoon told hi m as he stirred his wrists. "Dope boy magic baby"

         ᴑ   ᴑ   ᴑ

In about three and a half months Jamal and Spoon had not only Lake Worth on lock but had most of Palm Beach County on lock as well. The low prices that they were offering had dope boys going crazy. Business with Chico was thriving and going smoothly. They went from five bricks every two week to fifteen a week. Jamal moved Kim and Kayla into a beautiful house away from the hood that he purchased from Chico. They also shared the wealth with the rest of the South Side Boys. The Haitians was living large and you could tell by their matching Platinum chains and expensive cars. Every one was happy expect one person. Travis.

Travis, Buck and Man Man stood on the block in the neighborhood they were from. It was hot as hell outside, but yet they were all dressed in black from head to toe and smoking a joint. Travis was aggravated because after Ray Ray's death, 100% been watching them like a hawk, hoping they would retaliate against the Haitians. Everyday it was a hassle with that officer. Sometimes 100% would just park his car on the block for hours, which made it impossible for the young man to make any money on the block. Now to top it all off, the only day 100% wasn't parked on the block there was absolutely no buddies coming through and he owed his sister money. As Travis hit the joint, he realized his phone hasn't been ringing either. Business all around has been relatively slow for the past couple of months. He hasn't been making nearly as much money as he use too. Something was wrong and it wasn't just because of 100%.

"What the fuck is going on man?" Travis wondered as he stood on the block with the others. "Ain't no money come through all day.

"Shit them Haitians got the hood on smash," Buck reminded him. "That's why"

"Word on the street that boy Jamal got it," said Man Man. "I'm talking bricks on deck dawg"

"I'm fucking tired of them niggas man," said Travis. "If 100% wasn't on a nigga bout that club shit I would have been flamed they ass up!" He stated. "Now they out chea taking food out a nigga mouth but its cool tho cause sum' gotta give," he said as they looked at the car coming towards them. "Now here this girl come with her bullshit"

"Come on Travis," Shay complained after letting down her passenger window. "I ain't got all day"

"What's up Shay?" Man Man asked causing her to smile. "How you doin?"

"Hey Emanuel," she responded. "I'm fine"

"She ain't friendly nigga," said Travis as he pointed at buddy coming down the street. "There go Doug man . . . go get money or something"

"Uh Uh Travis who you suppose to be?" Shay asked with an attitude. "That boy could say hi if he wants too?"

"Naw it's straight," said Man Man before going to serve the buddy. "Fuck that nigga"

"Fuck you too nigga!" Travis said as Man kept walking. "You ain't saying shit!"

"What's wrong with you," Shay questioned as Travis entered the car. "That boy should whop yo' ass"

"Stay out of this Shay," he told her. "That nigga keep trying man"

"Whateva boy," she said. "You got that fo' me?"

"Yeah her yo go sis," he said handing her some money. "That's only sixty five tho"

"Uh last time I checked you owed me seventy two," she said as she stuffed the money in here Gucci bag. "What's the problem; you need me too drop it fo' you?"

"*Naw I don't need you to drop it for me* . . . I know how to cook dope," said Travis. "It's this pussy ass nigga Jamal," he informed her.

"Him and the rest of them south side niggas got shit jammed up out chea"

"Who the fuck is Jamal?" She asked. "Where he from"

"He moving bricks and shit with them Haitians on the south side," said Travis. "But Ima put an end to that soon"

"Jamal, Jamal, Jamal," she said as she snapped her fingers. "That name sounds familiar"

"How does that name sound familiar?" He asked. "Cause it shouldn't"

"Boy shut up," she snapped. "You worried bout the wrong thing?"

"Whateva man a nigga just looking out for ya," he told her as he watch Man Man walking back to the curb with the others. "These niggas ain't shit but snakes out chea"

"Well I don't need you to look out for me," said Shay. "I'm grown"

"I swear man if you wasn't my sister I would have been punch you in that slick ass mouth of yours," he told her before stepping out the car. "Straight up"

"If you say so just have my money Monday," she said in a sarcastic tone. "And ill see ya'll at the club tomorrow okay"

"Who said you could go to the club?" He asked. "You no how it goes down out there"

"I ain't worried bout how it goes down," Shay said showing of her pink baby .9 she pulled out her bag. "And besides Top 6 back in town performing tonight so you knows Ima be there . . . bye!"

"Hey them Haitians gon' be at the club tomorrow night?" Travis asked the others as Shay rode off.

"Shit the Top 6 concert is tonight . . . the whole hood gon be out there" said Buck. "Why?"

"Because nigga," he said with a smirk on his face. "I got a plan"

۹   ۹   ۹

As Shay stopped at a red light she fell into her thoughts. The Jamal her brother was talking about had her puzzled. The named rung a bell in her head . . . she knew a Jamal but couldn't quite figure out from where. Then the Hurricane Chris' song "Hey Bae Bae" came on the radio as the light turned green. The catchy chorus caused her too momentarily brush the thought off as she sang along, **"When you see me in club holla hey bae bae hey bae bae,"** then it struck her. She met him in the club. She was sure of it because he said he was Haitian and had that South Side Boy chain. She quickly grabbed her cell phone from her purse and searched her contact list until she found the name Jamal. Even though she thought he was cute she wasn't really interested in him like that until now.

"Hello?" Jamal answered. "Who this?"

"I don't think you remember me," she said. "My name is Shay you met me at the club"

"Shay, Shay, Shay," Jamal pondered. "Naw I don't remember"

"Well it was a while ago"

"Then why you just now calling me"

"Cause you got something I want"

"Yeah and what's that?"

"We can talk about that when I see you"

"And when is that?"

"You're going to the Heat Box tomorrow right?"

"Live and affect," said Jamal. "Heard the Top 6 concert gone be hot"

"Then look for a red bone with a fat ass," she told him. "I'll be wearing a pink dress okay"

"I got ya," said Jamal. "You remember what I look like?"

"I don't forget a face," she said before hanging up. "Smooches"

Shay knew that her brother would have a fit if he found out she was talking not only to a nigga from the hood, but to a nigga he was beefing with. As far as Shay was concerned she didn't care. The connect she had was taxing her twenty a kilo and that was hurting her cash flow. Shay needed lower prices and the one who had such prices was feeling her, so she had no problem with giving up some pussy to get what she needed.

"Who was that?" Spoon asked sitting in the passenger seat of Jamal's Porsche.

"Some hoe named Shay," said Jamal. "She said I met her in the club a while back"

"A while back?" Spoon asked. "Then why is she just now calling?"

"She says I got something she wants," said Jamal. "I hope its some dick cause she sounds sexy as fuck"

"I know that's right," said Spoon as they dapped up. "But be easy though nigga it could be a set up"

"Oh I already know bro," said Jamal. "She talking bout look for a redbone in a pink dress with uh fat ass.

"She better be sexy talking like that," said Spoon grabbing a joint from the ash tray then lighting it. "But like I said bro be easy"

"I got you my nigga," said Jamal as he turned on the street they were going to. "But I'm saying tho you think Jean Louis gon' be home bro?"

"Yeah man I told him we were coming," said Spoon exhaling the smoke then passing the joint. "Don't worry"

"I aint worried?" Jamal told him. "I just don't know bout this shit man"

"Just trust me Jay," Spoon told him. "This voodoo shit really works bro"

"Shit for five stacks my nigga it better work," said Jamal as they exited the car.

All the drugs that been flowing through the hood caused the crime rate to double. Shootings, robberies, murders . . . you name it. Task force has been jumping out on every block in the hood especially the block where the Zoes posted up at. On one occasion jump out found half a brick in a rental car whose doors were left unlocked. That day made the block an area of high interest. Spoon came up with the bright idea of paying the voodoo priest to put a spell on their product so troll would never find it in their possession. Jamal thought the idea was stupid sense he didn't believe in voodoo or hocus pocus as he called it.

The two pulled up in the drive way that belonged to a very small light green house in Lake Worth. "The yard had many black cats roaming around. One even hissed at Jamal as they made their way towards the door. As Spoon went to knock on the door Jean Luis opened the door surprising both Jamal and Spoon. The middle aged man had a bald head and wore a thick full beard with a long gold tee. He also talked with a heavy accent. The dark living room Jean led them to, had skulls hanging from the ceiling; on the shelves were lit candles and jars filled with oils and spices. The place was very dusty and smelled like cat food. The whole vibe of the place gave Jamal the creeps.

"So what can I do for you guys?" Jean asked as he sat on the couch.

"You tell us you the voodoo priest," said Jamal.

"Oh really," Jean chuckled. "I see this guy don't believe"

"Excuse him he rude," said Spoon in Creole. "We want you to make it so police can't find our dope"

"Yeah I can do that for you," said Jean in a strong accent. "Give me eight thousand dollars"

"I thought it was five?" Jamal asked. "Man this shit better work Spoon this man taxing us cause he know we get money"

"Come on Jamal man chill," Spoon said in a firm but low tone. "Fo' this man put voodoo on our asses"

"Let me tell you something guy," said Jean feeling insulted. "My power is very strong . . . If you don't believe now my friend one day you will"

"Yeah sure," said Jamal. "Can we hurry this up I got things to do"

Jean received his money then began to do his magic. He said a few prayers and blew out a few candles. Spoon watched in amazement as Jamal just shook his head. He didn't understand why Spoon took intrest in such none sense, but if it would help keep police off their asses then why not. Jean made them bow their heads as he did one last prayer.

"I'm done now," said Jean. "Your problem is solved"

"Done?" Jamal asked. "You mean that's it?"

"Yes sir," Jean said prideful. "But you still got to avoid police"

"Aww man this shit a joke," said Jamal. "Spoon you owe me four stacks"

"Voodoo is no joke my friend," said Jean. "What I do is very serious"

"Sure buddy," said Jamal as he made way towards the door. "Let's go Spoon"

"Thanks Jean for all your help man," said Spoon before following Jamal.

"Yeah thanks for nothing," said Jamal.

"Your dreams are trying to tell you something Jamal," said Jean finally annoyed by Jamal's slick comments. "Be careful"

"What you said?" Jamal asked stopping dead in his tracks.

"Your dreams are trying to tell you something," he repeated with a smirk. "Be careful"

"I don't know what your talking bout," said Jamal as he stormed out the house towards his car and Spoon followed in confusion. "This guy is crazy"

"You will believe my friend," Jean shouted form his house door as Jamal and Spoon entered their vehicle. "You will believe"

"What he talking bout?" Spoon asked as they rode off. "What dream?"

"I don't know man," Jamal lied. "I told you this shit was stupid"

"Hold on," said Spoon. "So you telling me you don't know what he talking bout?"

"That what I said right?"

"Sure," Spoon said sarcastically. "What ever you say"

"You know what Spoon fuck you," said Jamal. "How bout that?"

"Naw bro fuck with me dawg," Spoon chuckled as he lit up another joint. "Fuck with me"

CHAPTER 11

The next morning Jamal woke up with Kayla in his face calling his name. Kim who just got home from work was sound asleep. Kayla was hungry so he picked her up and walked down stairs to their beautiful kitchen. He fixed them cereal then sat in the living room as they ate and watched cartoons. As usual Kayla neglected her food and ate Jamal's. While feeding Kayla his phone rang. Lil' Boosie's ring tone "I love my Niggas" meant Ken was calling.

"What's up big bro?" He answered.

"Chillin man," said Ken. "What the play is?"

"Nothing much," said Jamal giving Kayla another portion of cereal. "Just feeding Kayla"

"Oh yeah?" Ken asked. "Let me speak to my niece"

"Hold on," said Jamal as he handed Kayla the phone. "Say hi to your Uncle Ken"

"Hi Uncle," she said with a mouth full of food. "I'm eating"

"What's up baby?" Ken asked. "Hello . . . heelloo?"

"Yeah I'm hear bro," said Jamal after taking the phone from Kayla since she was to busy to talk. "She said she eating"

"Okay tell her it's cool," he chuckled. "But I'm sayin' tho what's the beat is for tonight?"

"You already no bro," said Jamal. "Ima be at the Heat box . . . live and affect"

"Okay that's what it is then," said Ken. "I gotta hit the mall up to get fresh tho . . . you rolling with me?"

"Yeah that's a bet," Jamal agreed. "Ima go head and get ready"

"I got to handle some shit first so I'll be on ya in an hour," said Ken. "Oh yeah bring Kayla outside fo' we go"

"Oh shit," Jamal remembered. "I gotta bring her to Mommy's house anyway"

"Irite then I'll just take you," said Ken before hanging up.

Getting Kayla ready was always a hassle. Jamal chased her around the house like a mad man as Kim enjoyed her sleep. When he finally got her in the tub she cried during the whole bath. He hated this part of parenting. While getting him self ready, Kayla sat in the living room and watched "Dora the Explorer." When Ken pulled up outside, Kayla started to cry again when Jamal turned the TV off. Jamal didn't like spanking her but today she was really asking for it.

"Damn Ken," said Jamal after strapping Kayla into the backseat. "When you put these rims on?

"Yesterday man," said Ken. "I ain't like the other ones so I switch up the game a lil"

"Uh lil is right bro . . . they look the same," said Jamal. "I ain't even notice them at first"

"They look different in my eyes," said Ken wondering why his little niece wasn't her cheery shelf. "What's wrong Kay you not uncle friend no more?" He asked turning around to face the little girl who sat there with a frown on her face, and arms crossed. "Huh baby?"

"Naw she just being bad," Jamal informed him. "She mad cause I ain't let her finish watching Dora on TV"

"Oh fo' real," said Ken turning around to face her again. "Since mean daddy wont let you watch Dora I got you"

Ken exited the car and popped its trunk. When he returned Kayla's face lit up with happiness when she saw the latest edition to her Dora doll collection. "Here you go baby," he said handing her the doll form the front seat. "That's for you"

"Oooohhh pretty," said Kayla as she ran her fingers through the doll's hair. "Daddy look"

"Uh huh baby its pretty," Jamal said not bothering to look. "You stay spoiling her bro," Jamal told him. "Every time you see her you bring her something"

"Shit what you expect nigga?" He asked as they rode off. "That's my niece"

Jamal loved the bond Ken had with his daughter; no matter how much he complained about him spoiling her. Ken loved her like she was his own daughter. It was a surprise to Jamal that his older brother didn't have a child of his own yet since he loved children so much. He knew if anything was to happen to him Ken would have no problems in playing the father roll.

"I hope we ain't going to the Palm Beach mall," Jamal reminded him. "You already know we hot out there"

"I know bro," said Ken. "We going to the one in B-Town (Boynton). He said. "But first I got to meet up with Fat about some work"

"Come on bro," Jamal complained. "You know we got Kay in the car"

"Chill lil' bro I got you," said Ken. "Ima drop her off first"

ɞ ɞ ɞ

Meanwhile at the house, Kim was making her third trip to the toilet to throw up. For the past couple of days, she has been experiencing morning sickness at home and at work as well. Her period was late so that could only mean one thing. Before coming home she stopped at a 24hour Walgreen's to buy a pregnancy test. She waited until Jamal left to take it so he wouldn't be all up in her business, like he usually was. If she was pregnant she wanted to tell him at the right time.

She followed the step by step instructions then waited for the results. The two minute wait felt like forever. The thought of bringing another life into this world was exciting. A baby would be unexpected but not surprising due to their unprotected sex life together. The wait was finally over and the results were in.

ɞ ɞ ɞ

While Kayla played with her new doll, Jamal and Ken talked about business and how packed the club was suppose to be that night. Jamal also told his older brother about the mysterious girl in pink.

"Shit that's what's up bro but be careful," said Ken. "I mean you the man to be right now so a lot of niggas wouldn't mind knocking you off"

"Yeah I feel ya bro . . . Spoon told me it could be a set up too," said Jamal. "Don't worry tho Ima be on point"

"Yeah you do that," said Ken. "We need you out here"

"Well you guys better get right then," Jamal warned him. "I'm almost done with this shit"

"What you talking bout," asked Ken. "What you mean almost done?"

"I'm leaving the game man," said Jamal. "I'm thinking about moving to Haiti or something"

"We only been in this shit a few months man," said Ken. "You just saying that"

"Know I'm not bro," Jamal told him. "I already got close to a mill saved up so why not?" Jamal questioned. "Besides I got to think about my family but don't worry tho . . . Spoon still out here"

"Yeah that's what I'm afraid of," Ken said causing them both to laugh. "But its whateva bro," Ken continued as he gave Jamal dap. "If that's what you wanna do then do it"

When they made it to the hood Ken called Fat to tell him he'll be on the block in thirty minutes but he didn't answer. "Man I ain't tryna ride around with a half a brick all day," said Ken. "This nigga Fat been acting crazy lately"

"Acting crazy?" Jamal asked. "What you mean?"

"I don't know man," said Ken. "Like ever since that day 100% took him in fo' questioning he been acting scary"

"Damn fo' real?"

"Yeah bro he ain't acting like the Fat Zoe we know," said Ken as they pulled up to their mother's house.

Jamal called Junior to come outside and get Kayla. As the phone rung he asked, "You think he talking?"

"Hell naw man Fat ain't bout that life," said Ken not really sure himself. "He knows how the game goes"

"I hear ya but I don't know bro," said Jamal before their little brother answered the phone. "Bring yo ass outside man"

They sat in silence thinking about Fat until Junior came outside and exchanged a few slick comments with Jamal about the way he spoke to him on the phone. Junior grabbed Kayla and her belongings as the two older brothers said their goodbyes to the little girl. Ken's phone rung again and it was Fat telling him he was still on the block waiting. The two made their way to the block then parked. Ken tried calling Fat to tell him that he arrived but again no answer.

"Damn what the fuck wrong with this nigga?" Ken wondered as he continued to call Fat. "He playing"

"What he ain't picking up again?" Jamal asked as he replied back to Kim's I love you text. "Where he at?"

"I don't fucking know man," said Ken putting the car in drive. "But I'm leaving"

Immediately after they pulled off, an unmarked white Expedition that was observing them from a far started tailing them. Ken almost died when looking in his rearview mirror. "Damn Jay there go troll," he said to Jamal who was still focused on his text messages.

"Oh shit you fo' real?" He asked dropping his cell phone between his seat and the passenger door.

"Yeah they behind us bro but don't look back," said Ken trying to keep calm. "Fuck I got all that dope in the trunk too man"

"Just chill dawg he ain't turn on his lights yet," said Jamal looking in the side mirror. "But if he do, hit it man"

Ken drove cautiously, making sure not to exceed the speed limit. Every turn he made the Expedition followed. "Fuck bro this cracka still on us," said Ken in a tone that dripped in fear as his heart tried to escape his chest. "I bet 100% somewhere round here too"

"We straight bro just keep driving," said Jamal whose heart already escaped his chest and landed in his lap. "Okay, turn here, I know a girl that stays on this street"

The unmarked car was still on their trail when Ken made the right turn. When they stopped at a stop sign, a white Suburban with flashing police lights pulled up in the middle of the interception. Four officers dressed like SWAT team jumped out of the vehicle and stormed the car the two brothers were in. The brothers had no time to react and besides the quick actions of the officers had them paralyzed in their seats.

"Get the fuck out the car!" The officers yelled as they pulled the men out the vehicle and then proceeded to kick them as they lay on the ground. "Stay down!"

"Come on man stop fucking kicking me," Jamal yelled as he covered his face. "I'm down man I'm down!"

Ken tried to fight back but was no match for the big army boots and night sticks that were inflecting pain to his body. "Okay boys that's enough," said 100% who was driving the Expedition the whole time. "Put these assholes in cuffs"

"Well I guess today is my lucky day," He continued after the officers sat the brothers on the curb handcuffed. "I've got both of the Pierre brothers together"

"Damn 100%!" Jamal snapped. "Why you always fucking with us fo'?"

"Come on Jamal don't ask questions you already no the answer too," 100% joked. "Word on the street is you the man with the dope so why not *fuck with you*?"

"Where ever you getting your false information from," Jamal denied. "You could tell him to suck my dick right after you done"

"Very funny," 100% chuckled as he hopped on the trunk of Ken's car to sit. "But what I find really funny is how you guys manage to buy all these nice cars with no jobs?" He questioned. "Like take this one for instance," he continued. "It's nice and I really like the new rims by the way Ken," he commented. "But it's very expensive and Jamal your Porsche I fucking love it man," said 100%. "How much drug money did that run you?"

"Man how bout you suck–," Jamal began but was interrupted by the cocky detective.

"Hold up hold up . . . let me guess," said 100% while signaling him to stop with his hands. "Suck your dick right?"

"This right cracka," said Jamal as the sarcastic detective hopped off the car and approached him. "Suck my-"

Bam! As Jamal tried to repeat himself again, 100% interrupted him once more but this time with a right hook to the jaw. "No you suck my dick you fucking Haitian!" He yelled as Jamal spit blood onto the floor. "You boys go head and search the car," he ordered the officers who were laughing. "I would ask for you guys permissions," he told them. "But why bother huh?"

The officers began to rip apart Ken's Charger as 100% watched with a grin on his face. The odds that an officer would neglect to search the trunk of a car, is one out of every ten times; and the two brothers hoped that this was one of those times. They could feel their heart's every beat as they sat and watched.

"What we gon' do?" Jamal whispered to Ken in Creole. "The dope in the car"

"What can we do?" Ken asked as he shrugged his shoulders. "We got to take the charge"

"Hey shut up!" said 100%. "I don't wanna here that Creole shit, speak English"

Jamal looked up and gave 100% a "fuck you" look. "Last time I checked this was a free country"

"Yeah it is," 100% chuckled. "But not for you"

After five minutes of thoroughly searching the car, the officers came up empty handed. "They're clean sir," said one of the officers. "Nothing"

"You heard him man we clean!" Ken shouted. "I got a license, my tag straight so let us go!"

"Shut up!" The detective said kicking him in the stomach out of frustration. "Check the trunk I no these fools got something"

Each step the officer took towards the trunk was like in slow motion to Jamal. He felt helpless as he looked back and forth at the officer opening the trunk and 100% grinning, because of his police intuition telling him something was inside that trunk. Jamal wanted God to come down and save him and his brother, who was lying on his side gasping for air. If that didn't happen, he just wanted a chance to run but 100% was hovering over him like a UFO. As the officer searched inside the trunk, Jamal felt like his chest was sinking inward and his bones were turning into jelly. After all a half of brick of cocaine was fed time all the way. When the officer through Ken's Louis Vuitton bag on the ground Jamal thought his life was over.

"That's what I'm talking about," said 100% as he walked over to the bag and unzipped it. "You boys are going a way for a long time"

When he finished dumping the bag Jamal's payers were answered. "What the fuck!" The detective shouted as he looked inside the bag. "All that's in here is some dirty laundry!"

Jamal had a dumbfounded look on his face when he saw the dirty clothes on the ground. He looked at Ken who just shrugged his shoulder in confusion. No one had a clue where the clothes came from. "All this cop work for some dirty ass laundry!" 100% shouted as he threw the bag into someone's yard. "Get these fucking Haitians out of my sight!"

Jamal felt like the world's weight was lifted off his shoulders when one of the officers released him and his brother from the handcuffs. They quickly tried to get in their car and ride off but 100% stopped them. "This ain't over," he told them in a chilling tone. "I ain't stopping until you punks are in jail or dead and that's a promise"

The threats of the detective went in one ear and out the other. The brothers just wanted to get in their car and leave. As they rode off Jamal couldn't help but wonder what just happen then it struck him. "I believe," he said as he slowly shook his head. "I believe"

"Believe what bro?" Ken asked. "You okay?"

"Voodoo bro," said Jamal. "Me and Spoon paid Jean to put some on the dope"

"Good fucking thinking bro!" Ken said as he hit the stirring wheel with joy. "We almost went to the county rocking Rolexes (Fed bands)!"

"Shit don't thank me, it was Spoon's idea." said Jamal. "I ain't even think the shit would work."

"Then remind me to thank him when I see him," said Ken. "But where you think the work at?"

"I don't know bro?" said Jamal. "Pull over so we could look in the trunk"

When the two pulled over to the side of the road, Ken popped the trunk and there it was. Half a kilo of cocaine, seating in the middle of Ken's trunk. The two slowly turned their heads, looked at each other in shock then looked back at the dope.

"Yeah bro," said Ken. "Remind me to thank Spoon when I seen him"

CHAPTER 12

It was Friday and once again the main event for the night was the Top 6 concert at the Heat Box. The place was packed from wall to wall and the line outside went damn near around the corner. Ken had managed to get the DJ to play one of their songs, so the entire club was vibin' to the sounds of the South Side Boys until Top 6 arrived. Females were fighting for a chance to get into VIP and chill with the Haitians from Lake Worth as they popped bottles and made it rain as usual. Spoon was geeked up and wasted as he grabbed female body parts. Jamal was enjoying his self as well but his mind was set on finding the mysterious girl in pink. Ever since the day she called, he tried to put a face with her name but had no luck. After all he's been to so many clubs and met so many women.

"This bitch jumping Jay!" Fat Zoe said as he put one of his arms around Jamal's neck and the other in the air, holding a bottle of Hennessy and spilling liquor everywhere. "Ima fuck about three of these hoes tonight!"

"Chill out bitch," Jamal said as he gently shoved Fat off him. "You spilling liquor all on uh nigga"

"My bad bro," Fat slurred clearly showing he had a little too much to drink. "But G shit tho Ima fuck about three hoes tonight . . . straight like that!"

"Yeah you go head and do that bro," said Jamal wiping himself off with a napkin as he went to go stand next to Spoon. "Drunk ass nigga"

Since the incident earlier with 100%, Fat was suspect in Jamal's eyes. Fat told Ken he was inside the house buying food from the old lady on the block, and that he didn't even hear his phone ringing. Ken took the story and ran with it but Jamal wasn't buying it. Something just wasn't right in his opinion.

"Hey my nigga," Spoon said interrupting Jamal's thoughts. "What's wrong with you?"

"Ain't nothingg," Jamal lied. "Wassup with you tho . . . you okay?"

"Man my nigga I'm straight," Spoon yelled in a tone clearly showing he was drunk. "We got bitches; money, cars, ice and our music getting played in the club nigga we living . . . know what I'm saying!"

"Man you wasted," said Jamal as they shook hands before the DJ cut the music and came on the microphone. "But I feel ya tho"

"Are ya'll ready for this performance?" The DJ asked causing the crowd to scream. "Then give it up for TOP SSSSIIIIIXXX!"

The crowd went crazy when the music group from their hometown hit the stage. People started pushing and shoving as they rushed the stage. Bouncers had to restrain people who tried to get on stage with Top 6. The danger level in the club went from 5 to 10 in seconds. When the music started playing a fight broke out near

VIP as Jamal and Spoon watched. The bouncers quickly grabbed the young men and carried them towards the exit. The crowd was already getting out of hand and Top 6 wasn't on stage for a minute yet until one of the rappers interrupted the performance.

"Hey hey cut the music," One of the rappers with long dreads said. "Ya'll stop all that fighting and enjoy the concert man" he continued. "We don't need no drama, no shootings or anything like that ya dig?"

The rappers words brought a sense of peace in the club and you could feel it. The mean mugs and frowns turned into smiles. Instead of a death trap the club was about to turn into a party. Before the rapper ordered the music back on he had one last thing to say, "Oh yeah shout out to them South Side Boys man, we like the music!" When Spoon heard those words he went crazy. "Oh shit bro he talking bout us!" He yelled causing Jamal to laugh.

❦   ❦   ❦

Outside the club Travis, Buck, and Man Man were parked in the parking lot as they puffed puffed passed a dirty and listened to Lil' Bossie. They were all dressed in black and had their hand guns on their laps. Hidden behind the car's dark tents, they watched as some club goers went home early.

"Nigga you sure that's Jamal's car?" Travis asked as he passed Man Man the joint from the back seat. "I wanna do this and peal"

"Yeah nigga I'm sure," said Buck as he looked at the red Porsche parked a few cars in front of them. "He the only one in the hood with a damn Porsche"

"Good," said Travis. "When he comes out it's over"

"Didn't Shay say she was going to the club tonight?" Man asked from the passenger seat as he hit the joint.

"Why you worried about Shay for?" Travis asked as he burnt a hole through the back of Man's head with his eyes.

"Huh . . . man I ain't worried about yo sister," said Man Man caught of guard by the question. "And besides last time I checked she was grown"

"Watch yo mouth nigga," said Travis in an aggressive tone. "I know you like my sister man . . . don't size me I'm telling you" he threatened him. "Bro I'll shoot you"

"Nigga what you said?" Man asked as he turned around in his seat to face him. "You gon shoot me?"

Travis pointed his .9mm in Man Man's face. "Nigga you wont be the first," he said as they mean mugged each other. "Try me"

"Ya'll boys chill the fuck out man," said Buck. "Ya'll steady on that fuck shit"

"Naw it's this nigga," said Man Man. "He ain't gon keep sizing me bro"

"Just keep my sister name out yo mouth," said Travis placing his gun back on his lap. "Then we won't have no problems"

۰   ۰   ۰

Top 6 performed seven songs then left. The slow songs that the DJ was now seducing the crowd with meant that the club was about to be closed. This was usually the time for the males to try their final attempts at talking a female into coming home with them. If they were lucky they would find one who was wasted and ready. Jamal was kind of upset the mystery lady was yet to show her face.

"Damn what's up bro?" Ken asked. "That hoe ain't show up yet?"

"Naw man that hoe stood me up dawg," Jamal chuckled feeling like he was at the prom with no date.

"Man . . . fuck that hoe," said Ken. "Maybe it was for the best"

"Maybe"

While the brothers where chatting a chocolate skinned female that was a dime piece all the way approached Jamal. "What up baby?" She asked. "You taking me home?"

"Shit there you go lil' bro," said Ken. "You get to smash tonight anyways"

Just as Jamal was about to take the female up on her offer, his words were snatched out his mouth when he saw a beautiful milk chocolate female wearing a stunning pink dress. She was standing by the bar waving off guys that tried to holla.

"Uh I can't baby," Jamal said. "But my bro here got you"

"Damn that bitch look right bro," said Ken noticing what his brother was staring at. "That's her?"

"Hell yeah I think that's her," said Jamal as he walked off. "Ima fuck with ya"

"You do that bro," Ken said to Jamal who threw up a finger to jester okay. "And make sure you on point too!" He yelled glancing at the girl again. "Damn she looks familiar," he said to himself as he put his arm around the chocolate girl's neck. "So you still need someone to take you home?"

Walking towards the beautiful female who was now buying a drink, Jamal then realized where he first met Shay. It was surprising to him that he could forget a face as pretty as hers. "So I'm sayin' tho," he said. "Why you over here standing by yo self?"

"Sorry but I ain't interested" said Shay neglecting to turn around. "Bye"

"Well that's too bad," said Jamal before gentle grabbing her ass. "Cause I am"

"Uh uh boy you don't know me like that," She went off before turning around and realizing it was Jamal. "Oh my goodness I ain't know it was you," she said giving him a hug. "Why you play so much?"

"Damn ma what you was bout to swing on me?" He asked with both hands now on her ass.

"No it's just you know how these niggas be in here," she explained before taking a sip of her drink. "I was starting to think you weren't here"

"Naw I been chillin' in VIP with my dawgs," he said pointing at his friends in the VIP room surrounded by females.

"Oh looks like you guys like to have fun," she said.

"Yeah that's how we do it," said Jamal. "So what's up with us tonight?"

"You tell me baby daddy" she seductively said as she sipped her drink through her straw. "You said you like to have fun right?"

"Yeah that's right," Jamal chuckled as he grabbed her hand. "Let's go"

As the couple made their way towards the exit, Spoon who was drunk bumped into Jamal yet again falling into his arms. "Dam Jay that bitch bad," he said referring to Shay as Jamal helped him up. "Don't worry I ain't gon tell Kim?"

"Damn Spoon you straight?" Jamal asked. "You can't drive like this"

"Man what you talking bout?" He slurred. "I ain't fucked up"

"I got him," said Ronny. "We came together"

"Man I said I'm straight!" Spoon said before falling into Ronny's arms. "Let me go"

"Hey Jay let me hold the Porsche," Ronny asked. "I got a run to make and I ain't tryin' to use the Lexus"

"Ok then I got you," said Jamal before going in his pocket and exchanging keys. "Just don't let this fool drive"

"I got you," Ronny assured him. "Ima take him home now"

"Alright then be safe bro," said Jamal giving him dap before leaving out the club. "Let's go ma"

"Where you parked at?" He asked Shay when they made it outside. "Cause my dawg parked in the back"

"Well I parked in the front," she said. "Ima just follow you"

When the lights turned on the clubbers shielded their eyes as if they where vampires. Fat and Troy had their hands full with three bad bitches so they said their good byes and left. Ken managed to talk the chocolate skinned girl into coming home with him. Ronny himself had his hands full with Spoon.

"Hey man the party over already," Spoon asked as Ronny helped him to Jamal's car. "Why so early?"

"Come on Spoon lets get you home," Ronny said trying to hold him up. "Remind me not to go clubbing with yo ass again"

"Ronny man," Spoon slurred. "I fuckin' love you bro"

"Man how many beans did you pop?" Ronny asked. "Cause yo ass rollin"

As every one left the club and made way to their cars, the North Side Boys were scanning the area for Jamal. Travis was anxious for revenge as he griped his gun tightly. The music screamed murder and was hardwired to his brain, so he was ready to do just that, murder. Little did he know Jamal and Ronny switched cars for the night.

"Ya'll see that motherfucka yet?" Travis asked. "I'm tryin' to do this shit man"

"Naw man not yet," said Buck. "He must be with a bitch or something"

"Shit he betta not be," said Travis. "Cause whoever he with gettin' hit up too"

"Hold up bro," said Man spotting Ronny practically dragging Spoon to Jamal's Porsche. "Is that him?"

"Naw that's not them," said Buck. "I think that's Ronny and that nigga Spoon"

"What the fuck dawg!" Travis snapped. "What happened to Jamal?"

"I don't know bro . . . that's his car tho," said Buck. "They probably switched up"

"Well that's just they luck huh?" Travis asked as he stepped out the car. "Ya'll wait here while I go handle these niggas"

Ronny rested Spoon against the hood of the car as he searched for the keys in his pockets. Finally finding them he unlocked the passenger side door to put Spoon in. Just as soon as he grabbed his drunken friend, Travis crept up behind him and let off three hot ones, two slugs to the back of his head and one to the neck. Ronny died instantly as his body fell to the ground. The loud shots and screaming from a few female clubbers caused Spoon to momentarily snap out his drunken state of mind and try to grab his gun from his waist line, but it was too late. Travis let off two more shots hitting Spoon first in the arm and then the shoulder, knocking him to the ground. "Turn yo pussy ass over," said Travis as he rolled Spoon over with his foot. "This for Ray nigga," he said firing one in his chest.

Q   Q   Q

Jamal and Shay checked into one of Chico's many five star hotels by the Lake Worth intercostals called "El Ladrillo". Thanks to Chico, the two hundred dollar a night fee was only fifth bucks since Jamal had VIP access to all restaurants, clubs and hotels Chico owed. The two stood on the balcony smoking weed as they watched the waves clash with the wind under a beautiful moon light.

"The water is so beautiful," said Shay. "It's so wild and free to do what it wants"

"So what you ain't free?" Jamal asked as he blew smoke into the wind.

"Boy please ain't shit free," said Shay after sucking her teeth. "You got to give to receive," she continued. "Everyone wants money, power and respect, so much that it enslaves us"

"I feel ya," said Jamal. "Shit crazy out chea . . . a nigga gotta find a way out"

"So you feel where I'm coming from then?" Shay asked pulling Jamal closer by his shirt, pinning her body between his and the railing. "Then what I got to do to receive?"

"What you mean receive?" Jamal asked as Shay nibbled on his ear. "What you really want from uh nigga?"

"I want a new connect," Shay whispered in his ear as she unbuckled his belt.

"A new connect huh?" Jamal asked. "Shit I'm down with new business but what's wrong with your connect?"

"Their prices ain't low enough," she said as she squatted down pulling his pants with her.

"And what makes you think my prices are any lower?" He asked before taking another puff from his joint as Shay's tough ring teased his manhood through his boxers.

"I don't know," she said as she pulled out his dick. "But something tells me I could get them as low as . . . fifteen"

"Damn girl that's too low," he said trying to conduct business as Shay slowly jacked his dick. "I could do eighteen"

"I think we could do better then that," she said before slowly putting his entire dick in her mouth.

Shay was determined to get what she wanted and deep throated Jamal's entire dick to get her point across. Each time his dick touched her tonsils, the better fifteen started to sound to him. Shay was a professional in the art of oral sex and Jamal could tell by the way she used her hands while serving him. As she sucked the head of his penis, one hand massaged his balls and the other jacked him off. Shay by far had the best head game Jamal ever experienced.

"Yeah I could do fifteen," he said on the verge of coming. "You got that"

"Hhhhmmm I thought you'd see it my way," she said tugging on his dick like a leash before walking towards the door. "Let's go inside and seal the deal"

Jamal followed the seductive dime into the room. When she removed her clothing her body was that of a goddess. Her long hair fell delicately on her soft milk chocolate skin and her breasts were just the perfect size. As she stood there Jamal followed her slick curves to her vagina whose hairs were neatly trimmed to resemble a landing strip.

"I hope you not the type of nigga who likes to make love," she said kneeling over the bed to show off her fat ass as she looked back at him. "Cause I like it ruff daddy"

"Shit don't worry baby," he said as he removed his clothing. "I could do ruff"

Jamal put on his rubber and slipped inside the extremely wet Shay. He spread her cheeks apart and began to fuck the air out of her. Shay griped the white sheets on the bed as she began to throw it back. "That's right daddy fuck me," she shouted as the muscles in her legs and arms tightened.

Jamal had his share of drinks at the club so he had no problem handling Shay. As he fucked her harder with every stroke, a clapping sound could be heard as if an audience was in the room applauding their performance. "Oww baby you in my stomach," she screamed. Jamal sexed her in many positions before Shay asked him to stick it in her ass. He wasn't to keen on the whole anal thing but after some more of Shay's profound head game to lubricate his manhood, Jamal couldn't resist. Shay screamed in a mixture of pain and ecstasy as she came multiple times, almost simultaneously. Shay was defiantly a chick who liked it ruff.

The two were sweating profusely but the fun was yet to be over. Jamal folded her into a pretzel, pushing her legs behind her head as he pounded her. "OOOWWW Daddy get yo nut please!" She begged for mercy as her head banged against the head board. Her words disabled Jamal to hold out any longer. He pulled out of her pussy, whose walls seemed to tighten when sensing his end was near, and came all over her. When he blew his load, it was like all the water behind the hover dam was released. "Yeah fifteen sounds good," he sighed as Shay sucked the rest of his children out of him.

CHAPTER 13

After a night of fucking like jack rabbits, the two were exhausted. They woke up around 8:00 am and both their phones were over loaded with missed calls. "Checking to see if Kim called you?" Shay asked as she went through her phone.

"How you know her?" Jamal asked afraid he was set up. "Please don't tell me you know her"

"Relax nigga I don't know her," she chuckled. "Your drunk friend said her name last night"

"Oh good . . . good," He said in relief. "But while you all in my business who been blowing you up all night"

"I aint gon lie, it was my boyfriend," she said. "That nigga so fucked up bout me it's scary"

"Shit I could see why," said Jamal. "You got some fi' ass pussy"

"Whatever boy," she laughed. "Well I guess it's true what they say then"

"What's that?"

"That ya'll Zoes are good in bed," she giggled.

"I guess so," Jamal chuckled. "But I'm saying tho I'll have them things for you tomorrow"

"That's straight but listen," she paused. "Um . . . I was hoping we could do this again sometime"

"I know that's right," Jamal smiled. "I hope you ain't catching feelings already"

"Whatever boy, don't get big headed now," she said playfully punching him on the arm. "Just make sure you have them three bricks for me like you said"

"Shit as long as that money on deck it ain't a problem," said Jamal. "Business is business"

Shay went to the bathroom to freshen up while Jamal went back to searching his phone. Ken, Troy and Fat called him dozens of times to no prevail. Sensing something was wrong he returned Ken's call. When receiving the news of Ronny's death and Spoon being in the hospital, Jamal's heart shattered into pieces. Unable to hold in his pain, Jamal stood up and punched a hole into wall. When Shay came out the bathroom, a furious Jamal was sitting at the corner on the bed with tears flowing down his cheeks.

"What's wrong Jay?" Shay asked. "You okay?"

"Some niggas shot up my home boys last night I got to go to the hospital," he said standing up to get ready to leave. "Call me tomorrow and I'll have them things for ya"

"Okay baby," she said giving him a hug. "You going to be alright?"

"I don't know," he said pausing to think about her question. "I don't know"

Shay watched him put on his shirt as he rushed out the door. She knew Jamal rolled with the boys her brother was beefing with, so chances were Travis had something to do with the shooting. She felt like a trader true enough, but what her brother and the Haitians were going through was none of her concern. Bricks for fifteen thousand instead of twenty was a come up and if it meant fucking Jamal to keep coming up then that's what it was; even if she had to do it behind Travis' and her boyfriend's back.

                    ٯ   ٯ   ٯ

Jamal raced to the hospital. Finally arriving he ran inside and asked the receptionist for directions. Jamal rushed to the waiting room where Fat, Troy, Ken and Spoon's older sister Lisa, were anxiously waiting.

"Oh my God Jay," Lisa said as she ran to hug Jamal and cry on his shoulder. "I'm so scared Ima loose him"

"He gon be okay Lisa," he said trying to hold back tears. "That nigga a solider"

Lisa was ten years older then her younger brother Spoon. Their parents died in a plane crash that was meant to land in Haiti, so a then twenty year old Lisa was left to raise Spoon by herself. Being that Jamal and Spoon had been friends since the sixth grade, she treated Jamal like a younger brother as well. Now in her early thirties, she rocked a stylish low trimmed hairdo, had dark slick skin, brown eyes and a cute face. She always dressed to impress but due to all the drama she wore blue jeans a white T shirt and Sponge Bob bedroom slippers.

"So what they saying?" Jamal asked. "Ya'll ain't see him yet?"

"He got out of surgery a few hours ago," said Ken. "We waiting for the doctor"

"Damn man I can't believe this shit," Jamal said still trying to make sense of things. "So Ronny really dead huh?"

"Yeah he dead," said Troy trying to fight back tears. "Them pussy as niggas killed him bro"

"Who man?" Jamal asked. "Who the fuck did this shit?"

"We don't know bro," said Fat Zoe. "We don't know"

While they were talking, the doctor walked into the room. "Excuse me, you may see him now," she said. "But you can't be to long because he needs his rest"

"Is he going to be okay," Lisa asked.

"I believe so," the doctor said looking at her clip board. "The bullet to his chest went right through missing his heart, but he lost a substantial amount of blood," she continued. "Despite that, his heart still pumped at a descent rate due to large amounts of pills we found in his blood tests"

"Lucky ass nigga," said Jamal.

"Yeah he's very lucky," said the doctor. "Please follow me"

Walking into the room, the sight of his best friend laying in the hospital bed with tubes up his nose and connected to all types of machines, made Jamal light headed. If he could he would switch places with his boy in a heart beat. "Oh my God Spoon," Lisa cried as she ran her fingers through his dreads. The others surrounded the bed looking at their wounded solider. Lisa's touch woke Spoon up. He slowly opened his eyes then gave a weak smile when he saw the familiar faces.

"What's up ya'll?" He asked in a weak voice filled with pain.

"What's up with you lil' bro?" Ken replied. "How you feeling?"

"Like I just got shot," Spoon proclaimed. "How you think I feel nigga?"

"I see you still got your sense of humor," Ken chuckled as the others gave off a weak laugh.

"I'm saying tho why every body sad?" He asked. "Its gon' take more then a few shots to kill me," he stated. "I could see why Lisa crying but why yo' bitch ass crying fo' Jay?"

"Fuck you Spoon," Jamal chuckled whipping the tears from his eyes.

As Spoon looked around he noticed a person was missing. "Where Ronny at?" He asked bringing silence back to the room. "Damn what that nigga couldn't come see me?"

"Spoon listen Ronny is gone," said Troy. "He died last night"

"He died?" Spoon asked now remembering he was with him last night. "Damn man we was at the club right?"

"Yeah that's where you guys got shot at," said Jamal. "Who the fuck did this shit man?"

"Who you think?" Spoon asked. "That pussy as nigga Travis," he told them. "All I can remember now is him saying this is for Ray, and then he shot me"

"What the fuck!" Troy shouted. "That nigga gots to die!"

"I agree," said Fat.

"So do I." said Ken. "Them boys got to get it"

"You guys are crazy," Lisa cried not believing her ears. "Isn't Ronny's death enough"

"Chill Lisa," said Spoon.

"No you chill!" She shouted. "You boys need to stop this . . . nobody else needs to die"

"Sorry Lisa but we got to handle this," said Fat heading for the door. "Spoon stay up man, we got this"

Despite Lisa's cries for reasoning, Ken and Troy said their good byes to Spoon before walking out the room behind Fat. Jamal stood in silence as Lisa shook her head at the young men's decisions.

"Yo Jamal," said Spoon sensing he was out of it. "You straight bro?"

"Uh yeah I'm cool . . . I'm cool," said Jamal snapping out of his deep thoughts. "How bout you . . . you gon be okay?

"Yeah you know me," said Spoon. "Ima always keep it G"

"Cool," said Jamal. "What about you Lisa?"

"Yeah Ima be fine," she said. "Jamal I can tell your different from the others, please don't get involved"

Lisa was right, he was different. He's wanted to escape the life he was living for the longest but it just wasn't happening. The clubs, the cars, the beef and cops had his chances to break free fading fast. Just when he was about to answer Lisa, Ken walked in. "What's up Jay you coming or not?" He asked. Jamal paused for a second to look back and forth at Lisa and Ken before answering.

"I'm sorry Lisa," he said. "But I'm already involved"

Q   Q   Q

Detective Stacks AKA 100% was sitting in his black ford Taurus eating Donuts and drinking coffee as he watched the Zoes walk out the hospital to their cars. "Punk ass Haitians," he said to himself before taking another bite out his donut. Sense he was in charge of the "Gang violence" unit and the Haitians were suspected gang members, he took it upon himself to visit Spoon. After they pulled off he finished his donut then walked into the hospital. The receptionist directed him to Spoon's room. When he walked in Lisa was tending to her bother.

"I was hoping you would be dead like your friend Ronny by the time I made it up here," he said. "Guess my prayers weren't answered huh?"

Spoon's facial expression turned into pure hate when he saw the cocky detective at the door way. "Who the fuck let you in here?"

"I'm the police," he said with a big smile on his face. "I can go where I want"

He then walked over to Lisa and extended his hand. "You must be Lisa?" He asked. "I know so much about you"

"Well I don't know you," she said looking at his hand in disgust. "And I would appreciate it if—"

"Lisa chill!" Spoon interrupted her before she could further insult the Detective.

"So what you doing here cracka?" Spoon asked him. "You already know I ain't saying shit"

100%'s smile grew brighter as he crossed his arms. "Yeah I figured that," he chuckled. "So instead of coming here to find answers . . . I came to tell you what I know"

"And what's that?" Spoon smirked. "Indulge me"

"I know you and your punk ass friends make me sick," he said as his blue eyes filled with fire. "You and those North Side Pussies are the reasons why I got paper work up my ass!" He continued. "And I'm willing to bet one of them niggers the reason you laying in that bed right now," he went on. "If it was me, I would have put one right between your eyes," he continued. "All the dope that's being moved, all the shootings that's happening are somehow, someway, connected to ya'll and trust me when I say this," he told him putting his finger in Spoon's face. "I won't stop until ya'll in prison or dead and I would prefer ya'll dead"

"Oh yeah," Spoon said feeling him self about to explode as Lisa looked on in disbelief. "You know what I know?"

"What's that?" 100% smirked. "Indulge me"

"I know you can suck my motherfuckin' dick cracka!" Spoon exploded. "You think you can come in here and threaten me cause you the bitch ass police?" He asked. "If you know so fucking much then you should know my money long cracka!" He stated. "So you could run that shit!"

"Marc stop!" Lisa said trying to calm her brother down. "You in no shape for this!"

"Naw fuck him!" He shouted. "This cracka gon' respect me!"

By this time 100% was furious. He's eyes were bloodshot red and the veins in his arms and neck were showing. "Oh I'm going to respect you huh?" He asked before grabbing Spoon by the neck, trying to chock the life out of him. Spoon who was sore from the bullet wounds had no power to fight back. Lisa tried to pull the enraged detective off her brother but her strength couldn't compare to his.

"Let him go!" She yelled. "Help . . . someone please help!"

Lisa's cries caused nurses and doctors to run in the room. When seeing 100% now literally in the bed on top of Spoon chocking him, they tried to pull him off as others went to get security. It took three doctors to pull 100% off of Spoon and two more security guards to help restrain him.

"Sir calm down!" Said one of the security guards as Spoon gasped for air and a crying Lisa tended to him. "Please sir!"

"Get your damn hands off me!" 100% shouted as he pulled his arms away.

"I want this cracka out of here!" Spoon shouted as 100% calmly adjusted his tie and the rest of his clothing. "Get him out!"

"Come on sir," said one on the security guards as he gently grabbed 100%'s arm. "Let's go"

100% pulled away. "You touch me again I'll shoot your arm off!" He told the guard before turning his attention back to Spoon. "Remember what I said boy in prison or dead"

"Fuck you!" Spoon continued to yell as the detective made his way out the door laughing. "Suck my dick!"

"Stop Spoon please!" Lisa cried. "He's gone!"

"Ima kill that cracka," he said breathing hard. "Just watch me"

CHAPTER 14

S ince they left the hospital, Jamal, Fat, Ken and Troy had been searching the hood high and low for Travis and his boys. Jamal and Troy who where in the backseat were both armed with the .223 assault rifles that Chico gave Jamal. Ken who was in the passenger seat had Troy's tech–9. Not being able to find them, Fat Zoe who was driving, suggested shooting up their mother's houses would be the next best thing. Coincidently Buck and Man Man stayed across the street from each other, on the same block Ray's mother's lived. Fat dropped Jamal off in front of Ray's house then drove down the street to Buck's and Man's homes so Troy and Ken could do their damage. Simultaneously they let their weapons rip. The gun shots could be heard miles away. At Buck's and Man Man's house nobody was home but at Ray's house Ms. Stubbs was in the living room watching television. When the bullets from Jamal's weapon went flying through the walls and windows, Ms. Stubbs hit the deck faster then a solider in Iraq. "Lord Jesus help me!" She yelled as she covered her head with her hands to shield herself from the falling debris and glass. When Jamal finished his hundred round clip he ran down the street and jumped into the car after the others.

"Yeah my nigga!" Troy shouted. "We did that!"

"Yo Fat hurry the fuck up man!" Ken shouted as he looked in the rearview mirror "Hit the I!"

"Chill out man I got this," said Fat as his foot mashed the gas pedal. "Straight up"

"Hey man this shit don't mean nothing," said Troy. "We just lettin' them niggas know we looking for them"

"Hell yeah," said Ken looking in the rearview mirror at his silent brother. "You straight lil' bro?"

"Huh?" Jamal asked. "Yeah I'm cool"

Mario's song "How Do I Breath" pulled Jamal away from his thoughts. Realizing it was Kim's ring tone, he answered as if he didn't know who was calling. "Who this?"

"Oh so my ringtone ain't programmed in your phone?" She asked.

"Yeah it is," he answered. "Wassup?"

"Then why you asking who this?"

"I don't know Kim," he said starting to get irritated. "I'm in the middle of something right now"

"Oh really?" She asked matching the tone in his voice. "Why you ain't come home last night?"

"Man why the fuck you questioning me?" Jamal quickly switched the subject. "Damn!"

"What you mean why am I questioning you?" Kim asked with a confused tone. "So I can't know why you ain't come home?"

"Well if you must know I was at the hospital all night," he lied. "Ronny is dead and Spoon got shot . . . anymore questions?"

"I'm sorry baby," said Kim in a concerned tone. "Are you going to be okay?"

"I guess Ima be cool," he wondered. "Shit just crazy right now"

"Well come home baby," she pleaded. "I'll call off work and we could talk"

"Naw Ima be cool Kim," said Jamal. ""Just go to work"

"Well then make sure your home in the morning Jay," she said. "I got something I want to tell you"

"What you got to tell me in person that you can't tell me on the phone?" He asked. "I ain't got time for this right now Kim"

"Just make sure your home Jamal," she said. "It's important"

"Whateva man," said Jamal.

"Well if you need me baby I'm here for you," She reminded him. "And I love you"

"Yeah okay," said Jamal rushing her off the phone. "I love you too"

They flowed with traffic speed as they silently sat in the car. All that could be heard were the bumps and sounds of the busy interstate as music play low in the background. Ken who was observing his brother through the visor's mirror decided to roll a joint.

"Damn Lil' bro why you snapping on my sister in law like that?" He asked. "Ya'll okay?"

"Yeah we okay," said Jamal. "I guess she just called at a wrong time"

"I feel ya," said Ken. "So you smashed that hoe from the club last night?"

"Yeah," Jamal said staring at the passing cars through the window. "I fucked"

"Damn," said Ken with a smile on his face, still focusing on rolling the joint. "That hoe was right"

"I know," said Jamal. "She fucks right too"

"I'm telling you bro I know her from somewhere tho," said Ken. "I bet she had something to do with this"

"I don't think so," Jamal answered. "She just wanted a deal . . . I'm supposed to drop three of them things off to her for fifteen a piece tomorrow"

"Damn Jay!" Ken said as Fat whistled in amazement. "That's cheap!"

"I'm trying to tell ya!" Troy added causing everyone to laugh. "That hoe must have a mean fuck game!"

"Whateva ya'll niggas just don't know, lil' mama gets off bad," said Jamal. "And besides fifteen ain't know big deal . . . I got it like that"

"I hear that," said Ken. "But just make sure you on point tho . . . cause I'm telling you I know her from somewhere"

❍   ❍   ❍

After killing Ronny and almost doing the same to Spoon, the North Side Boys sought refuge in a motel a few miles west of the hood. They spent all day getting fucked up and running trains on a sexy red bone with blond hair, who worked a at local strip club. "Damn hoe you could swallow a dick," said Buck as he sat on the bed and received oral sex from the stripper. Travis and Man Man who already had their fun, were watching the 5:00 news as they smoked a joint amongst themselves.

"Shut the fuck up Buck!" Man said. "We tryin' to watch the news!"

"Oww bitch you nasty," said Buck ignoring him as the stripper slowly licked him clean.

"Buck fo' real man . . . shut the fuck up!" Travis said after taking a long pull from his joint. "We ain't trying to hear that shit!"

"Damn what's up with ya'll?" Buck asked with a hand behind the girl's head. "A nigga can't enjoy getting his dick sucked?"

"Man fuck that mutt ass hoe . . . we already fucked her guts out," said Travis with his eyes still glued to the TV. "And besides she can't suck dick that good anyway"

"*Hoe* . . . who you calling a hoe?" The naked stripper asked after coming up for air. "This how I make my money and I ain't ashamed of it"

"That's good for you," said Travis whose eyes were still glued to the TV. "Now please shut the fuck up while I watch TV hoe"

"Whateva," she mumbled under her breath before going back to getting money. "Yo mama a hoe"

"What the fuck you just said?" Travis asked the stripper. "I ain't hear you"

"I think she said your mama a hoe," said Man Man laughing as if he just heard the funniest joke of his life.

"Come on Travis chill," Buck pleaded knowing what was about to happen next. "Let the bitch finish first"

Travis grabbed his .9mm that was on the floor by his chair before getting up and snatching the butt naked stripper to her feet by her long blond weave. "Bitch don't you ever disrespect me like that again!" He shouted as Man Man fell to the floor laughing, while Buck shook his head in disappointment.

"AAAAHHHH stop your hurting me!" She screamed. "I'm sorry!"

"Shut up hoe!" Travis said still with a fist full of her hair. "Since you like sucking dick so much here . . . suck on this iron dick!"

Travis took his gun and stuck it right in the stripper's mouth muffling her screaming. Tears rain down her cheeks as she chocked on the gun. "Yeah bitch how that iron taste in your mouth huh?" He asked as he dragged her to the door. He then picked her up and through her against the door by the neck. This time before putting the gun back into her mouth again he cocked it.

"Don't you have any manners?" He asked the terrified stripper who shook her head yes in response, unable to speak. "I should kill your mutt ass right now hoe!"

"Come on Trav . . . ," said Buck. "Don't kill the bitch"

"Naw I ain't gon' kill her," said Travis pulling the gun out her mouth. "I'm just gon' teach her a lesson," he said before throwing the stripper to the floor and opening the door. "Get the fuck out!"

She wiped her tears then slowly stood up to go grab her things. "Uh Uh . . . leave all that shit here!" Travis shouted. "They don't belong to you no more!"

"But what about my money and other stuff?" She asked. "I don't even have on any clothing"

"That ain't my problem," he answered. "You should of thought about that fo' you got slick out the mouth"

"Please don't do this . . . I'm sorry," she begged as Man laughed at the whole ordeal. "I can't go out there naked . . . and that's all the money I got"

"It's either you leave my fucking room or I put a bullet down your throat," Travis calmly said as he pointed his gun at her. "Your choice hoe"

"You better peal lil' mama," Man warned her. "That nigga dead ass serious"

The stripper looked around the room for a second. She felt like going to sit down and refuse to leave without her money and clothes, but Travis's gun quickly changed her mind. After walking out Travis slammed the door in her face. "Dirty ass bitch," he said. She cried like a baby as she walked across the parking lot trying to cover herself with her hands. Buck ran to the window to search for her.

"Man that's fucked up Trav!" Buck said. "I ain't even get to bust a nut!"

"Man fuck that mutt and yo nut," said Travis turning his attention to Man Man. "What's so funny nigga?"

"How she called yo mama a hoe," said Man now standing on his feet.

"I ain't think that shit was funny," said Travis looking him dead in the eyes.

"Well I did," said Man Man whose smile turned into an evil smirk when sensing he was serious. "What's up?"

"Hey ya'll boys chill out man!" Buck shouted as he turned up the volume on the TV. "That looks like our block on the news!"

Indeed it was their block. Not to long after the Haitians wet up their Mama's houses, police and news crews were at the seen to investigate the aftermath. "Those fucking Haitians just wet our shit up man!" Buck shouted as he watched a police officer mark the many bullets holes on his mother's house. Man Man ranted and cursed as Travis stood there in silence and griped his .9mm extra tight. His blood boiled as his breathing grew heavier. If this were the cartoons, smoke would be seen coming from his ears and nostrils.

"Damn nigga ain't you gon' say anything?" Man Man asked. "You don't see this shit?"

"What the fuck am I suppose to say huh?" He asked staring him down. "They retaliated so its time to do the same"

"You ain't saying shit but a word nigga," said Man. "I'm down with that!"

"Yeah me too," said Buck. "But Ima go to the house first and see If my mama straight"

The three men quickly left their motel room to their vehicle and sped off home. On the way there they saw the stripper walking down the highway with a white sheet that she stole from one of the motel rooms, wrapped around her. As she walked home in embarrassment, truckers and other motorist honked as they drove by her. Even though they were in a serious matter, Man managed to give off a slight laugh when the stripper flicked them off as they drove past her. "Shut the fuck up Man Man," said Travis not amused.

Finally arriving, the block wasn't as hectic as it seemed to be on the news. There were far less officers and the crowd of people they saw on the news had dwindled down to a few bystanders. The news crew had packed up their equipment and were about to leave when they pulled up. Travis was the first to get out the car. He ran towards the house to go check on his aunty Ms. Stubbs, but Shay who just happened to be walking out the door stopped him in his tracks.

"I wouldn't go in there if I was you," Shay warned him.

"Why not?" He asked.

"Boy don't act stupid!" Shay said. "Aunty knows you had something to do with this"

"Who me?" He asked. "How the fuck?"

"Whateva boy . . . I already told you," Shay said. "Stop fucking with them Haitians"

"Man fuck them Haitians!" He shouted. "I'm going in to check up on my aunty"

"Whateva suit yourself," she said before walking to her car.

As she sat in her car, Shay thought to herself for a minute. Though she knew her brother and his friends shot up Jamal's homeboys, she still felt that it was fucked up they had to bring retaliation to her aunt's house. Ms Stubbs was so scared about almost lost her life. ***Damn I feel like such a trader***, Shay thought to herself but the deal with Jamal was already set. To make up for her lack of loyalty she promised her aunt that she would pay for the damages to the house her self. As she continued to think about her wrong doings, she heard a knock at the windows that startled her. It was Man Man.

"What do you want?" Shay asked after putting down her window.

"So why you ain't been picking up my calls?" Man Man asked her. "I know you seen me blowin' you up"

"I was handling business," she said in a slick tone. "You know how I do . . . money comes first"

"Fuck you mean handling business?" Man Man asked. "Since when do you handle business so late?"

"Since when I was old enough to do what the fuck I wonted!" She snapped. "Anyways why are you over here asking me questions like I'm your bitch?" She wondered. "Did you tell Travis yet?"

"That's beside the point Shay," Man Man tried to reason. "Why you bringing that up?"

"Because Emanuel," she said before speeding off. "Until you man up and tell him I'm pregnant . . . this pussy is free to do what it wants and Ima kill the baby . . . bye!"

Man Man watched in anger as Shay's car disappeared around the corner. He loved her to death but her attitude had to go. Strangely enough, that's what he liked about her the most. She was independent, strong willed and the fact that she had cash didn't hurt either. That's what made Travis so defensive about his sister.

He worried that niggas were just attracted to her for her money and would rob her when chance was given. That was contrary for Man Man. He fell in love with her the first day he met Shay when he was a teenager playing video games at Travis's house. When her former boyfriend Bird was incarcerated, Shay was devastated and venerable. One late night Man Man called her to re-up . . . and a couple of joints and a lot of liquor later lead to . . . well you know what. Now a year later, Man Man is faced with the decision to tell his best friend that's he's about to be an uncle or Shay kills the baby and walks out his life. The problem is it wasn't that easy. If Travis found out they were going together behind his back one of them would die; seriously. Shay didn't understand that her brother was like Scar face was about his sister. There would be problems especially since Travis and Man Man fucked hoes together daily.

"Boy you don't get enough do you?" Buck asked him after walking back from his mother's house. "Why you keep fucking with that hoe?" He asked him. "You know how that nigga is about his sister," He reminded him with a chuckle. "You act like you love her or something,"

"Maybe I do," said Man looking him in the eyes not amused.

"Hold up bro," Buck said sensing the seriousness in his voice. "Don't tell me you fucking her?"

Man Man stared at him in silence. "You fucking tripping bro!" Buck snapped. "Trav home team man . . . that shit ain't right"

"I know but I really do love her bro," said Man Man. "We bout to have a jit man . . . she pregnant and I got to find away to tell him"

"*Shoot me dead then bury me,*" said Buck in disbelief. "You playing right?"

"Naw man I'm dead ass serious," said Man. "We been talking for about a year now"

"Damn a year?" Buck asked him as Travis stormed out his aunt's house, drawing their attention. "That's on you bro . . . I'm out of it"

Travis and his aunt had another argument the same magnitude as the one after Ray's death. She accused him of having something to do with her house being targeted like Shay warned him, and she was right. Ms. Stubbs had to be restrained once again by friends and family as she tried to attack her nephew. She told Travis never to return to her house or she would have him arrested. That's when Travis turned his back and stormed out the house.

"Man this shit ain't over . . . I want them niggas dead!" Travis shouted. "Starting with that fuck nigga Jamal!"

"I already know man!" said Buck. "As mad as ma dukes gon' be when she get home them niggas got to feel my pain!"

"Them niggas want us to know they looking for us!" Travis informed them. "Well guess what they ain't got to look no more"

As they stood there and talked amongst themselves, 100% pull up in his black Ford Taurus drawing their attentions. He had a smile on his face like he had not a care in the world. He calmly stepped out the car ignoring the evil stares that the young men gave him. If there was one person the North Side Boys hated more then the Haitians it was 100%.

"Well well well," 100% began. "If it isn't the North Side Boys"

"What you harassing us for 100%?" Buck asked. "We the victims"

"Victims my ass you guys just as responsible as the ones that did this to your houses," said 100%. "And I'm willing to bet it was them Haitians"

"Well if you so smart why you ain't over there fucking with them?" Man Man asked. "Instead of standing here bull shitting with us?"

"Because Emanuel there is no evidence," 100% told him. "See I know you guys and those Haitians on the south side are going through it . . . so it doesn't take a genius to figure out that all these deaths that's accruing on both sides is not a coincidence," he continued. "It's just I have to find a way to prove it and trust me when I say this . . . *I will prove it*"

"You know what cracka fuck you!" Travis said not begin able to hold his silence anymore. "You full of shit . . . me and my dawgs got some where to be and you holding us up"

"I was wondering when you were going to speak up," 100% said as they walked towards their car. "But don't worry though the clock is ticking . . . It's just a matter of time before I win"

The young men ignored the officer as they entered their car. Travis eyes were bloodshot red as he listened to the detective's threats. He didn't know if 100% was telling the truth or was just playing the usual police mind games as a tactic to get them to talk. Either way he didn't care; Travis wanted blood, more specifically Haitian blood and he wanted it now, retaliations was a must.

CHAPTER 15

The following morning Jamal came dragging in around 7:00 am. He was wasted and tired. After spending the day looking for Travis and his boys they went back to the hospital were Spoon told them about his mishap with 100%. Then they hit the liquor store for a bottle of Remy to take back to the studio to drink the pain away. Kim was snuggled underneath the covers watching TV when he walked into the room. Jamal didn't bother to take off his clothing or even say hi. He just walked over to his side of the bed and plopped down.

"Baby," she said turning around to snuggle up against him. "You okay?"

"Yeah I'm cool," said Jamal letting out a deep breath. "Besides the fact my dawg dead and Spoon being in the hospital . . . I'm cool"

"I'm so sorry baby"

"Don't be," said Jamal. "If anyone should be sorry it should be me"

"What you mean bae?"

"I mean I'm sorry we still outchea," he explained. "I feel like we still trapped in this hood shit"

"What you talking about baby?" She asked him. "You moved us out the hood into a beautiful house"

"That's not enough man," said Jamal. "I'm ready to leave this shit along," he continued. "I planned to get in and get out but it seems like that ain't happen," he confessed. "Ain't know telling when this shit gon' collapse on a nigga"

"So what you saying bae?"

"I'm saying I'm ready to leave," he told her. "Maybe we can go to Haiti, buy a big house and live like King and Queen" he said holding her tight. "I got enough cash saved up to do whateva"

"How much cash baby?"

"You know my style . . . enough to last me you and Kayla uh lifetime," he said. "I was thinking about giving this shit to Spoon and let him do what it do with it"

"I'm so happy to hear you say that Jay," said Kim. "Because I got something to tell you"

"Oh yeah . . . you did have something important to tell me," Jamal remembered. "Wassup?"

Kim sat up on the bed and looked Jamal in the eyes. Not knowing what his reaction would be she hesitated to tell him but she had too. She stayed up after coming home from work just to tell him. Things have been good and life was better then it was before Jamal went to jail but the feeling of something happen to him was still there. Kim hoped that having another baby would really make Jamal consider changing his life. She took his hand, then a deep breath before letting it out.

"Baby," she said. "I'm pregnant"

"Hold on what you said?" Jamal asked wondering if he heard her right. "Who's pregnant?"

"Me baby," she said with a smile on her face. "I'm pregnant"

Her words had Jamal speechless. Kim was pregnant which meant he was about to be the father of two. The news brought tears to his eyes as he hugged her. He was excited, after all kids are a blessing but now he seriously had to seize his chance to break before it was too late.

He fell asleep with Kim in his arms. When he woke up at around 12:00 pm she was still sound asleep. Kim was due back to work at 8:00pm so she needed her rest. Jamal sat at the edge of the bed and admired his beautiful queen as she slept. He really had a ride or die bitch at his side. She has always been there for him since day one, through the good times and bad. He owed it to her and his child to leave the game alone and get them out of harm's way.

Q   Q   Q

"Yo yo Dread" said Jamal into his phone as he drove down the street in Ronny's Lexus. "Wassup?"

"Nothing mon," said Dread. "Wha gwon?"

"Living man," said Jamal. "But listen . . . remember what we talked about?" He asked. "Well I got a proposition for you so Ima come check you out at around 6:00"

"Okay mon," Dread agreed sounding very satisfied. "Link me"

"Fa'sho," said Jamal before clicking over to the next call. "What's up big bro?"

"Yo man I could have been left," said Ken. "I hate waiting for people"

"Chill nigga I'll be there in fifteen . . . Ima call you back," said Jamal looking at his caller ID again then clicking over. "Wassup?"

"I'm here," Shay told him. "Waiting on you"

"Aight then," he said. "Just chill"

Jerome's Caribbean Food was one of Lake Worth's most popular Haitian restaurants. When Jamal walked inside, he could smell the food being cooked which made him hungrier then he already was. A few of the customers waiting for their food, were arguing in Creole about who was the best musical artists form Haiti, as they listened to a Kompa/Konpa song on a small radio. The debating started to get out of hand when one of the male customers started yelling at the top of his lungs. A male employee had to come from the back to calm him down. *Haitians are so passionate about their music* Jamal thought to himself before spotting Shay seating at a table she reserved for them. He walked over and greeted her with a kiss on the cheek. As usual she was beautiful. She had on a gray women's business suit and sported a briefcase with her. Her blouse was buttoned down low, showing off her cleavage. Jamal glanced for a second before talking.

"So wassup?" He asked. "You ordered yet?"

"Yeah it's coming," she answered him. "Rice and spinach right?"

"Yeah that's right," said Jamal looking at the briefcase. "So that's me right there?"

"Yeah it's all there," she said handing it to him. "I told you I'm bout business"

"I ain't never doubt you sweetheart," he told her. "Your shit in the car"

"Is it on point?" She questioned him. "I don't want you tryin' to bullshit me you feel me cause I'm—"

"Just chill lil 'mama . . . I ain't even on them types of plays," he assured her. "And besides if I was I wouldn't be able to get no more of that fi ass head of yours"

"Shut up boy!" She laughed. "You ain't have to say all that"

"Don't be ashamed man," he chuckled. "It's all apart of the game"

"Whateva"

As usual Jerome's services took forever. The two chatted until their food finally arrived. Shay was really discreet about telling him where she was from. In fact she lied and told him she was form Rivera Beach and had home girls in Lake Worth. When Jamal asked her how she knew he sold work, she told him that the whole hood knew. If Shay was that type of chick she could have set Jamal up anytime, but it was money over everything for her. She felt like a trader but her brother's beef with Jamal was their problem. Flipping the dope after cutting it a few times was hers.

The two enjoyed their meals and Shay being the boss bitch she was picked up the tab. Jamal escorted Shay to her car and hugged her before opening the door to let her in. Shay loved the way she got butterflies every time he gave her that million dollar smile. His gold teeth shined in the light. Shay gazed at him for a minute and realized he was a really handsome young man. In fact she was starting to have feelings for him. The pound game he put on her had Shay thinking about it every night. They said their finally good byes before she pulled off then Jamal's phone rang again. It was Ken.

"Yeah bro," Jamal answered. "I'm on my way now"

"Come on Jay you got uh nigga on hold man," Ken complained. "I got shit to do bro"

"I'm on ya man," said Jamal. "Just chill"

"I hate when you say that shit," said Ken. "Just chill . . . that ain't telling me nothing?"

❧　　❧　　❧

It's was 4:30 pm and the North Side Boys where just arriving to the hood. They were in a blue 2000 Toyota Camry with dark tents. They all had guns and all were in kill mode. Any where a Haitian was, is where he laid and Travis was going to make sure of it. He sat in the back seat as Buck drove and Man Man rode shotgun. Getting off at 10th Ave. North, Buck spotted Shay at a red light waiting to get onto the interstate going north.

"There go Shay right there," said Buck. "I wonder where she going?"

"I don't know," said Travis. "I was trying to re-up but she ain't pick up"

"She must ain't got none," said Buck. "You never know with her"

"Naw she going to West Palm," said Travis. "She got something"

"How you know?" Man asked causing Buck to shake his head.

"Fuck you mean how I know?" He asked him. "Only time she don't pick up is when she about to go cook up"

Jamal finally made it to Ken's studio. He was due to meet Dread at 6:00 and had forty five minutes to make it to 45th street in West Palm Beach, where Dread owned a Jamaican restaurant. Jamal had Ken waiting for him all day and knew he was mad but he needed Ken for two reasons, for back up to go see Dread and to tell him something important.

"Damn Jay," said Ken as he entered the car. "You sized me bro"

"My bad man," Jamal chuckled. "Stop crying"

"What the fuck took you so long?" He asked. "You trippin"

"I had to handle business," said Jamal. "Remember the hoe I took home the night Ronny died"

"Oh the bitch you giving them things to for the fifteen?" Ken asked while lighting a joint he rolled while waiting for Jamal. "What's her name?"

"Shay"

"Yeah that's it, I'm telling you bro I know her from somewhere," said Ken. "I just don't remember where"

"Whatever," said Jamal. "You wish you knew her"

"Yeah right nigga, she aint that bad," said Ken passing the joint. "But anyway . . . you know Ronny's funeral is coming up right?"

"Yeah I know," said Jamal. "His mama told me"

"Damn man I still can't believe it bro," said Ken. "My nigga gone"

"Tell me about it," said Jamal shaking his head. "RIP"

"That nigga Travis got to get it," said Ken passing the joint. "That's on everything"

"Check me out man I got to tell you something"," said Jamal changing the subject. I ain't just need you to go see this nigga Dread with me"

"What's up then bro," Ken asked. "What you got to tell me?"

"Kim's pregnant man," said Jamal passing the joint. "We bout to have another one bro"

"Naw man that's what's up!" Ken shouted. "I hope it's a boy this time!"

"Me to bro," said Jamal "But that's not it dawg"

"What you mean?" He asked. "What could be bigger then this?"

"Remember when I told you I was leaving the game?" Jamal asked. "Well I'm out dawg real soon"

"You still on that shit man?" Ken asked him. "We doing this music shit and besides you our connect man you can quit"

"Naw man I'm done bro," said Jamal. "Ima give Spoon the connect"

"*Give Spoon the connect*?" Ken asked. "So you dead ass serious huh?"

"Yeah man I'm done," said Jamal pulling two tickets he brought earlier that morning. "Me, Kayla and Kim moving to Haiti bro,"

"*Moving to Haiti*?" Ken asked. "And you got tickets?"

"Yeah, me and Kim did some talking," he informed him. "And we decided to do it on the 8th"

"The 8th of November?" Ken asked choking on the weed smoke. "That's ten days from now!"

"I know bro," Jamal reminded him. "Ima hire an account to sell the house, the cars . . . then do this last deal with Dread and I'm out"

Ken was at a lost for words as his younger brother further explained his plans to him. Jamal was dead ass serious. He had seven hundred thousand saved up also if he liquidated all his hard assets like his cars and house, he would be set for life. This last deal with Dread would guarantee it too.

The 45th street Flea Market was a place to be on the weekends. People went out there to mostly chill. You could get every thing from bootlegs, clothing and gold over there and that was just in the parking lot. When finally finding a parking spot after five minutes of searching, they stepped out and walked towards Dread's Jamaican restaurant. They wore all black and were strapped. There platinum chains and teeth drew a lot of attention mostly from the haters tying to plot but again they were armed so fuck it. When walking in the restaurant one of the Jamaicans wearing an army fatigue shirt and pants lead them towards the back where Dread was playing dominos with other Jamaicans. Their Bob Marley joints filled the room with smoke as they talked sporty and slammed the bones on the tables. When Jamal and Ken walked in, Dread stood up and greeted his guess.

"Jamal mon," he said shaking his hands. "Wha gwon?"

"I'm okay Dread," said Jamal. "Nigga just trying to get it"

"I feel ya," said Dread signaling everyone to leave so they could talk in private. "Sit down mon"

Dread was in his mid forties and looked like Ox off the movie "Belly". He sported a fade and had waves at the top that you couldn't help but admire. He was dark skinned and his lips were almost blue from smoking so much. He wore a number 24 Kobe Bryant warm up suit with matching head and wrist band. He also wore the jersey underneath like he really had a game to play in later. Dread was a real original gangster from Jamaica and had the rep in the streets to prove it.

"I'm surprised you called me," he said taking a puff from his joint. "I've been trying to link up for a while"

"I know," said Jamal. "I just had to wait for the right time"

"Bumboclot," said Dread seeing through his game. "Everyone has to be careful . . . ya know?"

"Then you feel me then?" said Jamal. "So you ready to talk numbers?"

"Lets talk," said Dread. "But if you can't do better than twenty I ain't fucking with it"

"Come on Dread This Zoe you talking to," Jamal reminded him. "I'm talking seventeen five"

"Seventeen five?" Dread asked scratching his chin. "What's the catch?"

"Ain't no catch," Jamal assured him. "You just have to get a hundred bricks"

"I don't got it like that," said Dread shocked at the order he was asked to buy. "How I know this aint a set up?"

"What the fuck Dread?" Jamal asked him feeling insulted. "You did your research on uh nigga and I did mines on you!" Jamal told him. "So you know its one hundred on my end . . . I'm trying to hook you up!" Jamal said as he got up to leave. "You trying me right now I'm out"

"Okay Zoe hold on," said Dread. "You in my place of business take it easy mon . . . sit down please"

"Dread you asked me to fuck with you," Jamal told him. "Don't try me like that"

"I like you mon . . . no fear," the OG chuckled. "Apologies"

"So wassup?" Jamal asked ready to walk out. "Can you do that or what?"

"Yeah," Dread agreed. "I could do that"

The deal with Dread was set. Jamal already placed the order with Chico in advance knowing Dread couldn't refuse seventeen five when the going rate on a brick was twenty two. Jamal told Dread he'll call him on Wednesday, to inform him where the disclosed location would be so they could meet. If the deal went down smoothly Jamal would bring in $1,750,000, minus $1,000,000 for Chico.

"So you really serious about this huh?" Ken asked him as they drove home. "You out the game?"

"Yeah man I'm out," said Jamal. "Ima give Spoon the connect for five thousand a month until his out""

"Damn ain't this a bitch," Ken chuckled." My lil' brother retiring before me"

"That's crazy huh?" Jamal asked. "I got a family to think about"

"I feel where you coming from," said Ken. "I support you one hundred percent bro," he assured him. "It's just the others and I gone blow up big in this rap industry and I just always pictured you there"

"Ima always be there," said Jamal. "Just more behind the scene you feel me?"

"I feel ya bro," said Ken as they gave each other dap.

"Ten days," Jamal said to himself out loud as he drove off from dropping Ken back to the studio. The first Friday of November was tomorrow and if everything went as planned Jamal, Kim and Kayla would be in Haiti living the life before Thanks Giving. Sunday was Ronny's funeral then the following Wednesday he would contact Dread to seal the deal. In the mean time Jamal would be handling other affairs pertaining to the move across waters. Everything was in order and his chance to break was in his grasp. The clubs, girl, cars, jewelry, police and the beef were all distractions trying to keep him from focusing on his goal but he stayed strong and had one person to thank for that.

CHAPTER 16

Jamal couldn't help but thinking about the time he swore to himself he rather die then stepping foot in the county jail again but today was an exception. As he sat in the lobby mostly filled with baby mama's waiting to see there man behind bars, Jamal tried to sort out his mixed feelings. He was happy to be seeing Brooklyn again but he still felt kind of uneasy about it, especially since he's been having nightmares with Brooklyn in them.

The deputy called everyone to stand in line then lead them to the visitation area. ***"It's colder then a bitch in here***," Jamal thought to himself as he sat on the ice cold metal bench. That's what he hated the most about the county jail. The cold was used as an instrument of control and Jamal hated being controlled. The room resembled a dungeon and the only thing between them and the inmates was a thick piece of glass. As he sat there and rubbed the goose bumps on his arms a little girl walked up to him and waved. Jamal waved back then looked up at the mother who smiled as she called her daughter over to her. She was young and very attractive. She couldn't have been older then twenty three Jamal thought. She had beautiful long hair and her skin was dark and smooth. Both the daughter and her were well dressed and looked like they were doing well but the look in the mother's eyes told a different story. Jamal knew that look all to well. The look of worry and pain use to be in Kim's eyes every visitation before Jamal went to trial. No matter how much money you pay for a lawyer . . . sometimes you just didn't know with these prosecutors and Jamal wasn't trying to put Kim through that ever again.

When the inmates walked in and searched for their love ones, Jamal's heart began to race. He watched as the little girl's face light up when seeing her daddy. Shockingly, the man kind of resembled him. The only major difference was he was taller then Jamal and had a darker complexion. When turning back around, Brooklyn was standing on the other side of the glass. Jamal looked like he saw a ghost as Brooklyn sat down and reached for the receiver.

"What's up baby boy?" He asked after Jamal picked up his receiver. "How you been son?"

"I've been good bro," said Jamal. "Just living man"

"I see that," said Brooklyn referring to Jamal's platinum chain. "Heard you doing big things out there son"

"Well you know people talk," said Jamal. "But things are good tho"

"That's what's up baby boy," said Brooklyn sounding like a proud father. "So what brings you here?" He asked. "I thought you forgot about me son"

"Naw BK don't say that man," Jamal chuckled. "How Ima forget about the person who help he out this shit?"

"What you mean helped you out?" Brooklyn questioned him. "I don't follow"

"I mean things have been very good," Jamal confessed grabbing his chain. "Remember when you told me to take heed of my chance to break"

"Yeah I remember," said Brooklyn.

"Well I did that shit and I'm moving me and the family to Haiti next week," he told him. "And I have you to think for that bro"

"That's wonderful man," said Brooklyn. "I'm happy to see a young black man make it out this shit," he stated. "Especially one who's like my son"

"Thanks Brooklyn," said Jamal. "That means a lot to me"

The two men talked and laughed for the majority of the hour long visitation. Jamal further filled him in on his plans to move to Haiti but stayed very discreet about his business on the street. He also told him he was about to be the father of two. Brooklyn told Jamal about his case and said things were looking up. The witness that saw the shooting said he didn't remember seeing Brooklyn with a gun on the deposition so he was keeping his fingers crossed. While Brooklyn continued to tell him about his good news, Jamal couldn't help but think about his dreams. The man who was in his nightmares was right in front of him. Jamal had to speak up and get his opinion.

"What you think about dreams?" Jamal interrupted him.

"What I think about dreams?" Brooklyn questioned. "Where did that come from?"

"What you think about em' man?" Jamal asked again. "You think they mean something?"

"I don't know man . . . I guess," said Brooklyn still unsure where Jamal was taking the conversation. "What you talking about?"

"Nothing really man," said Jamal trying to find the right words to express him self. "I just been having these crazy ass dreams with me or one of my homeboys dead and your always in them"

"Oh I feel ya now," said Brooklyn. "I think dreams especially nightmares are like a reflection of your life," he told him. "It's like all the bad you've done in the past is coming back to hunt up," he continued. "I have nightmares almost every night that remind me of things I've done out there," said Brooklyn. "I take em' as God's way of reminding you to tighten up fo' it's to late"

"That's real talk," said Jamal. "I never looked at it like that"

"Check me out Jay . . . a man is the creator of his own destiny," said Brooklyn. "You make what happens to you happen, one way or the other . . . those dreams are like tracks," Brooklyn continued. "What you're doing is the right thing man; take your family and leave"

The deputy in the control booth flicked the lights on and off which meant visitation was over. When Jamal glanced over at the little girl from earlier, she started crying when her daddy stood up to leave. "Don't cry daddy coming home soon," said the mother with eyes full of tears.

"Well it's about that time," said Brooklyn putting his fist against the glass. "Much love baby boy"

"Much love BK man," Jamal said connecting his fist with the man's through the glass. "Be easy in there"

"Yeah Ima be okay baby boy . . . you just be easy out there," said Brooklyn. "Get that family out of here man"

"Let's go inmate!" A Deputy shouted at Brooklyn. "Visitation is over!"

"That's my cue man I'm outta of here," he said before standing up. "See ya when I see ya"

Jamal with the phone still in his ear watched as Brooklyn walked off. Jamal admired him a lot. Brooklyn was one of the realest niggas he knew. He always looked forward to the next day no matter what situation he was in. When the lights flickered again, Jamal realized he was the only one in the room. After waiting in line to get his ID back, he left the jail never to return again. On his way to the car he saw the mother holding the little girl's hand while waiting for a taxi. The looks on their faces looked as if they've just came form a funeral. He could honestly feel their pain. When the little girl saw Jamal again she pulled away from her mother's clutch to run and hug him. Jamal took a knee then reached in his pocket and pulled out a bank roll with a rubber band around it. "Give this to mommy," he told her as the mother started to walk towards them. Jamal told the little girl to go before he stood up and walked off. When the child handed her mother the bank roll of cash, the look on her face was in pure shock, especially since Jamal never left the house with less then five stacks. "The man gave it to me mommy," said the little girl pointing at Jamal entering his car. Before the mother could say anything he rode off.

❈　　❈　　❈

The North Side Boys where still creeping through the streets of Lake Worth ready to kill. They all were anxious as they searched every block in the hood for the Zoes. They were no where to be found but the urge to retaliate wouldn't let them give up. The men were quiet. The only thing that could be heard was the music that subconsciously instilled the will to murder in their brains. Travis who was sitting in the backseat called Shay for the tenth time today with no luck. She's been ignoring his calls and he couldn't help but think if she was really trying to cut him off. Yeah she was right and he knew it. All this beefing made no money but fuck it, this was personal. Anywhere he saw one of them Zoes at, Travis promised to handle them right then and there, and he usually made good on his promises.

"Where you think they at man," Buck asked getting tired of driving. "We hit every block in this bitch"

"I don't know," said Man. "Them niggas just ain't out here"

"Cause they know what time it is," Travis chuckled. "This shit is beef"

"Hey yo Trav, we running low on work man," said Buck. "Shay ain't pick up yet?"

"Naw man . . . I think she still on her period from the other day," he said before his phone rang. "Shit . . . looks like you talked her up . . . hello"

"Why you blowing up my phone?" Shay asked with an attitude. "What's the problem?"

"What you mean man?" He questioned. "You know why I'm calling?"

"Naw man I told ya . . . you too hot right now?" She reminded him. "And besides you owe me money?"

"Man tighten up Shay!" Travis yelled. "You with the bull shit!"

"I'm dead ass serious Trav," she told him. "You bad business right now"

"Okay Shay I thought about what you said," Travis said calming down. "I'm done with this beef shit," he lied. "I ain't gone look for trouble . . . Ima let it come to me"

"Whatever Travis," Shay said not believing him. "Now you with the bull shit"

"Now Shay I'm fo' real," he said in a convincing tone. "I'm bout this money"

"Okay then Travis Ima give you one more chance," she said going against her better judgment. "Meet me in West Palm"

When making it to West Palm, Shay directed them to a house on Pine Wood where she knew a few locals. When they pull up in the driveway, Shay was in the yard sitting on her car's hood. Her and a few of her friends both females and males where chatting and smoking weed. Travis stepped out the car while Buck and Man Man waited. As Travis made way towards the bunch, Man Man burnt a hole through Shay with his eyes. The last time they spoke was the day the Zoes shot up their houses and she was ticked.

"So when you gone tell him?" Buck asked noticing who his friend was staring at.

"I don't know bro," said Man shrugging his shoulders. "I don't think I am"

"What the fuck you talking about?" Buck asked him. "You might as well tell him dawg . . . shit ya'll bout to have a jit"

"Man fuck that nigga," said Man Man. "I aint got to tell him shit"

"Whatever nigga," said Buck. "Just keep me out of it"

While the two where in the car talking, Shay and Travis walked away from the bunch for some privacy. She was hesitating to give Travis the brick he came for. He claimed he was done with the beefing but she just wasn't sure. After begging and pleading his case, Travis finally got his way. Shay sent one of the men inside to retrieve the order. Coming back with a black plastic bag, the man handed it to Shay. Before she handed it to Travis, she made him promise one more time that he would stay out of trouble in which he did, behind a sinister smirk. As he made way towards his car Shay said something.

"Hey who you came with?" She knowingly asked. "Them clown ass niggas of yours?"

"Who else would I be with?" He asked sarcastically. "Why?"

"No reason," she said while looking to see if she could see Man Man through the car window. "Never mind"

○   ○   ○

Jamal himself decided to just slide and think as he smoked his joint. Bob Marley's "Jamin" smoothed his thoughts. The visit with Brooklyn put a lot of things in prospective for him. Maybe Brooklyn was right. Maybe the nightmares were God's way of telling Jamal time was running out. What ever the case might have been, Jamal was glad his last days in the game were near. When stopping at a red light he realized he was in West Palm and in need of another Dutch to roll his weed. He pulled into a near by gas station and parked in a parking spot in front of the store. When stepping out a few females eyed him but he paid them no attention, mainly because his mind was on the coast of Haiti somewhere. While walking inside the store he had no idea he'd been spotted.

"There go that fuck nigga right there!" Man shouted spotting Jamal while causally looking out the window. "That's him going inside the store!"

"There go who?" Buck asked. "Who you talking about?"

"That nigga Jamal!" said Man. "That nigga at the gas station!"

"I don't see him," said Travis trying to get a glimpse from the back window. "You sure that's him?"

"Yeah bitch!" Man shouted while grabbing his gun from underneath his seat. "I know that's him!"

"Then let's go back!" Travis ordered grabbing his gun as well. "Turn this shit around!"

"Hold up ya'll boys," said Buck. "We got a fucking brick in the car"

"Man fuck that shit we going back to get that nigga!" Travis shouted. "Turn this shit around!"

Buck did as he was told. He jerked the wheel and quickly switched lanes until he made it to the turning lane to make a u turn. The young men where unaware that Buck's reckless driving drew the attention of West Palm Beach's finest. Unable to wait for the red light Travis forced Buck to run the light cutting off a few drivers on the road.

Jamal walked out the store with a couple of Dutch's still humming the tune to Bob Marley's song. When he made it to his car he searched his pockets and realized he left his phone on the counter inside the store. While walking inside the store he didn't see Travis and his boys pulling up directly behind his car. After receiving his phone from the old white man who owned the store,

Jamal made his way out. When stepping out the door, he noticed the strange Toyota with black tents he stopped dead in his tracks. Feeling alarmed, Jamal put his hand on his gun at his waist line then let his guard down when he saw a squad car get behind the Toyota, and turn on his light. Jamal sighed in relief but the only problem now was that he was blocked in.

"Damn man there go troll!" Man Man said watching the officer approach the car. "What the fuck we gon' do?"

"Aww man we going to jail!" Buck told them. "I'm bout to hit it!"

"You ain't bout to do shit!" Travis shouted as the officer tap on the driver side window. "I got this!"

When Buck let down his window the officer asked him to move up so Jamal could back out. Before Buck could do as he was ordered, Travis opened the backseat door on the opposite side of the officer with his gun drawn. When Jamal saw Travis with his gun pointed at him he froze. The shock caused him to react to late. Travis let off a shot hitting the Jamal in the arm. The force of the .9mm bullet knocked Jamal against the side of the Lexus as he tried to move out the way. Seeing this, the officer wrestled with his holster to free his gun but his hesitation caused him to catch three hot ones in the chest form Travis's gun. While Travis's focus was on the officer, Jamal started for the store entrance while holding his left arm. Seeing that Jamal was trying to get away, Man Man opened his passenger side door and let off shots from his gun, barley missing Jamal who leaped for safety. The glass door and windows shattered into piece due to Man Man's failed efforts as Jamal slid across the floor.

"Let's get this nigga!" Travis shouted singling Man Man to follow him. "I want him dead!"

The frightened customers all ran for cover during the gun fire. Jamal found his cover in the nearest isle to the entrance. Now with his gun drawn, he peaked around the shelves and saw the two gun men making way inside the store. Knowing if they entered the small store he would probably die, he began to fire. Travis and Man Man ran for cover against the building as they returned fire. The store owner who was hiding behind the counter grabbed his shot gun and aimed it directly at Jamal. Seeing that he had more to worry about then just Travis and Man Man, Jamal quickly stood up and literally leaped over the shelves into the next isle, falling onto a woman and her child. The blast from the shot gun had chips and other foods flying everywhere.

While the store owner searched for Jamal, Travis sneaked inside and shot the store owner twice killing him where he stood. Seeing his chance to get away, Jamal made way for the back exist while ducking down and firing behind him. Not seeing where he was aiming all shots missed. Travis started for him but Man Man grabbed him by the arm.

"What the fuck you doing nigga?" Travis shouted as he pulled his arm free. "He getting away!"

"Let's go man!" Man Man shouted hearing the distant sirens. "Troll coming!"

The two men rushed out the store and jumped inside the car before Buck sped off. Jamal found his way to the store's back alley. Hearing the sirens in the distant, Jamal tossed his gun inside the sewer drain and made his way to the main street where police officers surrounded him. Jamal quickly surrendered by putting his hands in the air and getting down on his knees.

The North Side Boys escaped undetected through the back roads. When they made it to the Interstate they where able to relax more but getting to the motel was the main objective. At this point

Travis was furious. Once again Jamal was able to slip through his fingers. He was starting to think that nigga had voodoo on him or something.

"A day of searching for nothing!" Travis shouted hitting the back of Man Man's seat. "Why the fuck you stopped me for!"

"Nigga what you mean why I stopped you?" Man asked while turning around to face him. "Police was coming!"

"Fuck the police!" Travis said sucking his teeth knowing Man Man was right. "Pussy ass crackas!"

"Travis dawg you trippin," Buck informed him. "Shay told you to chill out man . . . then you go and do this shit?"

"Nigga fuck Shay . . . this shit personal!" He shouted. "I told you anywhere I see them Haitians it's on!"

CHAPTER 17

Racism still excites especially in the hood. It's like police was designed as a barbwire fines to keep the young minorities form making it pass the city limits. The medals and awards that decorated Detective Stack's office represented a good carrier, but was a cover up for one filled with false charges and police brutality. Racism not only lived in him but in many other officers like him on the force. It was 12:00 am Friday morning and he was still behind his desk doing paper work. The Captain was on his ass like white on rice about the on going violence in the city. The property value was going down fast and the mayor wasn't having that. Jobs were on the line including his. Unable to concentrate he put down his pen and leaned back in his chair. Then he stood up and walked over to his board where he had a diagram with pictures of The South Side Boys arranged in a pyramid shape, Jamal's picture at the top. He not only hated them, he hated what they represented, which was a group of black men with power.

"Hey Stacks you won't believe this," said Officer McCoy barging into the office. "There was a shooting at a gas station in West Palm."

"So that's not are jurisdiction," said Detective Stacks. "Let them fucks up there handle that"

"Okay then," said Detective McCoy before pointing at Jamal's picture. "What if I told you your boy was involved?"

"You're kidding me?" Detective Stacks asked in disbelief. "He's in custody?"

"Yeah he is," said Detective McCoy. "But they're letting him go . . . something about a cop who was shot in the incident saying he reacted in self defense"

"He said what?" Detective Stack asked running both hands through his hair. "Your bullshitting me man?"

"I bullshit you not his at the hospital right now," said McCoy. "If we hurry we could catch him"

Detective McCoy was just as racist as 100%. He had blue eyes and short blonde hair. He was also tall and built like an ox. Unlike 100% who dressed formal to work, Detective McCoy dressed like jump out since he often worked the jump out unit. When they made it to the lobby the receptionist directed them to Jamal's room. Standing in front of the door, were a couple of officers from the West Palm Beach police department. They were just leaving from asking Jamal a few final questions when Stacks and McCoy arrived.

"Oh look its Lake Worth's finest," one of the officers joked as they walked off laughing. "Learn how to keep your monkeys in the jungle"

"Up yours," said Detective Stacks. "Fucking assholes"

When the Detectives walked in, the nurse was just finishing with Jamal. His left arm was in a pain and in a slinky. He wore just his white beater since his black t shirt was all bloody. When he saw the detectives he sucked his teeth as he stood up to leave.

"Wow Mr. Pierre where you going?" 100% asked him. "I just got here"

"Man what ya'll want?" Jamal asked. "I already told them crakas I don't know shit," he continued. "The officer that got shot said it was self defense," he informed them. "So what's the problem?"

"The problem is Detective McCoy and I both think you do know who tried to kill you," said 100% signaling the nurse to leave the room. "They weren't even wearing mask"

"Like I told you man I don't know shit," Jamal lied putting on his chain with his right arm. "Maybe it was just some random robbery gone bad"

"Come on Jamal run that shit past some rookie prick," said 100%. "You and I both know it was Travis and his boys"

"Naw it wasn't them," said Jamal. "And besides I ain't no snitch"

"*You ain't no snitch?*" Officer McCoy mocked him in frustration. "These people tried to kill you . . . how is that snitching?"

"Man listen here," said Jamal before making way towards the door. "The officers said I was free to leave so I'm leaving"

"You know something you Haitians humor me?" said 100% grabbing Jamal by the shoulder, causing him to sigh in pain. "You guy's think ya'll run the city when ya'll are nothing more then cattle," he continued. "Time is running out and when it does Ima slaughter you all"

"Ya'll ain't nothing more than sum racist ass crackas," said Jamal pushing 100%'s hand off his shoulder. "Ya'll lock uh nigga up on bullshit ass charges everyday," he told him. "I bet when ya'll heard I was involved in this shit ya'll rushed ya'll bitch asses over here huh?" Jamal chuckled before leaving the Detectives with their thoughts. "Do your jobs officers, cause I don't know shit"

Walking out the building the Detectives watched as Jamal entered his brother's Doge Charger and rode off. The Haitians success in the streets brought 100% closer to being jobless everyday. Jamal's cocky attitude was like adding logs to an already raging fire inside him. As he lit a Newport to calm his nerves he chuckled knowing that they would soon crumble before him.

"Ain't that 100% and McCoy, Ken asked. "What they doing here?"

"Yeah that's them crakas," said Jamal leaning the passenger seat back to get comfortable. "They came to talk that shit like always"

"Racist ass crackas," Ken mumbled. "So them niggas almost got you huh?"

"Yeah them and the store owner," said Jamal. "That shit was serious dawg . . . troll got hit up too . . . lucky for me he had on a vest," Jamal continued. "He said I reacted in self defense"

"Damn this shit serious," said Ken. "But don't worry tho, I got Fat and Troy trying to find out where them niggas ducked off at," Ken told him. "We got twenty stacks on they heads right now . . . we gon get em"

"Man I don't care but that shit," said Jamal as his phone rang. "All I won't to do right now is go home bro," he told him before answering. "Hello"

"What's up daddy?" Shay asked while lying in her bed listening to slow music. "What you doing?"

"Ain't shit . . . sweetheart just handling business," Jamal lied. "Wassup?"

"Nothing really," she said in a sexy tone. "Just wondering if you could come through"

"Damn I would love to but it's been a long day," said Jamal. "Maybe some other time"

"Aww that's a shame," she said while gently touching herself as the slow music seduced her. "Cause I'm over her listening to music and thinking about you"

"Yeah I'm sure," Jamal chuckled. "It's really been a long day tho"

"Well then promise me you gone come through tomorrow night," said Shay. "Please"

"Alright then," Jamal lied. "I promise"

"Ima hold you to that," said Shay before hanging up. "Bye daddy"

"Aight then," said Jamal. "Ima hit you up"

"Who was that?" Ken asked him. "Sounds like she ready"

"Oh that's Shay, said Jamal. "Remember the girl I'm giving them things to for fifteen?"

"Hold up you said her name Shay?" Ken asked. "That's the bitch in the pink dress right?"

"Yeah that's her . . . wassup?" Jamal asked sensing the shock in his voice. "What's wrong bro?"

"Man I think that's Travis's sister bro," said Ken as he hit the stirring wheel with his fist. "I thought I knew that hoe!"

"Man you lying?" Jamal hoped. "Tell me you bullshittin'"

"Man G shit bro," said Ken. "Call that hoe right na' and ask her if she got a nigga named Bird that's locked up?"

"I can't believe this shit," said Jamal hitting the send button on his phone. "Hold on bro . . . It's ringing"

"Yes daddy?" Shay answered. "You must have changed your mind?"

"Naw I just gotta ask you a question," said Jamal. "And be uh hundred with me"

"Anything daddy," said Shay in an uneasy tone. "What's up?"

"You got uh nigga locked up named Bird?" He asked. "Yes or no?"

"Why does that matter?" Shay asked. "What you been checking up on me or something?"

"Man just answer the question," Jamal snapped. "Yes or No?"

"Yeah that *was* my nigga," said Shay. "But what we got is business and—"

"So Travis your brother then huh?" Jamal interrupted her. "And I bet you knew we were beefing"

"Yeah that's my brother," she confessed. "But it ain't like that daddy"

"Fuck you mean it ain't like that!" Jamal shouted into his phone. "For all I know you could be trying to set me up!"

"*Set up you?*" Shay said matching his voice level. "Nigga please if I wanted to set you up I woulda been did that!" She told him. "That beef ain't got shit to do with me . . . I'm bout money!"

"Say what you want but that's just playing it to close," said Jamal. "Ima have to cut you off"

"*Cut me off?*" Shay shouted. "Pussy ass Haitian I hope my brother—"

"Man fuck you," Jamal calmly said before hanging up in her face.

"Hello . . . hello?" Shay yelled into the phone before throwing it against the wall. "Pussy ass nigga!"

Things were really getting out of hand. Jamal couldn't believe this shit. First he gets shot and now he finds out Shay was Travis' sister. **What the fuck was next?"** He thought to himself. To play it safe he decided to stay home and only come out for things pertaining to business.

ø   ø   ø

After the shooting the North Side boys went back to the motel. Every one was sleep expect for Man Man. He stared at the ceiling in deep thought. The controversy with The South Side Boys was the least of his worries. This whole Shay ordeal had his mind in knots. *Am I really that intimidated by this nigga to lose family?* He asked him self as he glanced at Travis sleeping on the couch. At that moment his pride made him decided to tell Travis about him and Shay tomorrow no matter what the consequences. So excited about his decision, he sat up in bed and called Shay again. He had to tell her. This was the only thing stopping him from being with the girl of his dreams for life; the only problem was she wasn't picking up. As a matter of fact, she hasn't been picking up all day. Fed up with being ignored he decide to go over and tell her the good news. He grabbed the keys off the table then quietly left the room making sure not to wake anyone.

The ride to Shay's house seemed like eternity because he couldn't wait to tell her. He wasn't even mad about her not picking up the phone all day. He figured she was still mad at him but it was over now. Everything was going to be okay again or at least he hoped. Standing at Shay's door, he took a deep breath before knocking. Shay who was getting ready to take a shower answered the door in her bath robe.

"What you doing here Emanuel?" Shay asked as she walked back to the shower. "Its 2:00 in the morning"

"I know baby," said Man as he closed the door behind him. "I got something important I want to tell you"

"Well its gon' have to wait until I get out the shower," said Shay. "Give me a minute"

As Shay was in the shower, Man Man made his self at home. He went into the kitchen and grabbed a soda. Walking into Shay's room he could hear slow music playing which made him curious. Brushing off the thought, he placed the soda on the nightstand and started searching the bed to see if he could find the remote for the TV. Now looking around the room, he noticed Shay's phone on the ground with the battery out. *"That's why it went straight to the answering machine,"* he thought to himself as he picked it up and inserting the battery. When he turned on the phone he placed it on the nightstand and then went back to looking for the remote. He was fine for a second then his curiosity got the best of him. Still hearing the shower running, Man Man walked over to the nightstand and searched through her phone. As he scrolled down her contacts list, he saw Jamal's name. Anger quickly consumed him. He hoped for her sake it wasn't the same Jamal he had in mind. ***"Maybe it's somebody else,"*** he told himself before going through her text messages. When he saw a text Shay sent to Jamal that read **I'm missing you daddy,** he snapped. Rushing into the shower, Man Man pulled the curtain back startling her.

"So that's why you ain't been picking up?" He shouted while waving the phone in her face. "You fucking him?"

"Boy get out my face!" Shay yelled while covering her breast. "Why you going through my phone anyway?"

"Answer the question Shay!" He told her. "You fucking him or not?"

"Why does it matter?" She snapped. "We don't go together!"

Shay's words were like a knife piercing through his heart. He stood there and looked at her for a second. This couldn't be the girl he fell in love with he thought. This Shay looked so evil. The pain was unbearable. The pressure he felt on his chest was killing him so he had to relieve it. Lunging at her, Man Man grabbed her by the throat and slammed her against the shower wall. Shay wanted to scream but the death lock Man Man had around her neck didn't enable her to do so. She kicked and scratched but he wasn't letting go. The look in Man Man's eyes was that of a demon's. Shay grabbed his dreads and pulled out a few by the roots leaving a patch in his hair. Feeling the pain, Man Man threw Shay onto the bathroom floor and kicked her in the mid section. "Pussy as hoe!" He shouted while rubbing his bold spot as Shay gasped for air. Man Man then dragged her into the bedroom where he continued to kick her in the stomach. When he stood her up he slapped her, sending Shay's little body flying onto the bed.

"Trifling ass bitch!" He shouted as she laid there on her stomach crying. "How you gon fuck this nigga with my seed inside you huh?"

Remembering her pink .22 hand gun was underneath her pillow, she quickly tried to grab it. Seeing her hand movement, Man Man jumped on to her back pinning Shay down. The sudden increase of weight on her back made Shay let go of the gun. Man then tossed it onto the ground then grabbed a pillow. He turned her around then placed the pillow on her face, applying pressure. Shay's screams for help were muffled as she hit Man Man's arms but he was just too strong. The lack of air was evident as she began to resist less. All she could hear was the slow music in the back ground. Every slap to his arms became weaker and weaker. Man Man held the pillow over her face until Shay laid there lifeless.

ꙮ   ꙮ   ꙮ

The next morning 100% pulled up to yet another crime scene. The Crime Scene Unit took pictures of Shay's naked body as others dusted the place for prints. Detective McCoy was examining her lifeless body when 100% walked into the room.

"Good morning," said 100% shaking McCoy's hand. "What we got here?"

"Suffocation, badly beaten, no sign of forced entry or rape," said McCoy as he read from his notepad. "Also we have dreadlocks in the bath tub and a soda can on the night stand"

"We got an ID on her?" 100% asked as he closely examined the girl's badly bruised face. "*Sssseeesshh* . . . someone was really mad at her"

"Tell me about . . . when we came in, slow music was still playing on the radio . . . looks like a crime of passion to me," McCoy said as he flipped through pages in his notepad. "Oh yeah here we go . . . Lashala Stubbs related to Travis Stubbs . . . NSB member.

"Good God . . . did you say Travis Stubbs?" 100% asked. "This shit could be gang related"

"Yes sir," Detective McCoy chuckled. "The Captain is going to be mad"

"No shit Sherlock," said 100%, "Does the brother know yet?"

"Yeah they just informed him," said McCoy. "He's suposly on his way now"

"Hopefully we could get him to crack on the Haitians," said 100%. "I'm willing to bet they were involved in this"

"*Hopefully*," said McCoy. "Your job depends on it"

"Thanks for reminding me," said 100% in a sarcastic tone. "What are you the Captain's bitch on the side?"

"Owww . . . low blow you prick," said McCoy playfully flinching at the detective. "Take that back."

As the Detectives exchanged wise cracks, an officer walked in to the room and informed them that Travis Stubbs was outside and out of control. "Oh this is going to be a long day," said 100% as they followed the officer. Outside Travis was shouting and swearing at two officers as they tried to restrain him from entering the house. "I want to see her!" He yelled before tossing one of the officers to the floor. When seeing this, three more officers joined in and wrestled him to the ground as 100% and McCoy observed. When the officers finally handcuffed him they stood Travis up and then sat him on the hood of a squad car so the Detectives could talk to him.

"I'm sorry for your loss," said 100%. "I want you to know Detective McCoy and I will do everything in are power to catch who ever did this"

"Yeah right 100% . . . that's my sister that's dead in there and ya'll got me in cuffs!" Travis shouted as tears ran down his cheek. "I don't need ya'll help I can do it myself!"

"Come on now Travis," said 100% trying to sound really concerned. "We can't have you taking the law into your hands now," he continued. "Instead why don't you help us catch these guys?"

"If I knew who it was I wouldn't be standing here right now," said Travis. "And besides I don't fuck with the police"

"Cut the bullshit man!" McCoy shouted as he pointed at the house. "For God's sake that's your sister in there!"

"You don't think I fucking know that?" Travis shouted. "Do you know how it feels to get a call at six in the morning talking bout your sister dead?"

"Look man . . . I'm really sorry that's why I'm trying to help you here," 100% lied. "Listen I know the Haitians did this it's no secret," he said in a low tone. "We could get them back Travis, just give me something"

"Man I don't know shit," said Travis looking down at the floor. "All I know is my sister is dead and someone gon' feel my pain"

"You know what have it your way," said 100% waving him off as him and Detective McCoy walked off. "Stupid kid"

The tears in Travis's eyes were evidence of a man who was clearly in pain but no matter how much it hurt, he just didn't fuck with the police. Instead he would rather serve justices in the street himself. If 100% was right then the Haitians had hell to pay. "Damn Shay this shit is my fault," he whispered to himself as the detectives look at him form the distance. All the times she told him not to beef with the Haitians he wished he would have taken heed. Now the beef has really hit close to home and Travis swore to him self that the Haitians had to die. He just couldn't let go . . . revenge was a must and he knew exactly what to do.

"You think that's was a good idea telling him the Haitian's did it?" Detective McCoy asked while looking at Travis holding his head down. "His going to go out there looking for trouble"

"Stubbs ain't cracking man . . . he'll take ten years on head no problem," 100% explained. "If he goes out there and kills one of them Haitians . . . he'll be doing me a favor"

Q   Q   Q

A few hours later Buck woke up to an empty motel room. Wondering where the guys were he called both of their phones but received no answer. Last thing he remembered was seeing Travis rushing out the room around 6:00 a.m. Figuring he had a buddy to go bust down he went back to sleep. Man Man on the other hand, he had no idea. Hoping his friends were okay he decided to take a shower. While drying off he heard the door slam and Travis yelling. Rushing out the bathroom in his boxers he saw him kicking things and punching holes in the wall.

"What's wrong dawg?" Buck shouted in confusion. "What happened?"

"They killed her man!" Travis said as he sat at the edge of the bed crying. "They fucking killed her!"

"Who man . . . who died?" Buck asked. "What you talking bout?"

"They killed my sister man," said Travis looking Buck in the eyes. "Shay is dead"

"Naw man say it ain't true," said Buck running his hand trough his dreads in disbelief. "Who did it?"

"Them Haitians nigga!" Travis shouted. "It's all on the line now, I ain't sleeping until they all dead," he said as he stood up and wiped the tears from his eyes. "Fuck all this crying shit bro," he continued. "I ain't going out like this"

"Hold on bro!" Buck said. "How you know it was them!"

"Fucking 100% practically told me when I was at the crime scene!" He shouted while grabbing his AK–47 from underneath the bed. "Where the fuck is Man Man?" He asked. "Call him and tell him to get down here . . . It's going down!"

"What we gon' do?" Buck asked as he grabbed his phone from the counter. "I'm bout whateva"

"Ain't that nigga's funeral tomorrow?" Travis asked. "The one I merked at the club?"

"Yeah that's right its tomorrow," said Buck. "Why?"

"You know why," said Travis. "We going to go pay our respects"

ϙ　　ϙ　　ϙ

When Buck called Man Man he was at the park sitting inside his car, listen to music as he smoked a joint. The lyrics in the song helped him think. After the murder he came back to drop of the Toyota then called a buddy to use his car. When Buck informed him that Shay was dead his Oscar a winning performance had Buck really feeling his pain. After Buck instructed him to meet at the motel they hung up and Man Man sat in silence. He couldn't believe he killed not only Shay but his unborn child as well. The guilt weighted heavy on his heart but how could she betray him like that, especially with Jamal. *"Fuck it . . . it is what it is,"* he told himself as he hopped of the bench. He figured if he played his cards right, Travis would never know and besides he already thinks the Haitians did it so he was in the clear. At least he thought he was.

CHAPTER 18

J amal woke up to a gloomy morning. Today was the day the south Side Boys had to lay a fellow solider down to rest. Jamal hated going to funerals but he had to pay his respect. His arm was still sore from the gun shot wound but the sling he wore was uncomfortable so he removed it. Kim and Kayla were sound asleep as he got ready. Kim wanted to come but Jamal declined, figuring it would be safer at home since he was beefing. As he stood in front of the bathroom mirror, he put on his black RIP shirt with Ronny's picture on it, then he placed his Haitian flag in his back left pocket. Looking at his fallen friend's image, he couldn't help but think about how he almost lost his life that night. That hit was meant for him but instead Ronny meet his faith. It was like death was around every corner searching for Jamal, so as of late his been home bound getting ready for the move to freedom.

Walking into the bedroom, he watched as his loved ones peacefully slept. They were his domain, his everything. Kim was so excited to move to Haiti. The look of excitement had been on her face everyday but when Jamal came home with a gun shot wound to the arm, she cried and worried that something might happen to him before they left. Jamal assured her that nothing was stopping them from moving. As he stood there and smiled, his phone rung and Ken informed him that they were outside. Jamal kissed his family good bye and left.

"Wassup ya'll boys?" Jamal asked as he sat in the backseat next to Troy. Know one answered instead they nodded. Everyone in the car was grieving and Jamal could feel it. They all wore black RIP shirts like his. He glanced at Troy and watched him try to fight back tears. Troy and Ronny had a relationship like he had with Spoon, so Jamal understood. Fat who was riding shotgun, looked hopelessly out the window as Ken smoked a joint. He understood them all. They grow up with Ronny and been through a lot together before Jamal even jumped off the porch. The authorities' harsh treatment of the black minority was a struggle with in it's self, so they were one another's hope through it all. Losing a homeboy was like losing a piece of that hope and Jamal could see it in their eyes. He hated seeing his boys like this but it came with the game. Jamal wished Spoon was here because he always found a way of making things feel better but his releases date from the hospital was a few days to late of the funeral.

As they drove through the hood towards the E street church, Jamal was shocked to see all the graffiti that coved the hood. They said messages like "FREE TOP 6," "LAKE WORTH" and "WE LOVE TOP 6". It was like a graffiti street team hit the hood.

"Yo ya'll boys see this shit?" Jamal asked as he looked out the window. "Who did it?"

"Man I don't know I'm just as shocked as you," said Troy also looking out the window. "This shit is crazy"

"Oh ya'll niggas ain't heard?" Fat Zoe asked while pulling out the day's newspaper. "Top 6 just got indicted for the RICO act"

"*The RICO act?*" Jamal asked in a confused tone. "How the fuck?"

"I don't know," said Fat Zoe. "They calling them niggas a gang"

"Them niggas ain't no gang," said Troy. "Top 6 is a rap group"

"Not according to the police," said Jamal as he read the paper. "They're linking the shootings at the mall, the club when Fat shot Ray Ray, and when Ronny and Spoon got hit up . . . all to Top 6"

"How they gone prove that?" Troy asked. "We did most of that shit"

"I don't know but shit crazy," said Fat Zoe causing Jamal to glance at him. "Shit crazy"

Though the others were lost in confusion, Jamal knew exactly what was happening. He's been telling Spoon about this since he'd gotten out of jail. It's been on the news repeatedly for the past few months. The on coming recession, and the protesters complaining about the violence, it all made since. Authorities were desperate and Jamal feared the core of the problem was soon to fall, which were them.

When they pulled up to the church it looked like a club scene. The line to get inside was almost around the corner. Every one was dressed in all black and pictures of Ronny were everywhere. It was like he was in there performing instead of lying in a casket. People who got tired of standing in line stood in the parking lot and played music by Top 6. Finally finding a parking spot, the young men stepped out the vehicle. People stopped everything they were doing when they noticed it was the rest of the South Side Boys. Little did the young men know everyone was a waiting there arrival.

They walked past the line and up the steps. The usher made way for them as they walked through the crowded church. The service was about over and the preacher was telling everyone where the burial site was going to be. The young men slowly walked down the isle towards Ronny's golden casket as everyone whispered and pointed. Even the preacher stopped talking when realizing it was them. Jamal felt like his spirit was lifted out his body when he saw Ronny lying in the casket, with a black suit on and his South Side Boy chain around his neck. His homeboy was dead and at that moment it really hit Jamal. Tears began forming in all of their eyes as they stood in front of the casket. They bowed their heads and closed their eyes in silence. Jamal could feel the many eyes focused on them and hear the whispers in the background. When he opened his eyes he watched Troy take his Haitian flag from his back pocket and drop it in the casket with Ronny before walking away. Ken and Fat Zoe followed suit, leaving Jamal standing in front of the casket by himself. He turned around and watched as the others walked down the isle before looking up at the cross that was placed in front of the church. He looked at it for a second then slowly nodded his head as he took off his chain and placed it in the casket with Ronny. "You're free now," he said with a smile as tears rolled off his cheek.

Jamal followed the rest of his friends out of the church as the preacher told everyone to bow their heads and join him in a final prayer. When they made it to the car Ken popped open the trunk and grabbed a Hennessey bottle. He opened it and poured liquor for his dead homey before taking a sip and passing it. They shared the bottle as they waited for Ronny's body to be carried to the hearse. When Jamal took another sip from the bottle he spotted 100% and McCoy parked down the street playing photographer.

"Who invited them?" Jamal asked motioning his head towards the car. "These pussy ass crackas just won't leave us alone"

"They ain't even trying to hide," said Troy. "Over there snapping pictures and shit?"

"Let's give them something to take a picture of then," Fat said before standing on the trunk of Ken's car to flick off the officers. "Fuck you!"

The rest of them all shared a laugh as they put their middle fingers in the air too. "Yeah it's funny now but we'll see who has the last laugh," said 100% as he took more pictures with his camera. The young men really needed a laugh at a time like this and it being at the expensive of 100% made it priceless. Their brief moment of escape was done when they heard a loud scream from inside the church. They turned and watched as the usher opened the church doors for the paul barriers caring the casket. The young men watched as people were prevented from approaching the casket by the ushers and the uniformed funeral escorts. Inside people had to be controlled as they went crazy for the fallen soldier. When the paul barriers put the casket in back of the hearse, people crowded the vehicle as it slowly rode off. Jamal and the others entered their car and followed as well. Jamal watched in confusion from the backseat as people came up to the window and shouted, "We love you" and "Top 6". *What the hell is going on?* He wondered. Why were these people calling them Top 6? None of it made sense.

"Can you believe this shit?" Detective McCoy asked as he watched the people crowd the two cars. "These people love them"

"It's pitiful," said 100% as he snapped more pictures. "Niggers with this much support behind them is a problem," he continued. "It's like these fucking Haitians took the city from us"

"Tell me about it," said McCoy. "Why you think they're calling them Top 6"

"People take the news from the newspaper and the news from the streets and make it one," said 100%. "Link a couple crimes the South Side Boys did to some hood celebrities, like Top 6 and magic, we have a gang"

"Not to mention bigger bonuses," McCoy laughed. "Maybe now I could buy that boat I wanted huh?"

Mean while the North Side boys were just arriving to the church in a green Honda Accord with dark tents. They were all dressed in black and both Man Man and Travis had choppers while Buck drove as usual. They parked at the side of the rode and watched the two cars leave the parking lot. "These niggas think they stars huh," Travis chuckled in the backseat as he held his AK–47 assault rifle. The hate he had for the Haitians was more then you could image. He couldn't wait to kill. The anticipation that was built up inside him had Travis rocking back and forth like a mental patent. He rapidly tapped his feet on the floor to relive his anxiousness. As they pulled off behind the long line of cars that now followed the hearse, Buck spotted 100% and McCoy pulling off as well in a white Crown Victoria.

"Damn ya'll look," said Buck as the officers rode past them. "Ain't that 100% bitch ass?"

"Yeah that's him and McCoy," said Man Man. "I told ya'll he was going to be out here"

"Who gives a fuck?" Travis shouted. "We doing this and that's it no questions about it!"

The A street Cemetery was where mostly every one from the hood was buried. The short ride there felt like miles because of the long line of cars that followed the hearse. The amount of people that were waiting for the arrival of the hearse was remarkable. It was like the entire hood was there to pay their respects. The Paul barriers were followed to Ronny's final resting spot by the immediate family. Behind them Jamal and the others were followed by a large crowd of men, woman, and children. The North Side Boys parked across the street and watched as the Paul barriers placed the casket on the restrains above the hole where it was suppose to be lowered. 100%

and McCoy parked their car and stood watch from a close distant as the ceremony continued.

"You sure you still want to do this?" Buck asked as Travis and Man Man put on there ski mask. "Them crackas right there"

"Hey what I said huh?" Travis asked as he checked his clip. "You just worry bout driving this car," he ordered. "These niggas killed my sister so they got to feel my pain!" He said. "Now let's go . . . move this shit!"

The preacher began to say a prayer when he was interrupted by the sounds of screeching tires and a loud car horn. When everyone turned around they saw a green car speeding down the road that divided the grave yard into sections. "Who the fuck is that?" 100% asked using his hand to block the sun so he could see further. Jamal and the others looked at one another in confusion, wondering what was going on. When the car stopped a couple yards away from where they were, the doors opened and both Travis and Man Man jumped out and opened fire with their automatic weapons as they walked closer to the gravesite. A stampede erupted as shots rang through the air. Bullets ripped through people as if they were paper. Jamal and the others sought safety behind nearby grave stones as they returned fire with their hand guns. 100% and McCoy hid behind grave stones as well as they called for back up.

Jamal could hear the bullets zipping past his head as he took cover. Portions of rock and marble were knocked off the grave stone that shield him by the second. The amount of deaths and injuries that were done by the time both Travis and Man Man finished their magazines was horrendous. Instead of running back to the car like Man Man, Travis ran and took cover behind a nearby gravestone and began to exchange clips. In his mind the gunfight was far from over. "Let's go nigga!" Man Man shouted as he dodged rounds from the Haitian's guns all the way to the car. When Travis was fully reloaded, he stood up and opened fire again ceasing the Haitians from shooting. Their hand guns were know match for Travis's high powered weapon. A squad car that arrived to the scene early drove full speed towards them. When seeing the car, Travis aimed his aggression towards it. The rounds from his AK–47 caused the car to swerve and crash into a grave stone. Now knowing police was near, Travis ran and jumped into the already moving car as Buck sped off.

"Let's get these nigga!" Ken shouted as they all ran to his vehicle. "Get the choppa . . . Get the choppa!"

When they made it to the Dodge Charger, Fat grabbed Ken's SK from the trunk before jumping in the passenger seat. Ken smashed the gas paddle as he made a u-turn causing his tires to scream. "Suspects going north bound!" 100% shouted into his walky-talky as he watched the Haitians pursue the Honda in the distant. Ken's hemi equipped engine roared, enabling him to hit a 100mph in seconds. "Catch em fo' they hit the I!" Fat shouted as he pointed at the Honda getting into the turning lane towards the interstate. Buck tremendously reduced his speed, due to the on coming traffic, allowing the Haitians to close in on them. "Run the light they coming!" Man Man shouted as he looked in the passenger side mirror. By the time Buck was able to run the red light, Ken was right on his ass. Ken's aggressive turn in the lane caused cars to swerve in efforts to avoid collusion. Both cars made it onto the interstate seconds behind each other.

Being that it was an early Sunday morning, traffic was light so both cars zoomed down the straight away. Shit was serious and what Fat Zoe had in mind next was on some Young Jeezy shit. "Yo unlock the windows!" Fat said before grabbing the SK and climbing out the window. His long dreads flapped in the wind as he sat on the window frame and opened fire shattering the Honda's back window. People looked on in disbelief as the two cars flashed past them. "Oh shit these Haitians crazy!" Buck shouted as they all ducked down in there seats for cover. Travis who was in the backseat put the barrel of his AK-47 out the window without looking and fired. The bullets from his gun hit the front of Ken's car shattering both his head lights.

Fat Zoe's heavy fire cause Buck to swerve from left to right to try and dodge the rounds. In a split second decision, Buck jerked the stirring wheel and cut across the interstate. Cars honked and hit their breaks as the Honda cut them off. "Yo switch lanes bro!" Fat shouted after climbing back in the car. As Ken maneuvered into the lane next to the Honda, Jamal put his window down so he could fire at the car as well.

"They catching up dawg!" Buck said as he looked in his driver side mirror. "What to do?"

"Bash they ass!" Travis shouted. "Knock em' off the road!"

When Ken pulled up next to the Honda, Buck did as he was ordered and rammed his car into the side of the Dodge Charger. Ken's car swerved into the next lane due to the impact. Furious, Ken jerked the steering wheel to the left and bashed his car into the Honda. Then almost simultaneously both divers jerked their steering wheel and bashed the side of their cars into each other. The Forest Hill exit was approaching fast and both cars were riding side by side as one. In Ken's lane a semi truck was ahead of him so he had a decision to make and fast. It was either rub metal with the Honda until he crashes into the back of a semi truck or get the fuck out the way and let the North Side Boys get away. "Watch out for the truck man!" Jamal shouted form the backseat. At that moment, Ken jerked the wheel and missed the semi truck by inches, allowing the North Side Boys to escape through the exit.

"Damn, damn, damn!" Ken cursed as he hit the steering wheel. "They got away!"

❡   ❡   ❡

Back at the grave yard the aftermath was "devastating," said a News reporter as she pointed to the spot where the shooting took place. CSI specialists were placing yellow markers by the many bullet shells. Ambulances were tending to the injured as police placed white sheets over the dead. 100% stood next to Ronny's casket as he shook his head at what he just witnessed. A shootout at a funeral and both suspects got away . . . the Captain was sure to have his head for this one. He put an ABP out for the South Side Boys so he could stick them with charges, if he was lucky.

"So is this what you meant by them killing the Haitians?" Detective McCoy asked sarcastically while walking up to 100%. "I told you it was a bad idea"

"Shut the fuck up!" 100% said grabbing McCoy's vest to pull him closer. "You don't tell nobody bout this understood?"

"Take it easy man!" McCoy said pushing the detective off him and then adjusting his uniform. "Who the hell am I going to tell?" He asked. "I'm in this with you"

"I'm sorry man," 100% apologized. "It's just the Captain is going to kill me for this"

"I know dude," said McCoy. "He ain't going to be happy and that's for sure"

◦   ◦   ◦

After the chase Jamal and the other retreated to the studio. Never in their life have they all been this furious. "We never even expect it!" Fat Zoe shouted as he put away the chopper in the attic. Jamal sat on the couch with his head in his hands as the rest of them argued amongst them self. It was like he was torn between love and hate. Never in his life has he been so mad but the love for his family had him reluctant to retaliate. Something had to be done in the name of not only Ronny but all the Haitians that were killed at the funeral. The actions of the North Side Boys, was the last straw.

In need of some fresh air, Jamal stood up and walked towards the door. Just as he reached for the door knob SWAT team kicked in door and rushed inside. "Get on the ground!" They shouted as the Haitians did as they were instructed. The officers handcuffed them then combed the area. When determining the premises was clear, they began their search for guns. Jamal prayed they didn't find the SK in attic. If that was recovered he would surly spend the rest of his life in prison. When the search was over they found four guns and an ounce of marijuana. After putting the evidence in plastic bags they carried the Zoes off in the patty wagon, and took them to the precinct where someone was awaiting their arrival.

Q   Q   Q

The ride back to the prescient was the longest ever. 100% could imagine the Captain screaming at the top of his lungs as him and Detective McCoy exited the car. All eyes were on 100% when he walked inside the busy Police department. He could hear the Captain inside his office screaming into his phone about the shoot out at the funeral, so 100% knew he was in trouble.

"Wow he sounds mad," McCoy joked. "I wouldn't want to be in your shoes right now"

"Ha, ha, ha" said 100%. "Thanks for your support"

"Stacks get the fuck in here!" The Captain shouted before storming back in his office and slamming the door.

"Good luck," said McCoy as he padded him on the shoulder. "I'm here for you"

"Up yours," said 100% as he walked towards the Captain's office.

The Captain was a short fat white man, with a temper problem. The stress of being head of the Lake Worth Police Department for ten years had him smoking cigarettes by the carton. The gang violence in the city had him over the edge. The mayor was breathing down his neck about it and now that the Feds were in town, he was on 100%'s ass to put an end to it and take down The South Side Boys.

"I'm getting calls every five minutes about this," said The Captain as he smoked a Newport behind his desk. "How in God's name do you let a shoot out happen in the middle of a funeral?"

"Captain they had AK-47's," 100% explained. "What you wanted me to do get shot?"

"No what I want you to do is your job!" The Captain shouted. "These Haitians are taking over the city and the mayor wants results!"

"With all due respect sir I am doing my job," said 100%. "I got an ABP out on the South Side Boys right now"

"For what?" The Captain asked. "They were the victims and everybody that was there is going to testify to that," he informed them. "Now listen the District attorney given me the go head to indict these asshole under the RICO act along with Top 6"

"Oh yeah about that," said 100%. "Why Top 6?"

"I don't know, too many deaths at their concerts, strong fan base, who cares, we just need to help make it stick," said the Captain. "The Feds will be assisting us with the take down as well and I'm appointing you in charge of the operation," he said. "We need informants and photos . . . take all the overtime you need because a lot of money is at stake here"

"Hey Stacks," said Detective McCoy entering the office. "Their here"

"Okay good," said 100%. "I'll be there in a second"

"No no go now," said The Captain. "I want these Haitians off my streets and out of my city"

"Okay Captain I'm right on it," said 100% as he started for the door.

"Oh yeah and Stacks," said The Captain before 100% walked out. "If you fuck this one up, you can kiss your job good bye"

100% couldn't believe it. His prayers were finally begin answered. The RICO act would put the South Side Boys away for a long time and save his job. It was like killing two birds with one stone. *"Maybe I'll get a promotion for this,"* he thought to him self as he walked towards the department's holding cells. Hitting a small city like Lake Worth with the RICO act would make national news for sure.

After the raid, the Haitians were each caged in one man holding cells. They were not yet informed what their charges were and they all were out raged except for Jamal. He sat in his cell calmly as the others cursed at an officer who was doing paper work at his desk. Unlike the others he felt like there was no need to be mad since they had nothing on them and if they did, bond wouldn't be an issue for none of them. Instead he sat there and waited for the real reason they were here and when it arrived Jamal took a deep breath.

"Looks like I finally got the famous South Side Boys right where I want em' huh?" 100% asked as he looked into each of the men's cells. "Trust me when I say you niggers days are numbered"

"Man fuck you cracka you ain't got shit on us," said Fat. "Them niggas came too our funeral and shot at us"

"I clearly understand that Mr. Fatsen," said 100% walking back over to Fat's cell. "But I witnessed you shooting back and we found guns in your possession"

"Okay I don't give a fuck what you witnessed!" Fat Zoe said. "We the motherfucking victims"

"Bull shit ya'll deserved what happened out there," 100% snapped. "You immigrants come to the United States and cause turmoil for everyone, there's less jobs and more taxes . . . ya'll taking up space," he explained. "More of you pieces of shit should have gotten killed at that funeral if you ask me!"

It wasn't surprising to Jamal that the land of the free could have such a racist person like 100% to enforce its laws. It was a reality that his experienced his whole life, but the comments about the funeral broke his silence. The fact that innocent people died today and 100% was only worried about his personal agenda outraged the young man.

"You as crooked as they come man," said Jamal still sitting on the bench in his cell. "You might as well take off that badge and put a white sheet over your head"

"Who's that?" 100% knowingly asked as he walked back over to Jamal's cell. "Is that the leader speaking?"

"Naw ain't no leaders over here," said Jamal. "You crackas call us threats to society when in all actuality ya'll treats to ya'll yourselves," he informed him. "Because a man has felon's its harder for him to achieve what the next man has and because the color of my skin I was born with a strike against me," he continued. "You cracks think ya'll can keep the poor in poverty forever but trust me Detective Stacks . . . ain't no holding us down"

"See you don't know what I know so I'm going to let time reveal the truth," 100% chuckled. "But as of now Mr. Pierre ya'll boys going to the county on some gun charges so sit tight"

"Don't make no difference to me," said Jamal. "We'll be out before the day is over"

"Oh trust me I know," said 100%. "I'm just graining them pockets so when I'm really ready to take you down ya'll cant do shit about it"

As the overly confident detective walked out of the room, Jamal wonder what he had up his sleeve next. Jamal was knee deep in the game and anybody could be a liability at this point. He honestly felt like his time was running out and just hoped he was safely out the country before it expired. As he sat there and thought about 100%'s last words, he heard someone entering the room again. This time it was two officers coming for Fat.

"Officer Stacks wants to speak to you," one of the officers said as he opened the door to Fat Zoe's cell. "Hands behind your back"

"What he wants to talk to me for?" Fat asked as he turned around. "He was just in here"

"I don't know sir," said the officer as he handcuffed Fat. "I'm just doing as I was ordered"

"What the fuck you think that's about?" Troy asked after the officers escorted Fat out the room. "100% just spoke to us"

"I don't know," said Ken from his cell. "He probably trying that police integration bullshit"

Unlike the others Jamal been very weary of Fat for while. To many incidents like the time Jamal and his brother were pulled over when going to see Fat, didn't make sense. It was either 100% thought he could break Fat or this nigga was snitching. Either way Jamal was going to address him about it.

CHAPTER 19

J amal was the first to bond out the county jail at around 8 p.m. that same day. Then he posted everybody else's bond. Since Fat was transferred to the county jail a few hours after the others, he was the last to get his bond posted. After being released, Jamal went home to rest after a long day of drama. As he lay in his bed with Kim in his arms, his phone rang. It was his brother Ken. When he answered his phone he glanced at his alarm clock that read 12:00 a.m.

"What's up bro?" Jamal answered. "What time they let you out?"

"At like eleven," Ken informed him. "The others out too"

"That's wassup," said Jamal. "What about Fat?"

"Yeah he out too," said Ken. "But that's not why I called"

"So wassup then?" Jamal asked. "What happened?"

"I need you to come to Mirage with me," said Ken. "We got to handle something"

"Man is you crazy?" Jamal asked. "After what happened today I don't feel like going to no fucking club"

"Naw man this bout business," said Ken. "Remember when I told you I had twenty stacks on them niggas head?" He reminded him. "Well some stripper hoe who's working there knows where they at"

"G shit bro?" Jamal asked. "How you know it ain't a set up?"

"Naw it ain't no set up trust me," Ken assured him. "I fucks with a bouncer over there and he just called me a few minutes ago to tell me about the hoe," he continued. "Just get up and get ready . . . I'm on the way now"

"Okay then," said Jamal. "Call me when you outside"

Club Mirage was one of the hottest strip clubs in Palm Beach County. The club was always packed on the weekends. When Jamal and Ken arrived, the valet took their car and they made why towards the entrance. The bothers where dressed in black and Ken wore his "South Side Boy" chain, letting every one no who they were. The news of what happened earlier that morning at the funeral had every one cutting their eyes to get a glimpse at them. When they entered the crowed club, Ken looked around for a few seconds then spotted the bouncer who called him, working the VIP entrance, that's when they made way towards him.

Big Zoe was a big ass Haitian who stood 6'7 and weighed 300 pounds. The red shirt he wore like all the other bouncers; looked like it had to be at least a 10x. *"I see why this guys a bouncer,"* Jamal thought to himself after finally making it through the crowded club. Ken and Big Zoe did a little time together in boot camp when they were juveniles. He helped Ken fight some niggas who tried to jump him in there, and ever since then they've been friends. When the girl came to him with information about the whereabouts of Travis and his boys, he had to call Ken and tell him.

"Oh what's up Ken?" Big Zoe asked as he gave him dap. "Long time know see man"

"You know how things go man," said Ken. "This my brother Jay"

"What's up bro?" Big Zoe asked giving him dap as well. "Anything you need in here just holla at me"

"Thanks," said Jamal. "I appreciate that"

"Okay then let's get down to business," said Ken. "Where the girl?"

"She over there," said Big Zoe pointing at the girl giving a guy a lap dance in one of the VIP booths. "The red bone with the blond hair"

"You sure she straight Zoe?" Ken asked as he watched the girl grind on her customer. "I don't wanna kill her ass too"

"Oh yeah she cool," said Big Zoe. "I wouldn't bring nothing to you I though wasn't straight"

"That's the play then," said Ken. "Lets go and holla"

When they made it the VIP booth, Big Zoe pulled the girl off her costumer and told him to take a hike. He started to protest but changed his mind when noticing how big the bouncer was. He slowly made way past them then walked off.

"Big Zoe how you gon' size me like that?" The stripper asked. "That's my motherfuckin' money"

"Fuck that nigga," said Big Zoe. "These the guys who wanted to talk to you," he told her. "And don't forget to break me off either"

"Whateva nigga I told you I got you," said the stripper. "You just better make sure they got the 20 stacks"

"Man these niggas bout business," he informed her while spotting someone trying to sneak in VIP. "Ima let ya'll talk . . . I got to handle this"

After Big Zoe rushed off the three started to conduct business. "So what you got for me?" Ken asked. "Where them niggas hiding at?"

"Hold on lil' daddy . . . slow your roll," the stripper told him as she picked up the rest of her ones off the ground. "How I know you niggas ain't gon' buck me on my 20 grand?"

"Man don't size me hoe . . . I get money," said Ken pulling two bankrolls from his pockets and tossing them at the stripper. "Now where them niggas at?"

"Damn ya'll niggas really serious huh?" She asked looking at the money in disbelief. "They out west Boynton at the motel 6"

"Okay so how we know this ain't a set up?" Jamal asked. "Why should we believe you?"

"Because they took all my shit and that nigga Travis put a fucking gun in my mouth" she continued. "I hope ya'll fucking kill them motherfuckas"

"Let us worry about that," said Ken as he walked off. "Let's go Jay"

After waiting for the valet to retrieve the car, they both entered and rode off. The news the stripper gave them had Jamal anxious for revenge but he didn't know what the next step was. Ken was driving in silence as he listened to music. Jamal reached for the radio to put the volume down.

"So what's next?" He asked. "What we do now?"

"What you mean?" Ken asked. "We get them niggas back"

"I know that," said Jamal. "But how . . . when?"

"Tonight nigga," said Ken. "I don't want them niggas to get smart and peal," he continued. "Fat and the others are already at the studio waiting for us"

"Shit I'm down," said Jamal. "But you think it's a good idea bringing Fat?" Jamal asked. "That nigga suspect to me"

"Man you still on that shit bro?" Ken asked. "I told you that snitching shit ain't in Fat's blood," he told him. "That nigga one hundred all round the broad trust me"

"Aight then," said Jamal turning his head to look out the window. "Whateva you say"

When the two arrived, Jamal saw Troy's black Chevy Tahoe parked in the drive way but didn't recognize the red Buick with dark tents. Obviously that had to be the car they were using to do the hit Jamal thought. When they walked inside the studio, Troy and Fat were smoking a joint as they loaded up their choppers. They were dressed in all black and had Haitians flags wrapped around their necks. It was clearly time for war and they knew it. Ken walked over to his desk to grab his things as Jamal stood next to the booth and stared at Fat. He just couldn't get that strange feeling about him out his gut.

"Here nigga," said Ken as he handed Jamal a gun and Haitian flag. "Fat and Troy gon' tote the choppas"

"You think that's a good idea?" Jamal asked as he tied the flag around his neck. "I mean we can't trust to many niggas,"

"What you talking about," asked Fat in an offensive tone. "You got something to say?"

"Nigga I don't bite my tough," said Jamal. "I think you a snitch!"

"Bitch I'm far from a snitch!" Fat shouted tossing his weapon on the couch. "And you betta remember that shit"

"Nigga all I remember is how many times 100% call you in for questioning!" Jamal shouted. "For all I know you could be a pussy ass informant!"

Jamal words caused Fat Zoe to rush him and swing. Jamal duck and wrapped his arms around the heavy set man. They bear hugged each until Ken and Troy finally pulled them apart. Jamal tried to grab his gun from his whist line but Ken stopped him by grabbing his hand and taking it from him.

"What the fuck you doing!" Ken shouted after push Jamal into the corner. "Ya'll motherfuckas gon' let these pussy ass crackas get in between us?"

"Man that's him!" Fat shouted as Troy tried to control him. "Ain't no fucking snitch in me bro . . . I know the game!"

"Yeah whatever nigga!" Jamal shouted as he tried to rush Fat. "You ain't fooling me bro!"

"Man shut up!" Ken said pushing Jamal back into the corner. "I told you that nigga ain't on that shit!"

"You better tell him again Ken," said Fat. "Before I handle his ass!"

"Man shut the fuck up Fat!" Ken shouted as he pointed at him. "He's as much your brother as he is mine!" He told him. "Ya'll niggas need to make up right now fo' we do this!"

Since they both were reluctant to make the first move, Ken grabbed Jamal by the shoulder and shoved him. Troy did the same to Fat as well. The two gave each other dap and vaguely apologized. Jamal just didn't trust Fat anymore but he wanted Travis and his boys so bad that he decided to go along with the hit; but if anything went wrong, Fat was sure to meet an early grave and Jamal promised that to his self.

Q   Q   Q

After the hit at the funeral, the North Side Boys spent the rest of the day in the motel. Travis sat in silence in front of the television with his vest on and holding his AK. He knew the South Side Boys would retaliate sooner or later and when they did he would be ready. So many thoughts were running thorough his head but the one that kept repeating it's self was the reality that Shay was really dead. Know matter how many times he tried to justify it, he still felt like it was his fault. The hit at the funeral only healed his pain momentarily.

"You think that nigga gon' be okay?" Buck asked Man as they walked to get ice for the bottle of Hennessey in their room. "He's been seating in front of that T.V. all day"

"I don't know man," said Man Man. "That nigga liable to do anything"

"Shit . . . you ain't lying," said Buck as he put his bucket in the ice machine. "What about you dawg?" He asked. "How you taking the whole situation?"

"It's killing me bro," he said trying to really sound sincere. "I still can't believe Shay gone"

"Me neither bro," Buck said as they left the ice machine. "If you ever need me dawg just holla"

"That's real nigga shit," said Man Man as they walked back to their room. "I appreciate it"

Jamal and the others rode in silence to motel 6. Death was on everybody's mind. Ken was the driver, Jamal rode shotgun and the two gunmen Troy and Fat Zoe were in the back seat. Jamal glanced at Fat a couple times through the rearview mirror because it was like he could feel Fat staring at him. They both were still angry about the altercation from earlier but right now revenging their friends' death was the agenda.

When they pulled into the motel 6 entrance, Jamal's heart begin to race. "Their room should be towards the back," said Ken as everyone cocked their guns. As they crept through the parking lot, they spotted Buck and Man Man walking back to their room. "There them niggas go right there," said Troy as they all pulled their Haitian flags from around their necks to cover their faces. Buck and Man Man were still in deep conversation and didn't even notice the Buick creeping up behind them. When they made it to their room door, Man Man glanced at the strange vehicle while Buck searched for the room key with his free hand, since he was holding the ice bucket. Thinking nothing of it, Man Man turned his attention back to Buck who was still going through his pockets.

"Damn nigga where the key at?" Man Man asked. "You just had it"

"I don't know bro," said Buck. "Knock on the door so Travis can open up"

While Man Man knocked on the door, Ken pulled up behind them. When both Man Man and Buck realized what was about to happen next it was too late. Fat opened the back seat door that was facing the building and stepped before opening fire. Man Man leaped to the ground for safety as the multiple rounds from Fat's choppa nailed Buck to the wall. Paralyzed in fear, Man Man watched as his friend's body slid down the wall leaving a trail of blood. When the gunman with a Haitian flag over his face pointed the gun at Man Man, Travis kicked the door open and fired his AK. Taking this as a cue to get away, Man Man stood up and ran for safety. Fat jumped into the back seat of the car as Ken and Jamal ducked down in their seats for cover. Troy on the other hand, stepped out of the other side of the vehicle and returned fire, catching Travis in the chest multiple times, sending him flying back into the room. Good thing for Travis he was warring a vest.

When noticing Man Man making a run for it, Troy took off after him while firing. Man Man made it around the corner before any of the rounds could hit him. He ran and hid behind a car as Troy combed the area for him. "*Damn I wish I had my gun*," he thought to himself as the gunman got closer. When he peaked over the hood of the car, he watched as Troy finished searching behind a car that was only a few yards away from the one he was behind. Not wanting to be gunned down where he sat, Man Man made a run for it. Seeing his prey, Troy aimed and fired. One of the many bullets from his high powered weapon knocked a chunk of Man Man's thigh off, sending him crashing to the ground.

When the Buick came around the corner, Jamal watched as Troy walked towards Man Man who was now dragging himself on the ground to get away. "Please don't kill me," Man Man begged as Troy stood over him and pointed his gun. So much rage and anger was built inside Troy. The loss of his best friend was something he would have to live with for the rest of his life. Killing Man Man wouldn't change that but it would surely help him cope with it. As he got ready to pull the trigger, Travis came flying around the corner in a blue Toyota. Doing about 60 mph he crashed into the back of the Buick. The momentum of the impact knocked the Buick forward, flipping Troy and sending him flying into the windshield and then falling to the ground. Fat exited the backseat and opened fire at the Toyota as Jamal ran to go help Troy. Travis shifted into reverse and smashed the gas as he ducked down in the driver seat. The back of the Toyota crashed into a parked car. When Jamal finally got Troy into the backseat, Fat ceased fire and jumped into the backseat as well before they sped off.

Travis who was still in the car shifted back into drive after the Zoes rode off. He started to chase after them but noticed Man Man lying helplessly on the ground. He stopped as he rolled down his window. "Help me Trav," said Man Man as he reached his hand out. Something inside Travis told him not to help. Something told him to go about his business but being that they were tight, he went against his feelings. He stepped out the car and helped Man Man into the backseat of the Toyota then sped off.

"Yo man get me to a hospital," he begged Travis. "Ima bleed to death"

"I ain't got time for that!" Travis shouted. "I got to find out where they went!"

"Come on Trav they gone man . . . I'm bout to die," Man Man cried. "I need help dawg"

Travis looked in the rearview mirror to see how bad Man Man was wounded. The backseat was drenched in blood. "You keep your mouth shut about this!" Travis shouted as he made a U–turn for the Hospital. When they finally arrived he pulled over in the emergency driveway and dragged Man Man out the vehicle. "Keep your mouth shut you heard me!" Travis said again before getting back into the car and speeding off.

❡   ❡   ❡

After the hit, the Zoes went back to the studio and waited for sunlight before going to their homes. They made plans to go see Spoon in the hospital later and tell him the good news. When Jamal made it home, he crept into the room careful not to wake Kim. He grabbed his towel from the closet and went into the shower. He needed to wash the stench of death off him. As the steaming water dripped over his body he promised himself the killing was over. Revenging Ronny's death was the ending cap. All he had to do now was seal the deal with Dread and take his family to freedom.

CHAPTER 20

L ater that morning 100% was just arriving to his office. Operation "6 Under" was the only thing on his mind. This was the biggest case of his carrier and he couldn't mess up his chance. As he stood in front of his diagram he scratched his head and wondered how he could possibly pull this one off. The South Side Boys had love in the community and in the streets as well, but most importantly the loyalty amongst them was strong. He was determined not to let that stop him in his quest to take them down. If he had to play dirty then so be it.

Q   Q   Q

That afternoon Jamal and the others went to go see Spoon. Jamal and Fat still had some hostility towards each other since the altercation and weren't talking. They just shot each other a few mean mugs here and there. None of them noticed 100% and McCoy observing them from a distance in their parked car as they walked in the hospital.

"So you really think we could get him to snitch?" McCoy asked. "I mean he's loyal"

"For his sake he better snitch," said 100%. "If he knows what's good for him"

Spoon was lying in his bed watching television when the Zoes walked into his room. He's been waiting in anticipation for their arrival. He knew the hit went down but he didn't know the outcome. He hoped all the North Side Boys got what they deserved especially Travis.

"So what's up?" Spoon asked. "Ya'll did that?

"Yeah we hit em up," said Ken. "We got Buck and hit Man Man but Travis got away"

"Damn," Spoon said in disappointment. "That's the main nigga I wanted"

"I know but don't worry," said Troy. "We still looking for em"

"I ain't worried," said Spoon. "I already know his days are numbered?"

Ken and Troy further explained how the hit went down to Spoon and how Travis got away. In the middle of the conversation Spoon glanced at Jamal and Fat because they were unusually quite. He could sense the tension between them as they both stood on opposite sides of the room like the other was contagious. Inquiring about the beef was the last thing Spoon should have done.

"What's up with ya'll two?" Spoon asked. "Ya'll beefin?"

"Naw it ain't nothing," said Jamal as he crossed his arms. "It's just a stench in the air"

"Ken get your brother," Fat warned. "Ima hurt em"

"Hurt who?" Jamal snapped. "What you wanna do Fat?"

"Ya'll tighten up man?" Ken intervened. "Don't start this shit again!"

"What that hell?" Spoon wondered. "What's going on?"

"The click ain't as tight as we thought it was," Jamal informed him. "That nigga working!"

"You got me fucked up nigga!" Fat shouted. "I ain't neva been a snitch!"

"Whateva nigga!" Jamal said. "Tell that to 100%"

"Jamal shut the fuck up!" Ken shouted. "You don't really know if Fat snitching or not"

"You know what Ken it's cool," said Fat before starting to walk out the room. "I'm out dawg . . . he ain't got to worry bout me no more"

"Fat hold on," said Ken as Fat moved away from his reach. "You see bro that's that fuck shit I'm talking about"

"Man fuck him!" Jamal snapped. "We don't need him"

Fat was outraged. Never in his life has he been accused of snitching and for Jamal to be the one pointing the finger was an insult to injury. He went outside to calm down and get some fresh air. "There goes our perk," said McCoy as they watched Fat pace back and forth a few times before walking off to go stand by the car. On his way to the vehicle, the detectives drove up and cut in front of him, stopping Fat in his tracks.

"Get on the ground!" The Detectives shouted while hopping out with their guns drawn. "Get on the ground!"

"What the fuck!" Fat Zoe yelled failing to comply with the detectives commands. "I ain't do shit!"

Fat Zoe began to resist when McCoy tired to grab his arm. As they tussled 100% quickly placed his gun back in his holster before joining. They both had a hard time restraining the man before finally getting him face down on the ground and handcuffing him. When the detectives picked Fat up, he still resisted so 100% gave him a solid punch to the ribs, knocking the wind out of him. Fat fell to one knee gasping for air before the detectives dragged him to the car and tossed him in the backseat.

Jamal and the others were still inside talking. They couldn't believe that Fat was working but Jamal mind was made up. No matter how much they pleaded with him he just wouldn't budge. Ken was mad at his little brother's stubbornness but blood is thicker then water . . . so you know how that goes.

When they left the Hospital Ken was happy Fat wasn't at the car waiting. He just didn't feel like braking up another fight. As he drove he glanced at his brother through the rearview mirror and shook his head. Ronny was dead, Jamal was moving to Haiti and now this. The click was falling apart and he hated it, his pride just wouldn't let him speak on it.

"You really think Fat a snitch?" Troy asked before hitting the joint. "I mean that nigga knows a lot"

"Damn straight I do," said Jamal. "It's too many coincidences"

"So what we gon' do?" Troy asked. "This shit serious"

"I don't know man," said Jamal. "But I ain't letting no one stopping me from going to Haiti," he continued. "So if we got to shut em' up then—"

"Hold the fuck up . . . that's Fat ya'll talking about man!" Ken interrupted them. "He's one of us and until you got proof he really working . . . ya'll ain't doing shit!"

No one protested because deep down inside they didn't want to believe it either. Instead they just drove in silence. One of they own, working with these pussy ass crackas was just not comprehensible. They've known each other all of their lives and the loyalty between them was too strong to fall prey, but sometimes that's just how it was. Your own blood would betray you in these streets and the three of them know that all to well. If strong enough evidence was ever found against Fat then the game was just going to have to be played the right way. Snitches get stitches but in Palm Beach they get killed!

Q   Q   Q

"Man where the fuck ya'll taking me?" Fat asked from the backseat. "The police station is in Lake Worth"

"Shut the fuck up," said 100%. "You'll find out soon enough!"

"Man I ain't do shit!" He told them. "Ya'll ain't even tell me why I'm under arrest"

"Because your not," said Detective McCoy. "You're going to tell us what we want to know," he continued. "One way or the other"

"Man If I ain't under arrest then let me go!" Fat Zoe shouted. "I keep telling you crackas I ain't no motherfuckin snitch!"

"I'll tell you what," said 100%. "You better think of something to tell us before we get to where we going," he threatened him. "Or you ain't going to like what we have in store for you"

The Detectives took Fat Zoe to the woods in a discreet area on the B line. Fat looked around in confusion wondering what the fuck they could possibly be doing out there. What ever it was, the knot in Fat Zoe's stomach told him it couldn't be good. They slowly drove down a dirt road for a few miles before stepping out. McCoy opened the back door and dragged Fat out the car by his arm. He then shoved him and told him to walk. When Fat protest he pulled out his gun and told him to walk again. Not wanting to be shot Fat did as he was ordered. They walked in silence a few miles into the woods before detective McCoy hit him in the back of the head with his gun. Fat who was still handcuffed grunted in pain as he fell to his knees. Then 100% gave him a stiff right hook knocking him to his side before they both proceeded to kick the defenseless young man in his midsection. After a few minutes of brutality, they helped Fat up to his knees.

"So Mr. Fatsen," 100% began crouching down to Fat Zoe's level. "Are you going to tell us what we want to know or what?"

"You crackas ain't shit," said Fat looking the detective in the eyes. "Ya'll got me in the middle of woods to do what . . . kill me if I don't snitch?" He chuckled. "Ain't no tears in my eyes or fear in my heart," he told them. "So you'll gon' have to do what ya'll got to"

"You niggers fucking amaze me," 100% confessed. "You're too stupid to see you can't win," he said. "Those are my street and if you lil' fucks think I'm going to sit back and let ya'll run free; you got another thing coming," he continued. "I'm going to give you one more chance," 100% told him. "Tell me something . . . anything and I will make sure you stay free"

Fat Zoe glanced at detective McCoy before locking his eyes back on 100%. It's a shame it had to end like this but snitching wasn't him in fact, it never crossed his mind. Instead Fat Zoe gathered all the saliva in his mouth and spit in 100%'s face. "Fuck you!" He said as the saliva hung from the detective nose. Keeping his composer 100% slowly whipped the spit from his face with his handkerchief.

"Okay then have it your way," he chuckled. "Give me the gun"

Detective McCoy walked over and handed 100% the gun. "You know even if you did snitch I was going to kill you anyway," he told the young man as he cocked the weapon. "I just don't like you Haitian fucker"

"Well that's too bad," said Fat Zoe looking down the barrel of the gun. "Cause you can't kill us all"

"That's true but I can try," said 100%. "I can defiantly try"

Right then and there 100% pulled the trigger, shooting Fat Zoe in the face. He died before his body even hit the floor. 100% and McCoy looked at each other in satisfaction as Fat's body lay lifelessly on the ground. Kidnapping, police brutality and murder was nothing new in their carriers. The sad part about it was the odds of them getting caught, was almost zero to none.

CHAPTER 21

I t's been two days, and the others have yet
to hear from Fat Zoe. Ken called his phone,
went to his house, asked around about him but still no Fat. He was
the only one that was really worried about his friend being missing,
since the others had it in their minds that Fat Zoe was really a snitch
and probably decided to high tail it out the hood before anybody
else found out. Jamal decided not to let the whole Fat Zoe ordeal
bother him, because right now he had more important things to
worry about. Today was the day he was supposed to set up a meeting
spot with Dread. As he rode in the backseat of Troy's Tahoe while
Ken rode shotgun, Jamal dialed the Jamaican's number.

"Jamal mon," Dread answered. "Wha gwon?"

"Just chilling man," said Jamal. "You already no why I'm
calling"

"Yeah mon," said Dread. "Everything cool on my end ya
know"

"Good . . . same thing over here too," said Jamal. "Meet me
behind the cemetery in my hood Friday 10a.m. sharp"

"No problem mon," said Dread. "Link me"

　　　◦　　　◦　　　◦

That same morning 100% was sitting at his desk drinking coffee. Taking down the South Side Boys had him on the edge. He thought he could break Fat Zoe but that proved otherwise. 100% feared his days as a law enforcement officer were nearing an end, until Detective McCoy walked into his office.

"Hey Stacks you wont believe this one," said McCoy. "The DNA results came back from forensics on the Lashala Stubbs case"

"Lashala Stubbs . . . Stubbs," 100% tried to remember. "Oh yeah, you mean Travis' Stubbs sister"

"Yeah and you wont believe whose DNA we got," said McCoy. "Emanuel AKA Man Man"

"Wow isn't he an NSB member too," said 100%. "You think he killed her?"

"Why else would his dreadlocks be on the bathroom floor unless the victim pulled them out?" McCoy asked him. "That's the only explanation"

"Well we need him off the street," said 100%. "Do we have an ABP out on him?"

"No need for that he's in the hospital," said McCoy. "Apparently he suffered a gun shot wounds to the leg"

"I'm willing to bet them Haitians had something to do with it," said 100% while standing up then grabbing his coat from the back of his chair. "Maybe a murder rap will get him to talk huh?"

"You better hope so," said McCoy as he followed 100% out the door. "Or you can kiss your job goodbye"

The Detectives headed towards the hospital where Man Man was being treated. Man Man being responsible for Shay's death was valuable information for 100%'s case. This was the leverage he needed to put the RICO act into effect. He knew the North Side and the South Side Boys were rival gangs so maybe Man Man wouldn't be to stubborn to talk when presented with a murder rap.

When they arrived to the hospital the receptionist directed them to Man Man's room. As they walked down the hallway, 100% could feel his blood pumping. What he needed to take down the infamous South Side Boys was only a few doors away. When they walked in, Man Man was lying in his bed watching TV. His leg was wrapped up and his arm was hooked up to an IV. When he noticed the familiar Detectives he sucked his teeth.

"Well were happy to see you too," said 100% in sarcastic tone. "How are you doing?"

"Worse now that ya'll here," said Man Man. "What ya'll want?"

"We want some answers," said 100%. "Plan and simple"

"Well I don't know shit," said Man Man. "I already told the other officers that"

"You see Man Man," 100% began. "I wouldn't leave Lake Worth to come here unless I really had something," said 100% before tossing a zip lock bag with dreads inside it onto the bed. "These look familiar?"

"What's that?" Man Man asked feeling like his heart was now inside his throat.

"I think you know exactly what that is," said 100% walking closer to his bed. "We found these dreadlocks at a crime scene," he informed him. "You know a Lasahla Stubbs?"

"Yeah I know her," said Man Man. "But what her death got to do with me?"

"Come on Emanuel don't play stupid with me!" 100% said grabbing a fist full of Man Man's dreads. "You got a fucking patch in your hair where those dreadlocks in the bag use to be!" He said before letting go of his hair as he shoved him. "If I were you I would corporate and fast . . . that is if you ever want to see day light again"

100% had Man Man backed into a corner and he knew it, the tears rolling down his cheek made it evident. Man Man looked out the window to hide the defeat in his eyes. Not so much the fact that he was caught was the reason why he was so emotional, but the agony of killing his true love was eating him up inside and he had to release it. He had to tell someone before it killed him or worst Travis killed him; in which he will surly do when finding out.

"I loved her," said Man in a weak voice. "I didn't mean to do it . . . I just couldn't stop"

"I understand that's why I'm willing to help you," 100% lied. "But if you don't tell me what I need to know then I can't do anything"

"What's in it for me?" Man Man asked.

"I'll see to it that you'll get the least possible sentence," 100% lied. "You have my word"

"What about protective custody?" Man Man asked. "I won't to be kept away from Travis while I'm locked up"

"We can do that too," said 100%. "Whatever you want"

"Okay," Man Man agreed. "I'll do it"

Those words brought joy to 100% heart. After Man Man signed a few papers, Detective McCoy placed a tape recorder on the table. "Talk loud and clearly," he said before pressing play. Man Man took a deep breath before he began. He told the Detectives everything they wanted to know and more. He told them about Ray Ray's, Buck's, and Ronny's death. He also told the detectives about other shootouts and how the Zoes had all the drugs. He gave them enough information to take the South Side Boys down forever. When it was over, a uniformed officer came in and read Man Man his rights as he handcuffed him to the bed railing. "You're doing the right thing Emanuel," said 100% before walking out the door. Man Man couldn't keep himself from crying, his life was over.

When the Detectives made it back to the precinct, 100% rushed into the Captains office. To his convenience the Captain and District Attorney were having a meeting when he walked in. After he played the entire tape for them, they both congratulated 100% on his excellent police work. The DA rushed back to his office to file chargers against both gangs. 100% was on the way to finishing the biggest case of his career.

CHAPTER 22

Travis spent the past couple of days in a motel located on Federal, south side Lake Worth. It was 7:00 a.m. in the morning and he hasn't eaten or slept scenes the incident at the motel. Instead he listened to 2 Pac's album "Me Against The World" as he sat at a glass table with his vest on and AK-47 in his lap, contemplating suicide. He also had a couple of handguns and a mountain of cocaine on the table. He buried his face into the cocaine and took another sniff. When he came up for air he had residue on his nose and chin. He then grabbed the bottle of Hennessey by his chair and placed it to his mouth and took another drink. In his mind he had nothing to live for. Ms. Stubbs hated him, Ray and Buck were dead and to top it off, he blamed the death off his only sister on his self.

"Man Fuck it!" He said grabbing his .9mm from the table. He looked at it for a second then place it to his temple. "Forgive me Shay," he said as tears began to roll down his cheek. As he got ready to pull the trigger, he heard a loud voice over a blow horn. "Travis Stubbs come out with your hands up!" Travis stood up with his AK in his had and ran to the window. When he looked outside, he saw 100% on his blow horn. Behind him were Federal agents and what looked like the entire L.W.P.D. "I repeat come out with your hands up or we coming in!"

At that very moment Travis took faith into his hands. He had extra clips for days and one more choppa on deck, so if they wanted him they would have to come in and get him. He used the butt of the rifle to break the glass before firing at 100%. 100% dodged bullets as he ran then took cover behind a squad car as the rest of the officers fired back. Travis jumped to the floor as rounds zoomed past him. When they ceased fire he crawled back to the window and opened fire again. Travis knew it was over be he wasn't going down without a fight.

"Put your weapon down and surrender!" 100% ordered. "Or we're coming in!"

"Fuck you cracka!" Travis shouted before firing again. "Come get me!'

The stand off lasted an hour before 100% made good on his threat. Travis flipped his bed over to use it as a shield. When the SWAT team kicked in the door, they tossed a couple of gas bombs before coming in. As they rushed in, Travis took out three of them before taking multiple shots to the body and head. When it was over 100% walked in the room and looked around. The room looked like a war zone. When he walked up to Travis' body he kneeled down and shook his head. "I told you we were coming in," he said sarcastically.

That same morning at around 10:00 a.m. Spoon was getting ready to be released from the Hospital. Lisa was ecstatic to have her little brother back. As she helped him get dressed, two FBI agents rushed in the room and through Spoon against the wall. "What's going on?" He yelled as he tried to wrestle the agents off of him. Unable to control the young man one of the agents gave him a stiff right punch to the rib, as the other one twisted his arm.

Lisa screamed for them to stop as they wrestled her brother to his stomach and handcuffed him.

"Why are ya'll arresting him?" Lisa cried as they lifted Spoon to his feet. "What did he do?"

"We have a warrant for his arrest," said one of the agents. "He's wanted for the RICO act"

"*Racketeering* . . . what the fuck ya'll talking bout?" Spoon shouted as they dragged him out the door. "Lisa, call Jamal!"

As the officers took Spoon, Lisa ran to her purse on the bed to find her cell. She quickly dialed Jamal's number. When he picked up she cried into the phone. "Calm down Lisa I can barley understand you," said Jamal trying to make out her words. Lisa took a deep breath then explaining what happened again. The news caused Jamal's heart to skip a beat. "Racketeering, how the fuck?" He wondered as the others looked on in confusion. Before hanging up he assured her everything was going to be okay and to stay close to her phone.

"Yo what's up with Lisa?" Ken asked from the passenger seat of Troy's Chevy Theo. "She straight?"

"Naw man," said Jamal from the backseat. "Spoon just got arrested for racketeering"

"What are you serious?" Troy asked. "Ain't that what they charged Top 6 with?"

"Yeah bro . . . that means they gotta be looking for us," said Jamal hitting the door with his fist. "This shit is crazy!"

"How the fuck?" Troy asked. "We ain't affiliated with Top 6, we don't even know them"

"We ain't got to know them man," said Jamal. "These crackas do what the fuck they want"

"Then what we gon' do?" Troy asked.

"I don't know," said Jamal as he shook his head. "I don't know"

Everything was going as planned until now. The deal with Dread was successful and they were on their way back to the stash house with over a million dollars in the back of Troy's Chevy Tahoe. Fat Zoe been missing for a couple of days and Jamal would put any amount of money he snitched. Little did he know Fat Zoe died for keeping it real. As thoughts scrambled his mind, his phone rang again this time it was Kim.

"Jamal baby they just kicked in the door looking for you!" Kim cried into the phone as she held a crying Kayla in her arms. "They destroyed everything baby . . . I'm scared!"

"Calm down baby . . . just go to my mama's house," he told her. "I got to figure this out"

"But baby," she pleaded. "What about you?"

"Just do as I say!" He snapped. "Ima call you later"

"Okay baby," Kim said. "I love you"

"I love you too baby," said Jamal before hanging up.

"Yo they just kicked in my door," said Jamal. "We got to get out the hood man . . . go to the stash house"

"Damn this shit is crazy," said Ken. "We hot as fuck right now"

Troy drove through the hood towards I-95, careful not speed. Everyone in the car was silent wondering what the fuck was going on! Kim and Kayla ran through Jamal's mind. He came too far to let them down now. He had to find a way out of this and quick so he called the only person he knew that could help him . . . Chico, but he wasn't picking up. When they stopped at a red light on 6th avenue and "A" street, the young men were surprised when they noticed the ramps to the interstate going north and south had check points.

"Oh shit ya'll boys look," said Troy. "What the fuck is going on?"

"Go the other way man," said Jamal looking around for any other signs of police. "We straight"

When the light turned green, Troy waited for a few cars to pass by before getting out of the turning lane, to go the opposite way, towards Dixie highway and 6th avenue. As they drove down the highway, Troy noticed a Helicopter hovering over them. "Damn I think they on us ya'll," he said pointing at the chopper. When they made it to Dixie Highway and 6th avenue, south bound turning lane, Troy nearly had a heart attack when he spotted three black Suburban's riding back to back coming down the road. Then the unexpected happened. The Suburbans stopped in the middle of traffic, blocking Troy's Tahoe from being able to turn. Next Federal agents jumped out with their guns drawn, running towards them. "Yo hit it hit it!" Ken yelled as Jamal watched in shock form the backseat.

Shit was real and Troy knew it. He smashed the gas pedal and rode over the sidewalk as the agents leaped for their lives. Jamal looked in the back window and watch as the agents scramble to their cars to pursue them. "They're coming dawg . . . turn!" Jamal yelled. Troy made a hard right turn on 10th avenue south and Dixie, almost flipping the SUV over. Pedestrians watched as the

Black Tahoe zoomed past them towards the tracks. The truck went airborne when hitting the hill the tracks were on. As they sped across each intersection, they watched as L.W.P.D patrol cars formed road blocks down each street.

"Man they try'na trap us in!" Ken yelled as he looked out the window. "We got to get it on feet!"

"Man what about the money?" Jamal asked. "It's over a million in here!"

"Fuck the money!" Ken shouted. "These crackas coming man!"

Trapping them in was exactly what the police were trying to do. They had road blocks set up on every street to trap the suspects in the city. Coming up on a dead end, Troy made a hard left turn on "C" street, barely dodging a patrol car's efforts of trying to cut them off. Up ahead were two more police cars parked bumper to bumper, with two officers standing in front of them with their guns drawn. "Run through that shit!" Ken yelled. Seeing that the SUV had no intentions of slowing down, the two officers fired at the vehicle before leaping out the way. The Tahoe rammed through the patrol cars like a bulldozer before making a right turn. When Jamal looked behind him the three black Suburbans were hot on their trial.

"Damn these crackas everywhere!" Troy shouted. "How the fuck we gon' get out?"

"Turn on "B" street!" Jamal shouted. "We could hit it down the alley!"

As Troy made a right turn on B street Jamal grabbed one of the duffle bags filled with money, so he could run with it. Up ahead was yet another road block. This one was made up of three patrol cars and five officers. With the black Suburbans still behind them, stopping here would be risky Troy thought, so he decided to pick up more speed. "What the fuck man we can't ram that shit, slow down!" Jamal yelled from the backseat. Ignoring his cries, Troy kept going, reaching a speed of 110 mph. The officers took aim and fired at the vehicle. Ken and Jamal ducked down in their seats as the bullets ripped through the car. One of the rounds caught Troy in the arm causing him to lose control. The officers leaped for safety seconds before impact. The SUV swerved right before ramming through the cars and then crashing into a light pole. Troy died instantly. Ken and Jamal got out the vehicle and made a run for it as the officers continued to fire. Ken returned fire as he ran behind Jamal who still had a duffle bag in hand. Jamal scaled a gate into someone's front yard with no problem but Ken wasn't so lucky. As he went to jump the fence, Ken took a hot one to the leg causing him to fall against it. His cries for help caused Jamal to look back but it was too late. The officers had him surrounded as they yelled for him to drop his weapon. Declining to do so, the officers gunned Ken down like a dog. Seeing his own brother gun down made Jamal eyes widen in disbelief. The end was near and he could feel it but he had to keep going.

Jamal ran behind the house into the backyard and scaled it's back gate with three FBI agents from one of the black Suburban's, hot on his trail. Now in the back alley, Jamal ran for his life. The bag in his hand slowed him down but he refused to drop it. The agents let off a few shots causing Jamal to jump another back gate into someone's yard. He ran into the house through the back door that was left open. Running through the kitchen he entered the living room where he startled an old Hispanic lady watching TV. Running out the front door Jamal made into the middle of the street where a police officer was slowly cruising down the road. When spotting the suspect the officer jumped out and drew his gun. "Stop right there!" He yelled firing a shot in the air.

The gun shot stopped Jamal in his tracks with his back facing the officer. "Put your hands up!" The officer shouted as he called for back up. Jamal was breathing harder then a run away slave and sweating a ton. *"It can't end like this,"* Jamal thought to himself. He refused to go back to jail. "Drop your bag and put your hands up!" The officer shouted. Jamal put his left hand in the air then dropped the duffle bag before quickly grabbing his .45 from his waistline, then turning around and firing. The officer fired back hitting Jamal twice in the stomach as he endured three hot ones to the chest and neck. When they both ceased fired the severely injured officer fell against the car and slid to the ground as Jamal slowly fell to his knees. Jamal dropped his gun when observing his shirt had two big holes in it and was drenched in blood. Hearing a single siren coming down the street, he tried to get to his feet but collapsed to his side for his efforts. Now on his back gasping for air, he could hear foot steps walking towards him. When looking up he saw the devil himself standing over him smiling.

"Dead or alive Mr. Pierre . . . dead or alive," said 100% as he squatted down and took off his shades. "You really thought you niggers could run free in my city and get away with it?" He asked the young man fighting for his life. "Well news flash buddy it's over"

Destroying the South Side Boys is what 100% wanted to do for a long time. He pulled his gun out his holster and pointed it at the young man. Jamal stared at the gun and the man holding it. He was looking death in the eyes but all he could think about was how he'd let everyone down. His chance to break was gone and he only had his self to blame. The bullet from 100%'s gun extinguished the pain that was inside Jamal.

THE END